Satan's Counterfeit Gospel

Heidi Heiks

TEACH Services, Inc.
PUBLISHING
www.TEACHServices.com • (800) 367-1844

World rights reserved. This book or any portion thereof may not be copied or reproduced in any form or manner whatever, except as provided by law, without the written permission of the publisher, except by a reviewer who may quote brief passages in a review.

This book was written to provide truthful information in regard to the subject matter covered. The author assumes full responsibility for the accuracy of all facts and quotations as cited in this book. The opinions expressed in this book are the author's personal views and interpretation of the Bible, Spirit of Prophecy, and/or contemporary authors and do not necessarily reflect those of TEACH Services, Inc.

This book is sold with the understanding that the publisher is not engaged in giving spiritual, legal, medical, or other professional advice. If authoritative advice is needed, the reader should seek the counsel of a competent professional.

Copyright © 2016 TEACH Services, Inc.
ISBN-13: 978-1-4796-0748-8 (Paperback)

Library of Congress Control Number: 2016916088

Published by

DEDICATED TO THOSE

WHO WILL BE INSTRUMENTAL IN

FINISHING THE GOSPEL COMMISSION

"A revival and a reformation must take place, under the ministration of the Holy Spirit. Revival and reformation are two different things. Revival signifies a renewal of spiritual life, a quickening of the powers of mind and heart, a resurrection from spiritual death. Reformation signifies a reorganization, a change in ideas and theories, habits and practices. Reformation will not bring forth the good fruit of righteousness unless it is connected with the revival of the Spirit. Revival and reformation are to do their appointed work, and in doing this work they must blend."[1]

---

[1] Ellen White, *Review & Herald*, Feb. 25, 1902.

CONTENTS

Introduction vii

Chapter 1. The Nature of Sin / Man 13

Chapter 2. The Nature of Christ 58

Chapter 3. The Atonement, Completed at the Cross? 113

Chapter 4. The Man of Romans 7, Converted or Unconverted? 118

Chapter 5. The Real Gospel Stands Up 148

Chapter 6. The Final Generation/144,000 184

APPENDIX 257

INTRODUCTION

The task that has been set before me is not one that I asked for but has been heavily pressed upon me. The purpose here is to vindicate the real gospel and to clear an innocent party that has been wrongfully accused the world over for decades. Having accomplished this objective the reader now has in his possession the real gospel as presented from the Scriptures and fully backed through the writings of Ellen G. White. Therefore, it becomes imperative we unite on this platform of truth, fulfill the prayer of Christ in John 17 and speak with one voice, or risk the chance of being a castaway and shaken out of His Church when Christ begins to "thoroughly purge his floor" Matt. 3:12.

Unfortunately, there are actually two gospels being brandished within the Seventh-day Adventist Church. These two groups or classes of people are labeled as such:

1. The Conservatives or better known as the Independents.
2. The New Theology or better known as the Organized Church.

Yes, the organized church has been falsely misrepresented and labeled as the New Theology by the independents or the so called conservatives but this false accusation will be fully dismantled shortly.

Nevertheless, neither side advocates the typical position of the Evangelical Churches that claim Antinomianism, which means the law of God has been done away with. This class is so far removed from the truth that we will not even discuss them from this point on because both the independents and the organized church at large reject such a flagrant gospel. However, before we go any further, I want to dismantle a false accusation and state clearly that I am in no way in harmony with a gospel that teaches salvation in known or practicing sin and neither are any of my peers within the organized church.

The first class is the claimed, Conservatives or better known as the Independents. This class is largely spear headed by Dennis Priebe and Colin and Russell Standish, (Russell now deceased). Dennis Priebe's book, *Face to Face with the Real Gospel*[2] speaks for a rather large segment of leadership in this sphere. It is very important that it be realized that the beliefs expressed in this book are not just the beliefs of one lone individual; on the contrary, these views are held by some of the most influential conservative leads in the church. For example: Joe Crews (now deceased) advertises and sells the book, saying, "This book is an excellent study in righteousness by faith... False gospels are unmasked and the real gospel is presented." Ralph Larson also holds the same belief, (now deceased). Priebe used to work with Ron Spear, (now deceased) and was a regular write for the magazine, *Our Firm Foundation*. Robert Weiland and the 1888 Study Committee is also very much in harmony with this teaching as well as the Standish brothers. Together, these

---

[2] Dennis Priebe, *Face-to-Face With the Real Gospel* (Boise Idaho, Pacific Press Publishing Association, 1985)

men and others reach and influence a very large number of the claimed conservative segment of the church. Dennis Priebe has just come out with a new DVD series called; *Will the Real Gospel Please Stand Up*? The reader now has in his hands a reply to that request! Part of Priebe's advertisement reads:

> "Can you spot the impostors? Evangelist and educator Dennis Priebe shows how false gospels have permeated nearly every Christian denomination. This includes God's remnant church."

The second class representing, The Organized Church's understanding at large is by Gerhard Pfandl Ph.D. former Associate Director of the Biblical Research Institute of the General Conference of the Seventh-day Adventist World Church. This gospel has been labeled by the ultra-conservatives or independents listed above in the previous paragraph as the, New Theology. This baseless charge as stated previously will momentarily be proven to be utterly false. Nothing is worse for the genuine Christian or for a Church to experience, than to be falsely accused.

We will thoroughly investigate which gospel can withstand investigation and scrutiny of the Scriptures and Inspiration. My commitment and stance in the past and today is one and the same, I will call truth, truth and error, error and whichever camp that places me in, so be it. My comments when needed will be in brackets [ ]. Since this book is dedicated primarily to an Adventist readership, footnotes of Ellen G. White's sources will be displayed in an abridged format.

Knowing firsthand the issues and arguments on both sides of the debate minutely. My position as a former Bible teacher at *Hartland College* and editor for *The Firm Foundation Magazine* at Hope International along with my multiple visits to the office of the Biblical Research Institute of the General Conference has led me to see and understand the issues clearly. I will now simply present these facts along with my unbiased research, is my pledge to the reader and my commitment to the truth. We can only pray that the evidence will be carefully weighed again and the men presenting another gospel will make restitution with God and to the multitudes that have been misled by their teachings and come into line with the gospel of Jesus Christ lest we be found fighting against God Almighty still. This may be the last plea of forbearance before heaven acts in behalf of His church against those who stubbornly refuse to listen to reason and come into line with the teachings of His word and Inspiration. I believe that the time is just before us when God is going to act in a very forthright manner to cleanse His Church from all defilement. When He does, He will have a purified ministry presenting "the" gospel, a gospel that does not misrepresent His character and grace.

When men come to the place that they can no longer be taught and when their errors have been brought to their attention time and time again to no avail. And all the while they stand behind the pulpit dolling out their private humanistic teachings of another gospel to the unsuspecting flock then Heaven has outlined an unpleasant but necessary task to those who stand upon "it is written," the guardians of the people, to meet the threat. Ellen White met this unpleasant task and acted accordingly to our explicit counsel in I Timothy 5:20, found in Testimonies 2:14-15. Of all people, the beloved John had met this unpleasant task as well and acted accordingly, even by calling the culprit by name. We have his account and example of what must be done when "truth" is under siege openly in the church:

> 8. "We therefore ought to receive such, that we might be fellowhelpers to the <u>truth</u>.
> 9. I wrote unto the church: but <u>Diotrephes</u>, who loveth to have the preeminence among them, receiveth us not.
> 10. Wherefore, if I come, I will remember his deeds which he doeth, prating against us with malicious words: and not content therewith, neither doth he himself receive the brethren, and forbiddeth them that would, and casteth *them* out of the church." 3 John 8-10.

There is nothing more sacred and important in the entire Bible than for humanity to rightly represent their Lord's character of love and gift of grace to a perishing world.

> Let as many servants as are under the yoke count their own masters worthy of all honour, that the name of God and *his* doctrine be not blasphemed. I Tim. 6:1.

That can only be accomplished when we rightly understand in theory and experience the real transformation power of the real gospel of our Lord and Savior Jesus Christ on a personal level. Because, if we have the wrong doctrine, [gospel] we will have the wrong experience and that *will* prove fatal in the coming crisis.

Hence, the failure of the Jews on this very issue was the cause of Babylon's siege on Jerusalem and the captivity of Daniel and his colleagues. It was this same misunderstanding of the gospel in part, which produced in the conservative circles of the religious bigots and zealots in Paul's day that brought to fruition their conspired death wish for Paul:

> "Paul "returned again unto Damascus" (Galatians 1:17), and "preached boldly . . . in the name of Jesus." Unable to withstand the wisdom of his arguments, "the Jews took counsel to kill him."[3]

It was again the like-minded mentality of the so called conservatives (not the liberals) that were largely responsible for rejecting the 1888 movement by rejecting Ellen White's explicit counsel to them as well as to A.T. Jones and E.J. Waggoner that would have corrected their errors above and beyond her endorsements. Those endorsements rather than the teachings of Scripture and Ellen White have been credited and carried to greater heights by some in the church yet today and are being humanly interpreted to mean she endorsed everything Jones and Waggoner said. Even when it contradicts her own publically stated positions on the gospel that

---

[3] Ellen White, *Acts of the Apostles*, 128.

are 180⁰ diametrically opposed to the teachings of Jones and Waggoner! However, we will show and prove that Jones and Waggoner were grossly confused to some of the most basic fundamental teachings of Scripture and Ellen White. It is hard to understand why there is yet today an *1888 Message Study Committee*[4] still promoting Jones and Waggoner above and beyond Scripture and Ellen White!

Will history be repeated again? Or has the rebellion never subsided?

We are at the crossroads once again as the "destiny of the church hangs"[5] upon our correct attitude in response, unity and proclamation of the everlasting gospel according to the Scriptures and Ellen White in this late hour:

> "God is bringing out a people and *preparing them to stand as one united to speak the same things* and thus carry out the prayer of Christ for His disciples."[6] [John 17:20-21].

During this analysis I will make this study as brief and as clear as possible without being unnecessarily redundant. However, I promise that the reader will have sufficient documentation as to be able to make an intelligent and obvious evaluation of the facts presented and come to a clear conclusion as to who has and is presenting to the people the real gospel of our Lord and Savior, Jesus Christ.

Like John, I will fully expose the imposters and by the end of this book, we will have unmasked one of Satan's most subtle forms of legalism, a masterpiece of deception that is being widely promoted by some of the most constrictive leads in the Adventist Church under the so called, gospel commission. This most subtle form of legalism, the scourge of Adventism is coming to the conclusion that one is righteous on the basis of what the Holy Spirit does in him. This concept will be fully exposed by those that advocate such a heretical gospel. Paul allowed for no such mistake in this regard:

> "Knowing that a man is not justified by the works of the law, but by the faith of Jesus Christ, even we have believed in Jesus Christ, that we might be justified by the faith of Christ, and not by the works of the law: for by the works of the law shall no flesh be justified." Gal. 2:16.

After unmasking Satan's counterfeit gospel we will present the simplicity of the real gospel step by step. We will also unmask the private teachings and interpretations of *Last Generation Theology* (LGT) regarding the plan of redemption for the, final generation/144,000. Every honest, free thinking individual will no longer be tossed to and fro and will never again be confused as to what God does for us and in us and what He expects from us in return when the call is made to enter into the "solemn assembly" of Joel chapter 2, preparatory to receiving of the latter rain.

---

[4] See B.R.I.: *Primacy of the Gospel Committee – Report*:
 https://adventistbiblicalresearch.org/materials/independent-ministries-and-others/primacy-gospel-committee-report
[5] Ellen White, *Testimonies*, 1:181.
[6] Ellen White, *Testimonies*, 1:417. [Emphasis mine].

In this judicial analysis we will forthrightly provide each side's position from their own published sources and then the reader will see for himself who has left the platform of truth, the foundation of Scripture and Ellen White.

During this study, research and comparison I was introduced to two outstanding ministries converging and sharing the simplicity of the everlasting gospel in a deep but yet in a very simplistic format that all can fully grasp and experience for one's self. This was not by accident; therefore, having gladly received permission from all parties to include any or all of their material I have incorporated certain sections in this book as I know the reader will fully appreciate it as much as I have. There is an old saying, "No need to reinvent the wheel when it is already here." Such is the case here, in many respects. These two additional sources were taken from, *Pastor Frank Phillips*[7] and *Pastor Stephen Wallace*.[8] Both men are Seventh-day Adventist Ministers. Please visit these two wonderful ministries websites and their exceptional staff for their dedication and commitment to and for the truth. They have so much to offer that will help you connect all the dots and immensely further enhance your daily Christian walk step by step that cannot be found here due to space limitations. No one man is given all the light and the contributions that all parties bring to this study has resulted in bringing many discrepancies of the gospel among Seventh-day Adventist to a close. My primary role in this book was to honestly vindicate the real gospel and an innocent party wrongfully condemned. Also to expose the perpetrators of the false gospel in a hope to save their souls and their unsuspecting flocks lest we be found among the "superficial conservative class"[9] like the Jews of old that Inspiration has warned us about:

> "There are many who, when they are reproved, think it praiseworthy if they receive the rebuke without becoming impatient; but how few take reproof with gratitude of heart, and bless those who seek to save them from pursuing an evil course."[10]

This I have done with the object that all who read this book will *unify* with the brethren who have been shown to whom stands upon the real gospel of the Scriptures and Inspiration and present to the world a united front that God will be honored to claim as His own. In the APPENDIX the reader will find pertinent word definitions for better clarity and continuity.

We begin chapter 1 with an introduction by The organized church's response to the accusations leveled against her largely by the independents and her succinct rebuttal will be

---

[7] Frank B. Phillips, *His Robe Or Mine*, Justified Walk Ministries at www.justifiedwalk.com or email us justifiedwalk@justifiedwalk.com (269) 471-9224 PO Box 233 Berrien Springs, Michigan 49103-0233. Pastor Phillips has also been given an honorary Master's degree by Andrews University for his Biblical scholarship pertaining to the gospel of Jesus Christ.

[8] Stephen Wallace, "*Our Sinless Yet Sympathetic Savior*", revivalseminars.org. See also: americanchristianministries.org.

[9] Ellen White, *Testimonies* 5:463.

[10] Ellen White, *Patriarchs and Prophets*, 667.

taken from a PDF article[11] that may be viewed in its entirely on my website at www.thesourcehh.org.

---

[11] Gerhard Pfandl, *What Is New In The New Theology*, PDF, pgs. 1-11.

1
The Nature of Sin / Man

"WHAT IS NEW IN THE NEW THEOLOGY?

Gerhard Pfandl, Ph.D.

"The term "New Theology" was first used by M.L. Andreasen in 1959 in his **Letters to the Churches** which he wrote in response to the publication of the book **Questions on Doctrine** in 1957. In these letters Andreasen, who had been one of our most notable theologians for many years, attacked the denominational leadership for what he considered as selling Adventism down the river for evangelical recognition. What had happened?

ADVENTIST - EVANGELICAL CONVERSATIONS

In 1955, Walter Martin, a Southern Baptist clergyman, contacted the General Conference with a number of questions. Martin, at that time, was a Ph.D. candidate at New York University, researching for a dissertation on the subject "Non-Christian Religions in the United States."

In connection with his research, he was preparing a book against Seventh-day Adventists and wanted to ascertain as accurately as possible what we really believed and taught. This contact led to a series of official conversations with a group of evangelical leaders. The evangelicals involved were Walter R. Martin, George E. Cannon and, later, Donald G. Barnhouse. George Cannon was a professor of theology and Donald Barnhouse was then a popular radio preacher in Philadelphia, pastor of a large Presbyterian Church in the same city and editor in chief of *Eternity* Magazine.

The Adventist leaders who participated in these conversations were LeRoy Edwin Froom, W.E. Read, T.E. Unruh and, later, Roy Allan Anderson, then editor of *Ministry*.

The purpose of these discussions was to provide Walter Martin with an accurate account of the distinctive beliefs of Seventh-day Adventists for his book. The group met a number of times in the offices of the General Conference throughout the period of about one year.

M. L. Andreasen, who by then had been in retirement for some years, took exception to these discussions. To him, they represented a capitulation - a sell-out - on the part of the Adventist leadership.

A confrontation developed between him and high-ranking Adventist leaders, particularly the then President of the General Conference, Reuben F. Figuhr, with whom Andreasen exchanged a series of strongly worded letters, especially during the year 1957 (Roy Adams, *The Nature of Christ* [Washington, DC: Review and Herald, 1994], p.44).

When he was denied a hearing, on his terms, Andreasen went public with **Letters to the Churches**. In letter 1 on page 13 he wrote, "Whoever accepts the new theology must reject the Testimonies. There is no other choice." Under "New Theology" Andreasen understood primarily the teachings of Christ's sinless nature and the completed atonement on the cross as presented in the book *Questions on Doctrine*.

In time the term "New Theology" came to be used to describe people in the church who, among other things, believed (1) that Christ's human nature was sinless, (2) that man is born in sin, and (3) that the atonement was completed at the cross.

IS THE NEW THEOLOGY REALLY NEW?

There are Adventists who honestly feel that the "New Theology" is a masterpiece of Satan, and that those who accept it have apostatised.

The "New Theology" is a worldwide problem. It has been used by Satan in an endeavour to derail God's remnant church. We have confidence in the testimony of Ellen White that he will not succeed, but a huge number of God's people will sadly be lost as a result of the acceptance of this unscriptural theology (Colin & Russell Standish, *Deceptions of the New Theology*, [Hartland Publications, 1989], p.28).

It is further claimed that followers of the "New Theology" deny the Sanctuary Message and the relevance of the Spirit of Prophecy for the church today. Furthermore, the claim that the trend toward worldliness in the church is a result of the "New Theology".

In evaluating these claims, we must first of all state that the term "New Theology" is misleading, since it implies that it is something new which the

Adventist church did not hold prior to the 1950s when these perceived errors were supposed to have crept in."[12]

[Of the numerous contested issues that follow and that we will examine they will be presented as always coming first from the independents such as Dennis Priebe and the Standish brothers, which includes the 1888 Message Study Committee and all others who support their views. These men have largely led out in this endeavor against the church and have been the most vocal in their views and in their publications. Therefore, we will be quoting from them extensively throughout this discourse for they also have the largest following. Many of these independents have also publically declared that the S.D.A. organized church has repudiated the gospel endorsed by the scriptures and Ellen White and are in open apostasy. With that public accusation staunchly proclaimed many times over before us all, the only steps necessary then is to examine and show if that claim can be sustained first and foremost from the scriptures and then from the writings of Ellen G. White.

Therefore we begin with the issue regarding; The Nature of Sin and or The Nature of Man with Dennis Priebe stating his position]:

"The Nature of Sin

"In Geoffrey Paxton's challenging book, *The Shaking of Adventism*, he says that Seventh-day Adventists rejected righteousness by faith in 1888 because we rejected the historic doctrine of original sin. He identifies original sin as the foundational principle of Reformation theology.- Pages 98-114. Now original sin is simply the belief that we are guilty before God because of our birth as sons and daughters of Adam. We are guilty by nature, before any choice of good or evil enters the picture. Our condemnation comes from Adam; we are guilty because of our inherited depravity. "There in the desire to sin." "Sin is declared to exist in the being prior to our own consciousness of it." "There is guilt in evil desires, even when resisted by the will." – Desmond Ford, "The Relationship Between the Incarnation and Righteousness by Faith," in *Documents From the Palmdale Conference on Righteousness by Faith*, p.28.

According to this view, sin and guilt apply to nature, and the gospel must deal with the reality of guilt as a part of the nature of man which can never be removed until we are given new bodies at Christ's second coming, when mortality puts on immortality. In this view, weakness, imperfection and tendencies are sin. It is an interesting and significant point that the reformers built their doctrine of original sin on the premise of predestination, which teaches that God leaves some men to suffer and die in their sinful and guilty

---
[12] Gerhard Pfandl, What Is New In The New Theology, PDF 1-2.

natures while He elects to send His saving grace to others through the gospel. These two doctrines fit together naturally. Thus, it is a bit strange that while predestination has been rejected by many Christians today, original sin is still seen as the foundation of correct gospel teaching."[13]

"If we are to believe that sin is by choice, we must make a crucial distinction between evil and guilt. Guilt demands prior knowledge and willful rebellion. I am suggesting that God's condemnation is *always* based upon man's prior knowledge." [14]

The Standish brothers define The Nature of Man as such:

"The new Theology is predicated upon erroneous views of the nature of man. Indeed, this is one of the principal areas in which the new theology may be identified. . . .Man is not born with original sin. The concept of original sin was firmly etched in the Augustinian concepts of Christianity. He brought this notion with him from paganism. This concept holds that man is born, and even conceived, guilty because of Adam's sin. There is nothing that man can do nor God does to rectify this situation."[15]

[And they go a step further and declare that to accept such a view is apostasy from the truth and its proponents are presenting "another gospel." By definition we will let Priebe have the floor here as he has largely defined the divide and the issue at hand that will be addressed at this time:

"It is crucial that we define sin . . . as carefully as possible. If the primary meaning of sin is sinful nature, then we become sinners when we are born into this world. However, if the primary meaning of sin is sinful character, then we become sinners because of the choices that we make after we are able to choose between right and wrong. If sin is our nature, then we have no control over that, and we are sinners by nature. If sin is our character, then we do have control over the choices we make, and we are sinners by choice."[16]

Let's summarize:

---

[13] Dennis Priebe, *Face-to-Face With the Real Gospel* (Boise Idaho, Pacific Press Publishing Association, 1985) 12-13.
[14] Ibid. 30.
[15] Colin D. Standish & Russell R. Standish, *Deceptions of the New Theology* (Hartland Publications, 1989). 63.
[16] Dennis Priebe, *Face-to-Face With the Real Gospel* (Boise Idaho, Pacific Press Publishing Association, 1985) 66.

1. Priebe and the independents take the position that we do not become sinners, neither at conception nor at birth but it's a conscientious decision rendered by our choice *after* we are able to choose between right and wrong. This does not take place until what is commonly called by the independents, as the age of accountability. It is suggested that this takes place when the child is to be around 12 yrs. of age but no Scripture or Ellen White has ever been submitted to substantiate that supposition.

2. The organized church at large takes the position that we sin because we are sinners, our natures are evil. This takes place at conception and we have no choice in this matter, however, having a sinful nature does not and has not violated our free will or freedom of choice. Predestination finds no place in the Scriptures or in the gospel of Jesus Christ and the organized church at large has been falsely accused by the independents of incorporating this teaching into their gospel. After the fall of Adam and Eve they passed on to all of their posterity a fallen nature with a bent to evil that all are now born with inherent propensities of disobedience. A condition of alienation of which they were never created with when the Creator first formed man in His likeness. This fact has been correctly labelled by the organized church (Gerhard Pfandl) as "original corruption." The organized church at large rejects the Catholic definition of "original sin," the *part* that teaches "Adams guilt" or sins has been transferred to all his posterity. However, no argument is taken by the organized church at large when they also teach that we inherited "Adams stain" as well. The inherited stain refers to our sinful passions, to our tendencies or propensities to sin. Unfortunately, the independents have never presented the organized church's position accurately or honestly.

In order to bring closure to a topic that should have never been in dispute I will take each segment of our study in each chapter *when we are comparing the two gospels side by side* and present a list of the primary stated positions and beliefs from the Plaintiff or the independents from the sources presented and just viewed. They are as follows:

1. [They reject] "We are guilty by *nature*, before *any choice* of good or evil enters the picture."[17]

2. [They reject] "Our condemnation comes *from Adam*."[18]

3. [They reject] "We are guilty because of our *inherited depravity*."[19]

4. [They reject] "*Sin is declared to exist in the being prior to our own consciousness of it.*"[20]

---

[17] Ibid. 12-13.
[18] Ibid. 12-13.
[19] Ibid. 12-13.

5. [They assert] "*Inheritance does not* make us *guilty*, but the choice to exercise our fallen nature produces guilt."[21]

6. [They assert] "We become sinners because of the choices that we make *after we are able to choose between right and wrong*."[22]

7. [They assert] "God's condemnation is *always* based upon man's prior knowledge."[23]

8. [They assert] "We *do not inherit* guilt or condemnation."[24]

9. [They assert] "This death, the natural death that Adam died, was the *result* of sin, rather than the *penalty* of sin."[25]

10. [They assert] "This is one of the principal areas in which the new theology may be *identified*."[26]

11. [They assert] "This notion comes from *paganism*."[27]

12. [They reject] "That man is *born*, and *even conceived*, guilty because of Adam's sin."[28]

Now that we are clear on the position and understanding of the independents we turn our attention to the stated position of the Defendant or the Seventh-day Adventist Church at large that we are labeling the organized church. Because of the lack of transparency and the misrepresentation by some regarding this sensitive topic it has become necessary to provide the reader with an unbiased and full view of the big picture here in order for the honest in heart to see the foundation that Scripture and Ellen White have laid down for the everlasting gospel. This view will now be presented by former Associate Director of the BRI Gerhard Pfandl Ph.D. that many in the world church fully recognize and adhere to:

The Nature of Sin / Man

I. DEFINITION

"Original sin" like "Trinity" is not a biblical but a theological term. Yet, it expresses what most Christian theologians believe is a biblical concept. A Catholic catechism asks the question:

---

[20] Ibid. 12-13.
[21] Ibid. 56.
[22] Ibid. 66.
[23] Ibid., 30. Emphasis in the original.
[24] Ibid., 28. Emphasis in the original.
[25] Ibid., 31. Emphasis in the original.
[26] Colin D. Standish & Russell R. Standish, *Deceptions of the New Theology* (Hartland Publications, 1989). 63.
[27] Ibid., 63.
[28] Ibid., 63.

"What is original sin?" The answer given is: "Original sin is that guilt and stain which we inherit from Adam, who was the origin and head of all mankind."[29] We note that the answer clearly identifies two aspects of original sin: (a) inherited guilt and (b) inherited stain. The inherited stain refers to our sinful passions, to our tendencies or propensities to sin.

II. THE ISSUES AND QUESTIONS[30]

A major portion of Scripture is devoted to the subject of sin. "Next to the word God, the word sin is the most closely packed with meaning for the human race and for the universe."[31] But how should sin be defined? Is it an act, i.e., is sin simply "transgression of the Law" (1 John 3:4 KJV), or does sin also refer to a state of being? Is a corrupt nature in itself sinful or not? Should sin as a state of being be considered as the cause of individual acts of sin? How about children are they born sinners or do they become sinners only when they break the law? Is man a sinner because he sins, or does he sin because he is a sinner? What do we inherit from Adam? These are the questions and issues we will look at.

Adventists are divided in regard to how sin should be defined. E. Heppenstall, for example, wrote:

> "This state of sin into which all men are born is called original sin - not in the sense of inherited guilt, but of an inherited disposition to sin. It goes back to an original source, the sin of Adam and Eve, the first parents of the human race. Involved is the sinful condition of all members of the human race before they are actually guilty of committing sin themselves."[32]

In contrast to this position, D. E. Priebe said: "Sin is not basically what a man is, but the way man chooses . . . sin is concerned with a man's will rather than with his nature."[33]

Since these questions concern important issues, we will first look at the biblical evidence, then we will explore the history of the original-sin doctrine, and lastly we will investigate the understanding of this doctrine in the Seventh-day Adventist church.

III. THE BIBLICAL EVIDENCE

The Bible is very explicit in regard to the extensiveness (universality) of sin as well as to its intensiveness.

THE EXTENSIVENESS OF SIN

The universality of sin is set forth in direct statements of Scripture:

1 Kings 8:46 "there is no man that sinneth not."

---

[29] A Catechism of Christian Doctrine (London: Catholic Truth Society, 1958), p.19.
[30] For some of the thoughts and sources in this paper I am indebted to Norman Gulley, "Preliminary Considerations of the Effects and Implications of Adam's Sin", Adventist Perspectives 2:2(1988), 28-44.
[31] E. Heppenstall, The Man Who is God (Washington, D.C.: Review and Herald, 1977), p.107.
[32] Ibid., pp.107-108.
[33] Dennis E. Priebe, Face-to-face With the Real Gospel (Boise, ID: Pacific Press, 1985), p.17.

Psalms 14:3 "there is none that doeth good, no not one."

Ecclesiastes 7:20 "Surely there is not a righteous man on earth, that doeth good, and sinneth not."

Romans 3:10 "There is none righteous, no not one."

Romans 3:23 "For all have sinned."

Even the heroes of faith in Hebrew 11 who are described as perfect (Gen 6:9), as friends of God (Jas 2:23), or as men after the heart of God (Acts 13:22), were sinners. Noah was a drunkard (Gen 9:21), Abraham was a liar (Gen 12:13), and David was an adulterer and murderer (2 Sam 1). Thus they could join us and every other human being, but one, in repeating Isaiah's words (53:6): "All we like sheep have gone astray: we have turned everyone to his own way." The exception, the one - Jesus Christ - is mentioned in the last part of Isaiah's text: "and the Lord hath laid on him the iniquity of us all."

The fact that Scripture declares the universal need of atonement (John 3:16; Acts 4:12), of regeneration (John 3:3,5), and of repentance (Acts 17:30) also indicates that sin is universal. An additional proof is the fact that all persons are subject to death, the penalty for sin (Rom 6:23).

THE INTENSIVENESS OF SIN

How sinful is the sinner? How deep is our sin? Are we basically good, created in the image of God, but because of temptations we transgress God's law; or are we basically evil, with the image of God almost destroyed, and because of our evil nature we commit sin?

The Bible generally defines sin as an act, 1 John 3:4 "sin is the transgression of the law", or "sin is lawlessness" (NASB). In the Old Testament the most commonly used word for sin is *chata'* which in its most literal sense means "to miss the mark" as in Judges 20:16, "Among all this people there were seven hundred chosen men left-handed; everyone could sling stones at an hair breadth, and not miss (*chata'*)." In matters of morals, "missing the mark" refers to the fact that God's law is the standard of ethical behavior at which one must aim. Thus, when Joseph said: "how then can I do this great wickedness and sin (*chata'*) against God" (Gen 39:9), he was in effect saying, "how can I do this great wickedness and miss the standard of God's law." Missing the mark is not merely an accidental mistake, but a voluntary and culpable wrong act. C. R. Smith says:

> "The hundreds of examples of the word's moral use require that the wicked man "misses the right mark because he chooses to aim at a wrong one" and "misses the right path because he deliberately follows a wrong one" - that is,

there is no question of an innocent mistake or of the merely negative idea of failure."[34]

There are a number of other Hebrew words which express the idea of sin as an act, e.g., *shagah* "to go astray" (1 Sam 26:21), *chet'* "error" (Isa 1:18), or *pesha^c* "rebellion" (1 Kgs 12:19). And in the New Testament the most frequently used words for sin, *hamartano* (43x)[35] and *hamartia* (173x),[36] also have the underlying thought of missing a mark or aim.[37]

However, a great number of texts in both the Old Testament and the New Testament refer to sin as a state, or tendency of the heart. Jeremiah depicts sin as a spiritual sickness which afflicts the heart. He says that "the heart is deceitful above all things and desperately wicked: who can know it?"(17:9). David in Psalm 51 expresses the thought that he was born a sinner, "Behold, I was shapen in iniquity; and in sin did my mother conceive me." Not that his mother did anything wrong in connection with his conception or birth, she was an honorable woman, but he recognises that he was born with a sinful nature. He desires to be washed and cleansed from sin (vss.2,7) and asks God to create in him a clean heart (vs.10). The same thought is expressed in Psalm 58:3, "The wicked are estranged from the womb: they go astray as soon as they be born, speaking lies." Israel is called "a transgressor from the womb" (Isa 48:8). And "from the sole of the foot even unto the head there is no soundness (not a sound spot NEB) in it", says God in Isaiah 1:6.

The Hebrew verb *chashab* (to think) and its derivatives appear some 180 times in the Old Testament. They are used in connection with the thoughts and purposes of God, but especially in reference to the cunning and sinful devisings of man's heart. In Genesis 6:5 God looks down on the earth and sees that the wickedness of man is great, "every imagination of the thoughts (*chashab*) of his heart was only evil continually." Man's thoughts, says Isaiah, are "thoughts (*chashab*) of iniquity" (59:7). He therefore calls on the wicked to "forsake his way, and the unrighteous man his thoughts (*chashab*)" (55:7).

The New Testament is even clearer and more emphatic on these matters. In the Sermon on the Mount Jesus speaks of the inward disposition as evil (Matt 5:21-22,27-28). To the Pharisees he said: "O generation of vipers, how can ye, being evil, speak good things? for out of the abundance of the heart the mouth speaketh" (Matt 12:34). Evil actions and words stem from the evil thought of the heart: "For out of the heart proceed evil thoughts, murders, adulteries, fornications, thefts, false witness, blasphemies" (Matt 15:19). This sinfulness of the human heart, which we will call SIN, produces individual acts of transgressions which are sins. Thus by nature we are children of wrath (Eph 2:3) who are enticed to sin by their own lusts (Jas 4:1).

> "Paul's own self-testimony also is a powerful argument that it is the corruption of human nature that produces individual sins. He recalls that

---

[34] Charles Ryder Smith, The Bible Doctrine of Sin and of the Ways of God with Sinners (London: Epworth, 1953), p.20.
[35] Matt 18:15; Luke 15:18; John 5:14; Rom 2:12; 3:23; 5:12; etc.
[36] Matt 1:21; 3:6; 9:2,5,6; Mark 1:4,5; Luke 1:77; John 1:29; etc.
[37] R. C. Trench, Synonyms of the New Testament (Grand Rapids: W. B. Eerdmans, 1948), p.239.

"while we were living in the flesh, our sinful passions, aroused by the law, were at work in our members to bear fruit for death" (Rom 7:5). He sees "in my members another law at war with the law of my mind and making me captive to the law of sin which dwells in my members" (v.23). In Galatians 5:17 he writes that the desires of the flesh are against the Spirit. The word here is *epithumeo*, which can refer to either a neutral desire or an improper desire. There are numerous "works of the flesh": "immorality, impurity, licentiousness, idolatry, sorcery, enmity, strife, jealousy, anger, selfishness, dissension, party spirit, envy, drunkenness, carousing, and the like" (vss.19-21). In Paul's thinking, then, as in Jesus', sins are the result of human nature. In every human being there is a strong inclination toward evil, an inclination with definite effects."[38]

The only sinless human being in Scripture is Jesus. Of him alone we read that he "knew no sin" (2 Cor 5:21), that he was "separate from sinners" (Heb 7:26) and that "no guile was found in his mouth" (1 Pet 2:22). Thus he could be the lamb "without blemish or spot" (1 Pet 1:19).

TOTAL DEPRAVITY

Total depravity is the phrase used to describe the comprehensive effect of sin. It does not mean that human beings are as bad as bad can be, or that there is no trace of goodness left in them. The word *total* simply refers to the fact that man as a whole is infected with sin. No part of man is exempt. His body is affected by sin (Rom 6:6,12; 7:24; 8:10), his mind or reason is involved (Rom 1:28; 2 Cor 3:14-15; 4:14), and his soul or his emotions have been perverted (Rom 1:24-27; 2 Tim 3:2-4). Finally, also his will is affected by sin. The unconverted person does not really have a free will; he is a slave to sin (Rom 6:17). He, therefore, is unable even to understand and acknowledge the truth about himself as God sees it.

> "Man in his sinfulness cannot apprehend the truth of God. Each succeeding generation makes the same tragic mistakes. Man never seems to learn. Evil tendencies abound. Sin has produced a radical insanity of evil passions, selfish ambitions, wild desires, unreasonable emotions that are the curse of all men on the earth."[39]

Whether this innate sinfulness is to be understood as an inherited state of sinfulness deserving condemnation, or only as an inherited proneness to sin, will be discussed later. For now we must turn our attention to the question of origin.

THE ORIGIN OF OUR SINFUL NATURE

The doctrine of original sin is nowhere developed in any systematic fashion in Scripture. It is

---

[38] Millard J. Erickson, Christian Theology (Grand Rapids: Baker Book House, 1983), p.627.
[39] Edward Heppenstall, Salvation Unlimited (Washington, D.C.: Review and Herald, 1974), p.16.

based on isolated scriptural texts scattered all through the Bible. Theologians throughout history have pulled these texts together to establish this doctrine. One of the key texts used for this doctrine is Gen 3, the story of the fall. However, upon closer examination we find that Gen 3 refers to a number of results from Adam's sin - guilt (3:8), enmity (3:15), pain in child-birth (3:16), hard work (3:19), death (3:19), etc. - but human depravity is not specifically mentioned. This may explain why, apart from possible references to Genesis 3 in Isaiah 43:27 and Hosea 6:7, the Old Testament nowhere explicitly connects the fall with the universal sinfulness of man. It describes the reality of sin and states that man is a sinner from birth, but it does not explain how sin is passed on from generation to generation.

Paul is the only biblical writer who clearly connects the fall of man with our death and our sinful nature. In I Cor. 15:21-22 he teaches that death has its origin in Adam, "For as by man came death, by man came also the resurrection of the dead. For as in Adam all die, even so in Christ shall all be made alive." In Romans 5:12 he says that sin too comes from Adam, "Wherefore, as by one man sin entered into the world, and death by sin; and so death passed upon all men, for that all have sinned."

It is particularly the last part of Romans 5:12 which has caused considerable debate among interpreters. Does the phrase "all have sinned" refer to personal sins, committed by all, or to the fact that all men in some way sinned in Adam? As far as Greek Grammar is concerned, both interpretations are possible. If we choose the first interpretation, the meaning is that the result of Adam's sin was merely that he himself became subject to death, and thereafter, because "all have sinned", all men suffer the same fate. This seems to be the plain meaning of the text. The aorist *h'marton* "have sinned" is understood in the same way as in 3:23 "all have sinned and come short of the glory of God."

However, if Paul meant that all became subject to death, because of their own sins, the conclusion would logically be that all receive eternal life on the basis of the righteousness which they themselves achieved. But this is ruled out by Paul's statement in verses 17-19. Death came to all through the fall of one man (Adam), so likewise life is given to all because of the righteousness of one man (Christ).

The second interpretation, therefore, understands "all have sinned" to mean that "all men have sinned in Adam[40]. This is supported by an appeal to 2 Cor 5:14, the death of one was the death of all; so in Romans 5:12 the sin of one was the sin of all. Furthermore, this interpretation is strengthened by the immediate context in Romans 5; "many died through one man's trespass" (5:15), "because of one man's trespass, death reigned through that one man" (5:17), "by one man's disobedience many were made sinners" (5:19, RSV). Thus Paul seems to teach that Adam's sin produced in mankind not only the penalty of death, but also a real state of sin.[41]

> "Finally, the aorist *hemarton* "have sinned" is linked to the other two aorists in verse 12; "sin entered (*eiselthen*) into the world" and "death went through

---

[40] Anders Nygren, Commentary on Romans (Philadelphia: Fortress Press, 1949), pp.214-215.
[41] A.M. Dubarle, The Biblical Doctrine of Original Sin (London: G. Chapman, 1964, p.147.

(*dielthen*) to all men" All three are seen as historical aorists indicating what happened in Eden."[42]

How the sin of Adam resulted in the sin and death of mankind, and how Romans 5:12 is to be understood correctly, has been the subject of discussion for more than two millennia.

IV. HISTORY OF THE DOCTRINE OF ORIGINAL SIN

THE APOCRYPHA

During the intertestamental period Ben Sira (ca. 180 B.C.) the author of *The Wisdom of Jesus the Son of Sirach* (also called Ecclesiasticus) wrote, "From a woman was the beginning of sin; and because of her we all die" (Sir 25:24). And the unknown author of *The Wisdom of Solomon* (ca. 150-50 B.C.) stated that, "God created man incorruptible, and to the image of his own likeness he made him. But by the envy of the devil death came into the world, and they who belong to him will experience it" (Wis 2:23-25).

These are the earliest extra-biblical sources teaching that death is the result of the sin of Adam and Eve. However, a specific statement that the sin of the first parents is transmitted to each of their descendants - the idea of original sin - is nowhere to be found."[43]

THE JEWISH APOCALYPTIC LITERATURE

Jewish apocalyptic literature flourished between 200 B.C. and A.D. 150. These writings deal primarily with the future, the end of this world, rather than with the present. Frequently in the form of visionary experiences they describe the spiritual world of angels and cosmic powers; and they major on the purposes of God rather than on the actions of men. Among the best known examples are the *Books of Enoch*, the *Fourth Book of Ezra*, the *Apocalypses of Baruch*, the *Book of Jubilees*, and the *Assumption of Moses*. From Qumran comes *The War of the Sons of Light against the Sons of Darkness*.[44]

The idea of death as an inherited penalty is mentioned a number of times in these writings. Some authors put the blame for death on Eve, others on Adam.

Apocalypse of Moses (1st century A.D.)[45]

14:2   Adam said to Eve, "Why have you wrought destruction among us and brought upon us great wrath, which is death gaining rule over all our race?"

4 Ezra (100 A.D.)

---

[42] R.C.H. Lenski, St. Paul's Epistle to the Romans (Minneapolis: Minnesota, 1936), p.360.
[43] Johannes B. Bauer, Encyclopedia of Biblical Theology (London: Sheed and Ward, 1970), p.621.
[44] J. D. Douglas, ed., The New International Dictionary of the Christian Church (Exeter: Paternoster Press, 1978), p.52.
[45] All ancient quotations in this section are taken from James H. Charlesworth, ed., The Old Testament Pseudepigrapha 2 vols. (New York: Doubleday, 1983).

3:7   Ezra speaking to God says: "And you laid upon him one commandment of yours; but he transgressed it, and immediately you appointed death for him and his descendants."

2 Baruch (2nd century A.D.)

23:4   "When Adam sinned and death was decreed against those who were to be born, the multitude of those who would be born was numbered."

54:15   "Adam sinned first and brought death upon all who were not in his own time."

56:6   "For when he transgressed, untimely death came into being..."

Apart from death as the consequence of Adam's fall, 4 Ezra 7:118 seems to indicate that in Adam all his descendants fell, "O Adam, what have you done? For though it was you who sinned, the fall was not yours alone, but ours also who are your descendants." And in the *Life of Adam and Eve* (1st century A.D.) the sin of all generations is traced back to Eve, "And Adam said to Eve, what have you done? You brought upon us a great wound, transgression and sin in all our generations" (44:2).

In Rabbinic thinking man was created with a good impulse (*yetzer ha-tob*) and an evil impulse (*yetzer ha-ra^c*) which struggle for the mastery in man's heart. Thus in 4 Ezra 3:20-22 we read:

For the first Adam, burdened with an evil heart, transgressed and was overcome, as were also all who were descended from him. Thus the disease became permanent; the law was in the people's heart along with the evil root, but what was good departed, and evil remained."

Through the study of the Torah man could protect himself against the evil impulses of his heart.[46] Thus the Tannaim, the religious thinkers cited in the Mishnah, had God saying to man as it were: "If I created the Evil Inclination to tempt you into error, I also created the Torah to keep you from error."[47]

We see then in Jewish literature an attempt to grapple with the question of sin and its heredity, but an unambiguous statement concerning original sin and its propagation is lacking.

THE WRITINGS OF THE CHURCH FATHERS

The Gnostic controversy, in which the problem of evil played an important role, forced the Early Church to define the doctrines of the original state and of the fall.

The Greek Fathers

The Greek Fathers viewed man as having been created "neither mortal nor immortal, but capable of both; his destiny depended on how he exercised his free will."[48] When man fell he became mortal and corrupt. This physical corruption was seen to be propagated in the human

---

[46] William D. Davis, Paul and Rabbinic Judaism (Philadelphia: Fortress Press, 1980), pp.21-22.
[47] Nathan Ausubel, The Book of Jewish Knowledge (New York: Crown Publishers, 1964), p.506.
[48] J. N. D. Kelly, Early Christian Doctrine, 5th ed., (London: A. and C. Black, 1977), p.168.

race, but was not considered sin in itself. Neither did it involve mankind in guilt.[49] Romans 5:12-21 was generally interpreted in terms of the death to which man became subject. The sin in Romans 5:12d "for that all have sinned" was understood to refer to man's personal sin.

Irenaeus (died c.195), bishop of Lyon, viewed all men as being seminally present in Adam, the head of the human race. By virtue of this union, all men were conceived of as existing in Adam and hence as being personally involved in Adam's sin. "In the first Adam", he wrote, "we offended God, not fulfilling His commandment . . . To Him alone were we debtors, whose ordinance we transgressed in the beginning."[50] However, he denied that children share in Adam's guilt because sin always originates in the free choice of man.[51]

Origen (c.185-254), a theologian in Alexandria, at first taught the theory of an inborn sinfulness as the result of the fall of all individual souls in a previous, celestial existence. Later, however, he accepted the doctrine of inherited corruption, introduced by Adam's fall.[52]

To summarise: The Greek Fathers understood death to be the penalty for Adam's fall. They believed that all men were involved in Adam's sin and that it affected our moral nature. They taught that we inherit an evil and corrupt nature, but that no guilt is attached to it.

The Latin Fathers

Similar to the Greek Fathers, the Latin Fathers saw man's original state as one of supernatural blessedness. Adam and Eve, created immortal,[53] radiated perfect innocence and virtue, they were even exempt from the need of food.[54] Because of pride Adam fell and became mortal.

Tertullian (c.160-215), the founder of Latin theology, equated original sin with concupiscence (sexual lust) which, by inheritance, Adam passed on to his descendants.[55] He understood this in terms of the traducianist doctrine of the origin of the soul, which says that all individual souls were in some way contained in Adam from whom they ultimately derive. By his sin Adam is said to have infected the entire human race with his seed, making it the channel (*traducem*) of damnation.[56] He said:

"Every soul, then, by reason of its birth, has its nature in Adam until it is born again in Christ; moreover, it is unclean all the while that it remains without this regeneration; and because unclean, it is actively sinful, and suffuses even the flesh with its own shame."[57]

---

[49]Louis Berkhof, The History of Christian Doctrines (Grand Rapids: Baker Book House, 1975), p.128.
[50]Kelly, p.172.
[51]Julius Gross, Entstehungsgeschichte des Erbsündendogmas, 2 vols. (München: E. Reinhardt Verlag, 1960), 1:94.
[52]James Hastings, ed. Encyclopedia of Religion and Ethics, 13 vols. (Edinburgh: T. and T. Clark, 1956), 9:560.
[53]Gross, I:113.
[54]Kelly, p.353.
[55]Gross, I:117.
[56]Kelly, p.175.
[57]Tertullian, A Treatise on the Soul, 40 (ANF 3:220).

Ambrose (339-397) and Ambrosiaster (4th century) two other Latin fathers strongly emphasised the idea of man's solidarity in sin by virtue of the participation of all in Adam's sin.

Ambrose: "In Adam I fell, in Adam I was cast out of Paradise, in Adam I died. How should God restore me, unless he find me in Adam, justified in Christ, exactly as in that first Adam I was subject to guilt and destined to death?"[58]

Ambrosiaster: "It is therefore plain that all men sinned in Adam as in a lump (*quasi in massa*). For Adam himself was corrupted by sin and all whom he begat were born under sin. Thus we are all sinners from him, since we all derive from him.[59]

Nevertheless, neither of these writers seems to have considered this inherited sin as worthy of punishment. Ambrose explicitly distinguishes our inherited unrighteousness for which we shall not be punished from our personal sins for which we shall be punished.[60] And Ambrosiaster in his interpretation of Romans 5:12-21 attributes the death of all men to their imitation of Adam's sin.[61]

There seems to be a certain amount of ambiguity and uncertainty in their statements. On the one hand Ambrose speaks of man being subject to guilt in Adam (see above) on the other hand he denies that Adam's guilt is somehow transferred to us. Possibly this is an indication of the tension these writers experienced as they wrestled with the problem of original sin.

Pelagius (5th century) was a well-educated Briton, trained in law, who appeared in Rome around the year 400 teaching Christian perfection and calling for repentance and penitence.

According to Pelagius, Adam was created with a middle nature, i.e., neither holy nor sinful, but with a capacity for both good and evil. He was created mortal, but with an entirely free and undetermined will. He chose to sin yet his fall injured no one but himself. Pelagius denied any hereditary transmission of a sinful nature or of guilt, thus man is still born in the same condition in which Adam was before the fall. There are no evil tendencies or desires in man's nature. The only difference between Adam and man is that the latter has the evil example before him. Sin does not consist in wrong affections or desires, but only in a separate act of the will.[62] Sin's universality, said Pelagius, is due to wrong education, to bad example, and to a long-established habit of sinning. "By force of habit, sin attains a power akin to that of nature - sin becomes as it were 'second nature'".[63]

God's grace for Pelagius is primarily God's gift of man's good nature with its capability of freely choosing and doing the good. He saw grace in terms of "external gifts and natural

---

[58]Kelly, p.354.
[59]Ibid.
[60]Ibid., p.355.
[61]George Vandervelde, Original Sin (Amsterdam: Rodopi, N.V., 1975), p.10.
[62]Berkhof, pp.132-133.
[63]Vandervelde, p.12.

endowments, such as man's rational nature, the revelation of God in Scripture, and the example of Christ."[64]

Jesus Christ, according to Pelagius, is the fullest concretisation of the original grace of nature. As the direct image of God, Christ is a mirror of what man is and ought to be. By beholding Christ man becomes changed into His image because Christ's example effects a resonating response in man's deepest being, i.e., in his *memoria* - the noetic ontological link with his original nature.[65]

Pelagianism with its rosy view of human nature was condemned at various councils and finally anathematised at the Council of Ephesus in 431.[66]

Augustine (354-430),[67] the greatest of the Latin Fathers, was bishop of Hippo Regius in North Africa. He became the chief opponent of Pelagius.

Augustine conceived of four stages in the history of man: before the fall, after the fall, after conversion, in perfection. In the Edenic state man possessed a full measure of freedom. He could choose between good and evil and was thus able to refrain from sin (*posse non peccare*). This ability was not an innate ability, not a natural endowment, it was a gift of divine grace.

Since free will contains the possibility of a fall, the first sin was occasioned by free will. Through the fall man lost the gift of grace and with it the freedom which constituted the ability to choose the good. For when grace was lost, human nature was changed. His basic attitude changed. Whereas before the fall man's life was directed towards God, now it was directed toward self. Self-love was substituted for the love of God. The baser powers of human nature - concupiscence - assumed a dominating position. In isolated instances the will can overcome concupiscence but the direction of the will nevertheless remains the same.

Man after the fall no longer has the power to choose the good, he now has a compulsion to sin. He is no longer able not to sin (*non posse non peccare*). This does not mean he cannot do isolated good deeds, but the direction of his will is toward evil. Within this basic attitude towards evil man still has a free will, but man is free only to sin.[68]

Augustine believed that the whole human race was seminally present in Adam and therefore also actually sinned in him. He said, "In the misdirected choice of that one man all sinned in him, since all were that one man, from whom on that account they all severally derive original sin."[69] Through sexual procreation Adam transmitted his fallen nature (guilt and corruption) to his posterity. Thus man, separated from God, burdened with guilt, and under the dominion of evil,

---

[64]Berkhof, p.133.
[65]Vandervelde, p.13.
[66]Kelly, p.361.
[67]This section is based on Bengt Hägglund, <u>History of Theology</u> (Saint Louis: Concordia Publishing House, 1968), pp. 135-136, and Berkhof, pp.134-135.
[68]Kelly, p.365.
[69]Ibid., p.364. In this argument Augustine relied on the Vulgate translation of Rom 5:12 which says, "**in quo omnes peccaverunt**," i.e., "in whom all sinned." All modern translations recognise that the Greek "**eph ho**" has the sense of "because" or "considering that."

cannot will that which is good in the sight of God, i.e., that which springs from the motive of love to God.

Here we have the first clear definition of original sin as it came to be accepted by most Christians from then on.

Salvation for Augustine is all of God's grace, but this grace includes the regeneration of man. Man's will is altered and he can truly do that which is good and thus he can become God's co-worker in faith. Man is saved by faith, but this faith also does that which is good. Deeds that originate in love are thought of as being meritorious and will eventually be rewarded. But such merit can only be won by grace.[70] The actual basis of salvation, for Augustine, is grace alone (not man's free will), but that which is of note in the work of grace is not so much the "alien" righteousness of Christ which is imputed to us but rather the change which takes place in the life of the newborn individual.

To summarise: Like the Greek Fathers, the Latin Fathers before Augustine taught that death and original corruption are the result of man's participation in Adam's sin. Most of them, however, denied that man's corruption deserves punishment. Augustine, in the controversy with Pelagius, formulated the classical doctrine of original sin which includes death, corruption, and guilt.

FROM AQUINAS TO ARMINIUS

Thomas Aquinas (1224-1274) was the greatest philosopher and theologian of the medieval church. Building on the teachings of Augustine and Anselm (1033-1109), Thomas Aquinas defined original sin as the privation of original justice or righteousness.[71] God created man and woman in a state of original righteousness which included supernatural grace and the exemption from concupiscence and death. Furthermore, in this state of original righteousness, reason and the will of man were in submission to God. When Adam rebelled, the supernatural gift of grace was withdrawn and the interior harmony of his nature as well as his submission to God were lost.[72] This is the condition of original sin in which all men are born. Original sin for Aquinas included guilt since he viewed humanity as constituting a single body in the sense that a civic community can be spoken of as one body.[73]

In opposition to Thomas Aquinas the Reformers maintained that original sin is more than a mere absence of original justice. Like Augustine they saw original sin as a total corruption of human nature (total depravity). They considered even the first movements of the desires, which

---

[70]This is different from the Reformers who said that only faith in Christ and His merits justifies a man; human works do not enter in.
[71]Vandervelde, p.28.
[72]Ibid., p.29.
[73]Ibid., p.30.

tend in the direction of sin, to be sins - indwelling sins which make man guilty and worthy of condemnation.[74]

The Council of Trent (1545-1563) was one of the most important Councils in the history of the Roman Catholic Church. It was convened to halt the continuing success of the Protestant Movement. While the emperor hoped the Council would reunite western Christendom as a means of strengthening the imperial power against the Turks, the pope wanted the Council to anathematise every form of Protestant heresy. In the end the council provided the foundation for a revitalisation of Catholicism and the eventual success of the Counter-Reformation.

In regard to the question of original sin, the aim of the Council of Trent was to correct the teaching of the Reformers on the radical corruption of human nature by Adam's sin. The decrees of this Council represent the most comprehensive and definitive statement on original sin issued by the Roman Catholic Church.

Canon One[75]

"If anyone does not profess that the first man Adam immediately lost the justice and holiness in which he was constituted when he disobeyed the command of God in paradise; and that, through the offence of this sin, he incurred the wrath and the indignation of God, and consequently incurred the death with which God had previously threatened him and, together with death, bondage in the power who from that time "had the empire of death" (Heb 2:14), that is, of the devil; "and that it is the whole Adam, both body and soul, who was changed for the worse through the offence of this sin": let him be anathema.

Canon Two

"If anyone asserts that Adam's sin was injurious only to Adam and not to his descendants, and that it was for himself alone that he lost the holiness and justice which he had received from God, and not for us also; or that after his defilement by the sin of disobedience, he "transmitted to the whole human race only death" and punishment "of the body but not sin also, which is the death of the soul": let him be anathema. "For he contradicts the words of the Apostle: 'Through one man sin entered into the world, and through sin death, and so death passed upon all men; in whom all have sinned'" (Rom 5:12).

Canon Three

"If anyone asserts that this sin of Adam, which is one by origin, and which is communicated to all men by propagation not by imitation (*propagatione, non imitatione transfusum*), and which is in all men and proper to each, is taken away either through the powers of human nature or through a remedy other than the merit of the one mediator, our Lord Jesus Christ who reconciled us to God in his blood, "being made unto us justice, sanctification and redemption" (1 Cor 1:30);

---

[74]Berkhof, p.147
[75]These texts are from Vandervelde, pp.33-39.

or denies that, through the sacrament of baptism rightly conferred in the form of the Church, this merit of Jesus Christ is applied both to adults and to infants: let him be anathema. Because "there is no other name under heaven given to men by which we must saved" (Acts 4:12). Hence that voice: "Behold the lamb of God, behold him who takes away the sins of the world" (cf. John 1:29). And: "All you who have been baptised into Christ, have put on Christ" (Gal 3:27).

Canon Four

"If anyone denies that newly born infants are to be baptised", even though they may have been born of baptised parents, "or says that they are indeed baptised for the remission of sins but that they do not derive anything of the original sin from Adam that must be expiated in the bath of regeneration" *to obtain eternal life*; "and, consequently, that for them the form of baptism - 'for the remission of sins' - is to be understood, not in a true, but in a false sense: let him be anathema. Because the words of the Apostle:'Through one man sin entered into the world, and through sin death, and so *death* passed upon all men; in whom all have sinned' (Rom 5:12), cannot be understood in any other way than as the Catholic Church everywhere has always understood them. Because of this rule of faith", *from a tradition of the apostles* "even infants, who have not yet been able to commit any personal sins, are truly baptised for the remission of sins, that in them that which they have *con*tracted [*contraxerunt*] by generation may be washed away by regeneration" (DS, 223). *"For unless a man be born again of water and the Holy Spirit, he cannot enter into the kingdom of God"* (John 3:5).

Canon Five

"If anyone denies that through the grace of our Lord Jesus Christ conferred in baptism the guilt of original sin is remitted, or even asserts that everything having the true and proper nature of sin is not taken away but is only brushed over or not imputed: let him be anathema. For God hates nothing in the regenerated because "there is no condemnation for those who are truly buried with Christ by means of baptism into death" (Rom 6:4), who "do not walk according to the flesh" (Rom 8:1), but putting off the old man and putting on the new man "which was created according to God" (cf. Eph 4:22ff.; Col 3:9f.), are made innocent, without stain, pure, no longer hateful, but beloved sons of God, "heirs indeed of God and joint heirs with Christ" (Rom 8:17), so that absolutely nothing delays their entrance into heaven. It is the mind of this council and it professes that concupiscence or the tinder [of sin] remains in the baptised; but since it is left to provide a trial, it has no power to injure those who do not consent and who, by the grace of Jesus Christ, manfully resist. Moreover, those "who compete according to the rules will be crowned" (2 Tim 2:5). As for this concupiscence which the Apostle sometimes calls "sin" (Rom 6: 12ff.), this holy council declares that the Catholic Church has never understood it to be called sin as being truly and properly sin in those born again, but because it is from sin and inclines to sin. If anyone thinks the contrary: let him be anathema.

The Council of Trent rather than defining original sin described the results of it - loss of original justice and holiness, death, and bondage in the power of the devil (Canon One). Adam's sin and its results are passed on to his inheritance (Canon Two) by propagation not by imitation (Canon Three). Thus Adam's sin by virtue of the imputation of this single original sin to all men is inherent in each human being.

Original sin is taken away by baptism which is the application of Christ's death to adults and infants (Canon Three). Thus, even infants who have not yet committed any personal sin must be baptised (Canon Four) in order for the guilt of the original sin to be remitted (Canon Five).

Canon Five is particularly aimed at the teaching of the Reformers, especially at Luther who held "that concupiscence, understood as man's culpable bias to evil, remains in the Christian and constitutes sin in a true and proper sense."[76] Thus the Christian, according to Luther, can be described as *simul justus et peccator*: "just, because in faith he shares in Christ's redemption and, in the power of that faith, fights against the evil within; sinner, because precisely this evil, 'invincible concupiscence', continues to dwell in him."[77]

Like Luther, John Calvin (1609-63) believed that original sin is a hereditary depravity which produces in man the works of the flesh. This corruption, Calvin taught, is not, as Augustine thought, primarily found in the sensual appetites, but also in the higher faculties of man.[78]

Jacobus Arminius (1560-1609) was a Dutch Reformed professor at the University of Leyden in Holland who came to question some of the teachings of Calvinism.

According to Arminius we receive from Adam a corrupt nature but not Adam's guilt.

We begin life without original righteousness, unable without divine help to obey God's commandments, and destined for death. As a matter of justice, therefore, God grants to each person a special gift of the Holy Spirit (prevenient grace) which neutralises the corruption received from Adam. It makes obedience possible, provided the human will cooperates, which it still has power to do.[79]

Evil tendencies, said Arminius, may be called sin, but they do not in themselves involve guilt or punishment, neither are we accounted guilty because of Adam's sin. "God imputes to each man his inborn tendencies to evil only when he consciously and voluntarily appropriates and ratifies these in spite of the power to the contrary, which, in justice to man, God has specially communicated."[80]

Summary

During the first 1600 years of the Christian era, we find that three views dominated the history of the doctrine of original sin.

---

[76] Vandervelde, p.39.
[77] Ibid.
[78] Berkhof, p.147.
[79] A. H. Strong, Systematic Theology (Valley Forge: The Judson Press, 1967), p.601.
[80] Ibid.

1. <u>The Pelagian View</u>: In this view Adam transmitted neither corruption nor guilt to his descendants. His sin is only a bad example. Hence baptism does not remove sin or guilt in infants since they have none. Physical death is not the penalty of sin, but an original law of nature. Romans 5:12d, "death passed upon all men, for that all have sinned", means: "all incurred eternal death by sinning after Adam's example." Unitarians hold this view today.[81]

2. <u>The Augustinian View</u>: In this view Adam transmitted both corruption and guilt to his descendants. It holds that God imputes the sin of Adam directly (immediately) to all his posterity, because when Adam sinned all humanity was seminally present in him as its head. Romans 5:12d refers to physical, spiritual and eternal death for all men, because all sinned in Adam their natural head.[82] Luther and Calvin held this view and the Roman Catholic Church[83] and Lutheranism are its modern representatives.

3. <u>The Arminian View</u>: In this view Adam transmitted corruption but no guilt to his descendants. The state of sin into which man is born does not in itself involve guilt or punishment. Only when man consciously and voluntarily sins and he thereby ratifies his corrupt nature, then God imputes to each man his inborn tendencies to evil. Romans 5:12d is understood to mean that physical and spiritual death is experienced by all men because all consent to their inborn sinfulness by acts of transgressions. The Methodist Church is the modern representative of this view.[84]

THE POST-REFORMATION ERA

In the post-reformation era three further theories (variations) concerning the imputation of Adam's sin were developed.

The Federal Theory:[85] This theory originated with Johannes Cocceius (1603-69), a German theologian who taught at Leiden in Holland, and is also called "the theory of the Covenants."

According to this view, God entered into a covenant with Adam as the federal head of the human race, stating that if Adam obeyed he and his posterity would receive eternal life. However, if Adam were to disobey, depravity and death would be the lot of all humanity.

Because Adam sinned, God accounts all his descendants as sinners, i.e., God immediately creates each soul of Adam's posterity with a corrupt and depraved nature which always leads to sin and which is itself sin. Thus, a corrupt nature came upon the human race through God's covenant and not through Adam's sin.

In contrast to Augustine, who believed that all men sinned in Adam, the Federal theory teaches that Adam's sin is imputed to his posterity. Thus Romans 5:12 "death passed unto all

---

[81]Ibid., p.597.
[82]Ibid., pp.619-620.
[83]There is a difference between Catholicism and Lutheranism in regard to the question whether the Christian remains a sinner after baptism. Luther said man remains a sinner, the Council of Trent in canon five denied it.
[84]Ibid., pp.601-602.
[85]Strong, pp.612-613.

men, for that all sinned", means: "physical, spiritual and eternal death came to all because all were regarded and treated as sinners." The Reformed Church is a modern representative of this theory.

Mediate Imputation Theory:[86] Placens (1606-1655), professor of theology at Saumur in France, taught that all men are born physically and morally depraved due to Adam's sin. This inborn sinfulness which has descended by natural laws of propagation from Adam to all his posterity and which is the consequence, not the penalty, of Adam's transgression is the source of all actual sin, and is in itself sin. The soul is immediately (directly) created by God, but it becomes actively corrupt as soon as it is united to the body.

In a sense, therefore, Adam's sin (guilt) is imputed to his descendants, not immediately, as if they had been in Adam or were represented in him, but mediately through the corrupt nature which resulted from Adam's sin. In Romans 5:12, "death passed unto all men, for that all sinned", means: "death physical, spiritual, and eternal passed upon all men, because all sinned by possessing a depraved nature."

New School or New Haven Theory:[87] It developed at Yale University (New Haven, Conn.) under the leadership of Timothy Dwight (1752-1817) and Nathanael Taylor (1786-1858) and was directed particularly against Calvin's doctrine of predestination.

New Haven Theology taught that a newborn enters life with a predisposition to sin, but this predisposition was not called sinful since nothing but the voluntary act of transgressing a known law can, in this view, be called sin. Thus infants do not need a Saviour. Sin is not viewed as a state, but solely as an act, hence man does not sin until he reaches the age of moral consciousness. Physical death is the result of Adam's sin, whereas spiritual death is the result of one's own sin. In Romans 5:12, "death passed on all men, for that all sinned", means: "spiritual death passed on all men, because all men have actually and personally sinned."

To summarise: The Federal and Placean theories are akin to the Augustinian theory, the New Haven theory is similar to the Arminian position. In the Augustinian tradition man is born a sinner and therefore sins; in the Arminian tradition sin is confined to an act, thus man is a sinner because he sins.

V. THE DOCTRINE OF ORIGINAL SIN IN ADVENTISM[88]

THE EARLY DECADES

The fledgling Seventh-day Adventist Church was reared in the New England context and was initially influenced by the New Haven Theory of original sin.

George Storrs (1796-1867), a Methodist minister who left his church in 1840 over the question

---

[86]Ibid., p.617.
[87]Ibid., pp. 606-607. Some Presbyterians and Congregationalists support this view.
[88]This section is to a large degree based on Edwin H. Zackrison, "Seventh-day Adventists and Original Sin" (unpublished Ph.D. dissertation, Andrews University, 1984).

of natural immortality, became the central figure in the earliest Adventist treatment of original sin. His book, *An Inquiry: Are the Souls of the Wicked Immortal? In Six Sermons* (1842),[89] was widely circulated among Adventists and adopted by many.[90] Storr's views can be summarised in five main points:

1. Man is to be viewed as a holistic unit, indivisible. Whatever affects any aspect of man affects all of man, i.e., he does not have a soul, he is a soul.

2. In his original creation man was made neutral both in his character and his essential constitutive nature. He was neither holy nor unholy, mortal nor immortal. Character (good or bad) is the result of choices in relation to God's will. Mortality is the result of Adam's disobedience. By the same token immortality would have been the result of obedience and access to the tree of life in Eden.

3. The nature of the penalty for original sin, i.e., Adam's sin, is to be seen as literal, physical, temporal, or actual death - the opposite of life, i.e., the cessation of being. By no stretch of the scriptural facts can death be spiritualised as depravity. God did not punish Adam by making him a sinner. That was Adam's own doing. All die the first death because of Adam's sin regardless of their moral character - children included.

4. The role of the Atonement of Christ is to give a second probation, as it were, to the victims of original sin. Consequently, everyone can demonstrate his own faithfulness by obedience to God and eternal destiny is decided on the basis of personal sin, not Adam's sin.

5. Finally, the "corrupt" nature that all of Adam's posterity inherit from him is not to be perceived as depravity but as a dying nature - "dying to die", or doomed to die - mortality. Original sin does not mean spiritual death for man, rather it means a dying condition or state of man.[91]

Early Adventists accepted Storr's view of sin and death and publicised them in the pages of the *Review and Herald* in 1854 and 1855 through articles by J. M. Stephenson,[92] D. P. Hall,[93] and J. N. Loughborough.[94]

J. M. Stephenson, whose series of articles was later published in book form, believed that Adam's posterity was involved in his sin by proxy, or by their representative, not in actuality.

---

[89] L. E. Froom, The Conditionalist Faith of Our Fathers, 2 vols. (Washington, D.C.: Review and Herald, 1966), 2:307.
[90] J. White, Life Incidents (Battle Creek: SDA Pub. Assn., 1868), p.154.
[91] Zackrison, pp.224-225.
[92] J. M. Stephenson, "The Atonement," RH 6, Aug.-Dec., 1854.
[93] D. P. Hall, "The Mortality of Man," RH 6, Aug.-Sept. 1854; "Man Not Immortal," RH 6, Sept.-Dec. 1854.
[94] J. N. Loughborough, "Is the Soul Immortal?" RH 7, Sept.-Dec. 1855.

Due to the fall Adam became mortal and passed a "mortal, corruptible, dying nature" on to his children. Yet because it was Adam who sinned personally, his posterity are not held personally accountable even though they now share his condition. Accountability only comes with personal sin.

Thus no one dies for personal sin except those who are lost, but all die the first death whether they personally sin or not. Since infants have no personal sin, they are automatically covered by the perfect Atonement of Christ, even though they must die for original sin.[95]

> "Both Testaments represent man as being exposed to death for personal sins. But, inasmuch as all die for original sin, none can die for personal sin, without a resurrection to a second life; hence the Bible teaches that there will be a resurrection of the dead, 'both of the just and the unjust.' To be preceded by a second life, it must, in the nature of things, be a second death; hence while the penalty for personal sin is only one death, yet in reference to its relation to the penalty for original sin, it will be a second death."[96]

Like Storr, Stephenson used "original sin" to mean "Adam's sin." He saw the result of Adam's sin only in terms of a dying physical nature not as spiritual death or a depraved nature. He understood man's spiritual lostness only as the result of one's personal transgression rather than as the result of original sin.[97]

James White (1821-1881) was in basic agreement with this when he suggested that children are innocent and born in a state of grace. Though he admitted that they possess a fallen and corrupt nature, he did not believe that they are guilty because of it. "Christ has cancelled the guilt of Adamic transgression, and in the resurrection of the last day, all the effects of the fall on the innocent, or justified, will be removed, not before."[98]

In the early decades E. G. White (1827-1915) said little on the subject, though she differed from her husband in regard to little children.

> "Children are the lawful prey of the enemy, because they are not subjects of grace, have not experienced the cleansing power of the blood of Jesus, and the evil angels have access to these children; and some parents are careless and suffer them to work with but little restraint."[99]

The most prolific Adventist writer on the subject of Adam's sin during the early decades was Uriah Smith (1832-1903), long-time editor of the Adventist Review. Like Storrs and Stephenson, Smith believed that Adam had a middle nature - created without morality - and that the penalty of Adam's sin was physical not spiritual death. He understood spiritual death to be a reality of

---

[95] Stephenson, "The Atonement" RH 6:2 (August 22, 1854):10.
[96] Ibid.
[97] Zackrison, p.235.
[98] James White, "The Kingdom of God," RH 5:20 (June 13, 1854): 153.
[99] E. G. White, "The Duty of Parents to Their Children," RH 6:6 (Sept. 19, 1854): 46.

man's sinful existence, but he viewed this as a result of Adam's sin not as the penalty for it. This was in contrast to the generally held Protestant opinion that man's punishment was death - spiritual (state of sin), temporal (separation of body and soul), and eternal (eternal misery).[100] Smith's definition of "total depravity", i.e., "our inability to render, unaided by Christ, acceptable obedience to God",[101] reflects the moderate views of the New Haven theology.[102] The state of sin is really the actual sinning of the individual and only personal sins not his nature decide the fate of man.[103]

Thus, for early Adventists the result of Adam's sin was mortality - a dying nature - physical death. Sometimes Adventists referred to this as the sinful nature: "Remember that a dying nature and a sinful nature are identical."[104] Because of their adherence to conditional immortality, Adventists first studied original sin from an anthropological perspective.

A SHIFT IN UNDERSTANDING

The anthropological emphasis continued until the 1880s. At that time, particularly after 1888 when a new emphasis on righteousness by faith emerged from the Minneapolis General Conference, the focus of original sin studies shifted from anthropology to soteriology. As early as 1870 E. G. White had written:

> "The sin of Adam and Eve caused a fearful separation between God and man. And here Christ steps in between fallen man and God, and says to man, You may yet come to the Father; there is a plan devised through which God can be reconciled to man, and man to God; and through a mediator you can approach God."[105]

This theme of separation was taken up in 1888 by L. A. Smith, assistant editor of the Review, who argued for the moral effects of separation from God. He believed that the Fall of Adam affected the physical, mental and moral sides of man. Man sins because he is morally deranged; and all mankind are "heirs by nature" of this diseased moral nature.[106] By the turn of the century Seventh-day Adventists had come to consider original sin in terms of separation from God.

In regard to the moral derangement, early Adventists believed that it was acquired more by imitation than by physical inheritance, for it is not sin or guilt that the head of the race passed on

---

[100] Albert Stone, "Thou Shalt Surely Die," RH 22:24 (Nov. 10, 1863):190.
[101] U. Smith, "Perpetuity of the Moral Law," RH 14:6 (June 30, 1859):45.
[102] Zackrison, p.261. Cf. When . . . I say that mankind are entirely depraved by nature, I do not mean that their nature is itself sinful, nor that their nature is the physical or efficient cause of their sinning; but I mean that their nature is the occasion, or reason of their sinning - that such is their nature, that in all the appropriate circumstances of their being, they will sin and only sin. . . When the Apostle asserts, that mankind are by nature sinners, he must mean simply that such is their nature that uniformly in all the appropriate circumstances of their being, they will sin. (Nathaniel Taylor, Concio ad Clerum 2 [Ahlstrom, Theology in America, p. 224]), Zackrison, p.335.
[103] U. Smith, "What is the Penalty of the Law?" RH 9:23 (April 9, 1857):181.
[104] E. Goodrich, "Grace Through Unrighteousness," RH 16:19 (Sept 25, 1860):149.
[105] E. G. White, "Christian Recreation," RH 35:24 (May 31, 1870):185-186.
[106] L. A. Smith, "The Irrational Nature of Man," RH 65:45 (Nov. 13, 1888):715.

to his children but simply death, and a dying nature.[107] Ellen White, however, from the 1880s on clearly identified it with the inherent natural depravity of the heart.

> "Moral derangement, which we call *depravity*, finds ample room to work, and an influence is exerted by men, women, and youth professing to be Christians that is low, sensual, devilish."[108]

> "Bad habits are more easily formed than good habits, and the bad habits are given up with more difficulty. The *natural depravity of the heart* accounts for this well-known fact - that it takes far less labor to demoralise the youth, to corrupt their ideas of moral and religious character, than to engraft upon their character the enduring, pure, and uncorrupted habits of righteousness and truth. . . . In our present fallen state all that is needed is to give up the mind and character to its natural tendencies."[109]

> "They (Adam and Eve) were told that their nature had become depraved by sin; they had lessened their strength to resist evil, and had opened the way for Satan to gain more ready access to them. In their innocence they had yielded to temptation; and now, in a state of conscious guilt, they would have less power to maintain their integrity."[110]

> "Because of sin his [Adam's] posterity was born with inherent propensities of disobedience."[111]

> "At its very source human nature was corrupted. And ever since then sin has continued its hateful work, reaching from mind to mind. Every sin committed awakens the echoes of the original sin."[112]

> "There is in his nature a bent to evil, a force which, unaided, he cannot resist."[113]

There is a question as to whether E. G. White understands this depravity to be sin or not, i.e., is man guilty before he commits an act of sin simply because he is depraved or not? E. Zackrison seems to think not,[114] whereas R. Olson believes that our sinful nature (depravity) also needs forgiveness. In support of his position he quotes from 5 Testimonies, page 645, "God will be

---

[107]J. N. Andrews, "Institution of the Sabbath," RH 16:1-2 (May 29, 1860):10.
[108]Ellen G. White, Letter 26d, 1887, reprinted in In Heavenly Places, p. 196. (Emphasis mine).
[109]Idem, Letter 26d, 1887, ibid., p.195.
[110]Idem, Patriarchs and Prophets, p.61.
[111]Idem, Letter 8, 1895, reprinted in Nichol, ed. SDA Bible Commentary, 5:1128.
[112]Idem, "The Warfare between Good and Evil," RH 78:16 (April 16, 1901):241.
[113]Idem, Education (Mountain View, 1903), p.29.
[114]Zackrison, p.335, n.1.

better glorified if we confess the secret, inbred corruption of the heart to Jesus alone than if we open its recesses to finite, erring man."[115]

Following E. G. White's lead, a number of Adventist writers during the 1890s took a decided turn toward a more radical expression of original sin than in previous decades. E. R. Jones, a minister from Healdsburg wrote:

> "By one man's disobedience many were made sinners" (Rom 5:19). None will deny that this refers to the inherited depravity, the sinful nature and tendency in which, through disobedience, every single soul of Adam's race is born."[116]

F. J. Hutchins, pioneer evangelist and medical missionary in Central America described Adam's legacy in these words:

> "First Adam lost his innocence and left us sinful; second, he lost his dominion, and left us homeless, without an inheritance, third, he lost his life, and left us dying, our life forfeited, and only a process of time required to demonstrate the fact by the power of death."[117]

By 1894, M. E. Kellogg could write that it was Adam's sin that left man with a "sinful nature which made him subject to the second death - eternal death."[118] This view clearly suggested that Adam's legacy was not simply physical mortality leading to the first death, but also spiritual depravity deserving the second death. However, in spite of these clear statements to the contrary, the old traditional view of Storrs persisted in different circles[119] and Uriah Smith continued until his death in 1903 to reiterate and repeat the view that Storrs had introduced sixty years before.[120]

VI. OUR PRESENT POSITION

In 1988 the Ministerial Association of the General Conference published the book *Seventh-day Adventists Believe ...*, a biblical exposition of our twenty-seven fundamental doctrines. In the chapter on the nature of man sin is declared to include: 'the transgression of the law' (1 John 3:4, KJV), a failure to act by anyone 'who knows the good he ought to do and doesn't do it' (Jas 4:14, NIV), and 'whatever is not from faith' (Rom 14:23)."[121] On the question of original sin it says:

> "Paul said, "In Adam all die" (1 Cor 15:22). In another place he noted, "Through one man sin entered the world, and death through sin, and thus death spread to all men, because all sinned" (Rom 5:12).

---

[115] Robert W. Olson, "Outline Studies on Christian Perfection and Original Sin", Insert to Ministry, Oct. 1970, p.29.
[116] E. R. Jones, "In the Flesh," RH 67:1 (Jan 7, 1890):2.
[117] F. J. Hutchins, "The True Object of Life," RH 69:7 (Feb. 16, 1892):98.
[118] M. E. Kellogg, "Life from the Dead," RH 71:42 (Oct. 23, 1894):644-645.
[119] See the Sabbath School Quarterly, Second Quarter (April 25, 1896):12.
[120] U. Smith, "The Resurrection of the Wicked," RH 70:27 (July 4, 1893):434.
[121] Seventh-day Adventists Believe . . . (Washington, D.C.: Review and Herald, 1988), p.89.

> "The human heart's corruption affects the total person. In this light Job exclaims, "Who can bring a clean thing out of an unclean? No one!" (Job 14:4). David said, "Behold, I was brought forth in iniquity, and in sin my mother conceived me" (Ps 51:5). And Paul stated that "the carnal mind is enmity against God; for it is not subject to the law of God, nor indeed can be. So then, those who are in the flesh cannot please God" (Rom 8:7,8). Before conversion, he pointed out, believers were "by nature children of wrath", just like the rest of humanity (Eph 2:3)."

> "Although as children we acquire sinful behavior through imitation, the above texts affirm that we inherit our basic sinfulness. The universal sinfulness of humanity is evidence that by nature we tend toward evil, not good."[122]

Thus the general consensus of Adventist scholars, as expressed in this book, defines sin as an act (1 John 3:4) as well as a state (Ps 51:5; Eph 2:3). We inherit a sinful nature (SIN) which, unless checked by the Holy Spirit, entices us to commit individual acts of transgression (sins).

The clearest expression of the hereditary nature of our innate sinfulness is found in Ps 51:5, "Behold I was shapen in iniquity; and in sin did my mother conceive me." The Seventh-day Adventist Bible Commentary observes concerning this text:

> "David recognised that children inherit natures with propensities to evil (see Job 14:4; Ps 58:3; PP 61,306; MH 372,373; GC 533). He did not seek to excuse his sin, but sought to stress the still greater need of God's mercy because of his inborn tendency to do evil." (see PP 64).[123]

SIN AS SEPARATION FROM GOD

The underlying cause of our sinful state (original corruption) is our separation from God. The first action of our first parents after their first sin was to hide (Gen 3:8). And mankind has followed in their footsteps ever since. Through the fall the close fellowship which Adam and Eve had enjoyed with their Maker was destroyed. In sinning man broke his relationship with God.

> "Man's removal from the garden of Eden was symbolic of that broken relationship. From then on he had to exist distant from God. And every human being, except one, has been born into this state of separation from God. Therefore, "babies die, not because they have actually sinned or are punished by God, but because they are now part of this alienation from the source of life. All men are born self-centred, not God-centred."[124]

Self-centredness was the issue in the fall of Satan, "I will ascend above the heights of the clouds; I will be like the most high." (Isa 14:14). It is also the heart of the original sin problem.

---

[122] Ibid., pp.90-91.
[123] F. D. Nichol, ed., Seventh-day Adventist Bible Commentary 7 vols. (Washington, D.C.: Review and Herald, 1954), 3:755.
[124] E. Heppenstall, Salvation Unlimited, p.12.

Through the fall, Ellen White says, Satan conformed to his own nature the father and mother of our race.[125] Is it any wonder that we are born as self-centred rebels? As any parent knows, children are by nature egotistic, everything belongs to them and revolves around them; children have to learn to share, to be altruistic in their actions. As Heppenstall points out:

Original sin is not per se wrong doing, but wrong being. So there is a causal connection between the first sin of the first man and the self-centredness of his posterity. The consequence of Adam's sin was total.

> "Accordingly, original sin is a state of the whole self in relation to God. It is never simply a physiological or biological problem. Trying to locate sin or the transmission of sin genetically simply misses the real problem. The issue is a spiritual one and not something in a gene. Sin is not transmitted genetically from parents to children. Sin must not be reduced to something physical."[126]

The last part of this quote makes an important point. SIN is a spiritual problem not a physical defect, though our physical degeneration is certainly one result of Adam's sin. But "bad habits and practices are developed, they do not come via the genes."[127] Whatever inherited character defects we may have, like death they are the result of the fall - the outgrowth of our separation from God. Our sinful nature is located primarily in our mind not in our bloodstream. Thus Ellen White says:

> "In order to understand this matter aright, we must remember that our hearts [minds] are naturally depraved, and we are unable of ourselves to pursue a right course."[128]

In another place she writes:

> "Through sin the whole human organism is deranged, the mind is perverted, the imagination corrupted. Sin has degraded the faculties of the soul. Temptations from without find an answering chord within the heart, and the feet turn imperceptibly toward evil."[129]

The most important effect Adam's sin had was man's separation from God. Cut off from the tree of life, man's physical nature began to die. Cut off from the presence of holy beings, man's spiritual nature (his mind) became deranged. Man became self-centred and proud (the pride of life, 1 John 2:16); his eyes, which had beheld the glory of creation, now showed him what he desired to own and to control (lust of the eyes); and because of the close interrelationship between body and mind, the natural drives like sex and appetite turned into the unnatural perversions of the flesh (lust of the flesh). Death, sickness, and our corrupt and

---

[125] Ellen G. White, Desire of Ages, p.114.
[126] E. Heppenstall, The Man Who Is God, p.122.
[127] Ibid., p.124.
[128] White, Counsels to Parents, Teachers, and Students, p.544.
[129] Idem, Ministry of Healing, p.451.

depraved nature are all the results of our separation from God - the source of life and of all goodness.

ADAM'S GUILT

The Augustinian theory of original sin, which to a large extent has become Roman Catholic doctrine, includes the idea that Adam's guilt is inherited by every newborn. Babies, therefore, must be baptised to wash away this inherited guilt.

Adventists generally deny that we inherit Adam's guilt. The *Seventh-day Adventist Encyclopedia* states: "SDAs believe that man inherited a sinful nature with a propensity to sin, and their writings either reject or fail to stress the idea that men inherit the guilt of Adam's transgression."[130]

Some Adventist theologians, however, do include Adam's guilt in their definition of original sin. Robert Olson, for example, says: "We inherit guilt from Adam so that even a baby that dies a day after birth needs a Saviour though the child never committed a sin of his own."[131] He bases this on such statements by E. G. White as these: "As related to the first Adam, men receive from him nothing but guilt and the sentence of death."[132] "Adam sinned, and the children of Adam share his guilt and its consequences."[133] However, she also says: "It is inevitable that children should suffer from the consequences of parental wrong-doing, but they are not punished for the parent's guilt, except as they participate in their sins."[134]

There is a question, therefore, whether Ellen White's statements refer to an actual imputation of Adam's guilt to his descendants or simply to the consequences of Adam's sin. In other words, just as death comes to all men because Adam sinned, so guilt comes to all because we are born

---

[130] Don F. Neufeld, Ed. Seventh-day Adventist Encyclopedia (Washington: Review and Herald, 1966), p.748.
[131] Olson, ibid., p.28.
[132] White, Letter 68, 1899 (6BC, 1074). The immediate context of this statement is the education of children: "Parents have a more serious charge than they imagine. The inheritance of children is that of sin. Sin has separated them from God. Jesus gave his life that he might unite the broken links to God. As related to the first Adam, men receive from him nothing but guilt and the sentence of death. But Christ steps in and passes over the ground where Adam fell, enduring every test in man's behalf. He redeems Adam's disgraceful failure and fall by coming forth from the trial untarnished. This places man on vantage ground with God. It places him where, through accepting Christ as his Saviour, he becomes a partaker of the divine nature. Thus he becomes connected with God and Christ.
[133] Idem, Faith and Works, p.88. This statement appears in an Article in Signs of the Times, May 19, 1890 entitled "Obedience is Sanctification." The whole paragraph reads as follows: "We have reason for ceaseless gratitude to God that Christ, by His perfect obedience, has won back the heaven that Adam lost through disobedience. Adam sinned, and the children of Adam share his guilt and its consequences; but Jesus bore the guilt of Adam, and all the children of Adam that will flee to Christ, the second Adam, may escape the penalty of transgression. Jesus regained heaven for man by bearing the test that Adam failed to endure; for He obeyed the law perfectly, and all who have a right conception of the plan of redemption will see that they cannot be saved while in transgression of God's holy precepts."
[134] Idem, Patriarchs and Prophets, p.306. This is E.G. White's commentary on the statement in the second commandment which says: "Visiting the iniquity of the fathers upon the children unto the third and fourth generation of them that hate Me."

sinners and commit sin ourselves. A. L. Moore denies that Ellen White teaches inherited guilt. He says:

> "White's concern appears to relate to the consequences of separation from God and enslavement to Satan - which is inherited from Adam. A cause and effect chain is seen in which sin separates from God and leaves the soul with guilt."[135]

It may be useful to distinguish between Adam's guilt and our guilt as a consequence of our inherited sinfulness. We do not inherit Adam's guilt, but as a consequence of Adam's fall we are born distant from God, out of harmony with his will, in a state of sin which is condemnable, and therefore we are guilty before God. E. G. White may be referring to this guilt.

VII. CHRISTOLOGICAL IMPLICATIONS

We have seen that sin is more than an act, that it is a state which we inherit because of Adam's separation from God. M. J. Erickson has well said:

> "Sin is not merely wrong acts and thoughts, but sinfulness as well, an inherent inner disposition inclining us to wrong acts and thoughts. Thus it is not simply that we are sinners because we sin; we sin because we are sinners.[136]

Now, if every man is born a sinner, separated from God and in need of salvation, then how could Christ be born a man and still be sinless? Early Adventist sources show a wide divergence on the question of Christ's nature. In 1888 G. W. Morse replying to the question: "If Christ did not possess our carnal nature or evil passions, how could he be tempted in all points as we are?" Said:

> "The only point of difference between his opportunity and ours, for resisting temptations, is found in the fact that *he possessed no natural trait of, or tendency to, sin*, whereas we do. It must be born in mind that Christ came to this earth to start from the stand-point that Adam did, and not from our stand-point."[137]

Two years later 1890 E. J. Waggoner, editor of the Signs of the Times, wrote in his book *Christ and His Righteousness*:

> "The fact that Christ took upon Himself the flesh, not of a sinless being, but of sinful man, that is, that *the flesh which He assumed had all the weaknesses and sinful tendencies to which fallen human nature is subject*, is shown by the statement that He "was made of the seed of David according to the flesh."[138]

In fairness to Waggoner, we must remember that Seventh-day Adventists at that time believed that inclinations and tendencies to sin were not sin in the proper sense of the word.

---

[135] A. Leroy Moore, The Theology Crisis (Corpus Christi, TX: Life Seminar, 1980), p.109.
[136] Erickson, p.578.
[137] G. W. Morse, "Scripture Questions," RH 65:35 (Aug. 28, 1888): 554.
[138] E. J. Waggoner, Christ and His Righteousness (Oakland, 1890), pp.26-27.

On the one hand, the answer to the question asked of Morse must avoid making Christ a man just like us. For the corporate solidarity of the human race with Adam made it impossible that one of the human race could rise above the basic sin-problem, i.e., the separation from God. "Only one from outside the race could enter it and bring change."[139] On the other hand, it must avoid making Christ so much unlike man that he cannot be identified with us. "He must be one with us in nature but not one with us in sin (whether sin as separation from God, as nature, or as acts)."[140]

> "The two sides of the problem were met in Christ's miraculous conception (Luke 1:35), when He took all the limitations of our humanity, except sin (Heb 4:15 Greek). He [Christ] for our sakes laid aside His royal robe, stepped down from the throne in heaven, and condescended to clothe His divinity with humanity and became like one of us except in sin."[141]

Jesus was both like and unlike Adam in his human nature.

> "It was not the Adamic [nature], because it had the innocent infirmities of the fallen. It was not the fallen, because it had never descended into moral impurity. It was, therefore, most literally our humanity, but without sin."[142]

The statement in Romans 8:3 that Jesus came "in the likeness of sinful flesh" does not mean he <u>had</u> sinful flesh, otherwise the word "likeness" would be inappropriate. The Greek word *homoiomati* refers to "likeness" not "sameness."[143] Jesus was neither a sinner by nature nor a sinner by acts. Thus he was the unique substitute - the spotless Lamb.

SUMMARY AND CONCLUSIONS

A survey of the history of the doctrine of original sin indicates that this particular biblical teaching has been understood in a variety of different ways. Most influential were the Pelagian, Augustinian, and Arminian interpretations.

Until the end of the eighteenth century Augustinian theology dominated the churches' understanding of original sin in America. The New Haven theologians in the nineteenth century, in their opposition to the Calvinistic Federal theology, developed a doctrine of original sin similar to the Arminian position.

> Seventh-day Adventism born in the milieu of New England acquired a hamartiology similar to the New Haven theologians who viewed man's inheritance as neither his responsibility nor properly called sin. There is a clearly discernible connection between the New Haven theology, the conditionalism of George Storrs, and the understanding of original sin in early Adventism.

---

[139]Gulley, p.39.
[140]Ibid.
[141]White, Youth's Instructor, Oct. 20, 1886.
[142]Seventh-day Adventists Believe . . ., p.47.
[143]W. F. Arndt and F. W. Gingrich, A Greek-English Lexicon of the NT 2nd ed. (Chicago: University Press, 1979), p.567. s.v. "homoioma." Concerning Rom 8:3 the authors say that the word **homoiomati** brings out the idea that "Jesus in his earthly career was similar to sinful men and yet not absolutely like them."

Early Adventists taught:

> 1. Adam in his unfallen state had a middle nature - capable of becoming morally good or corrupt.
>
> 2. Original sin was understood to refer only to Adam's transgression.
>
> 3. The penalty for Adam's sin was seen only in terms of a dying nature - physical death. This dying nature was also called a sinful nature.
>
> 4. Spiritual death (depravity) was seen as a consequence not as a penalty of original sin. It could be overcome.
>
> 5. Because sin was defined in terms of transgression of the Law, depravity was not considered to be sin but rather as the natural bent or inclination to sin.

Ellen White's writings from the 1880s on slowly directed the church's view towards a more biblical understanding. By the end of the century it was recognised that Adam's legacy was not simply physical mortality leading to the first death, but also spiritual depravity deserving the second death.

Seventh-day Adventists today generally define sin as a lack of conformity to the will of God, either in act or state. They believe that children are born with a sinful, depraved nature as a consequence of Adam's sin and the resulting separation from God. This sinful state means that if a baby dies a few hours after birth he/she is subject to the second death, even though he/she has never broken any commandment.

> "If this were not so, then babies who died would not need a Saviour. Christ allowed for no such exception when He said, 'I am the way, the truth, and the life. No one comes to the Father except through me.' (John 14:6)."[144]

That each newborn possesses the guilt of Adam's sin has not been commonly accepted among Adventists. Nevertheless, the term original sin is used by Adventist authors - "not in the sense of inherited guilt, but of an inherited disposition to sin."[145] For the sake of clarity and to avoid confusion, I would suggest that we use the term "original sin" for the Augustinian concept of imputed guilt and corruption; and the term "original corruption" for the state of sin into which each member of the human race is born.

---

[144] Gulley, p.34. We cannot agree with Erickson (p. 639) who believes that there is no condemnation until one reaches the age of responsibility. He says, "If a child dies before he or she is capable of making genuine moral decisions, there is only innocence, and the child will experience the same type of future existence with the Lord as will those who have reached the age of moral responsibility and had their sins forgiven as a result of accepting the offer of salvation based upon Christ's atoning death." This line of reasoning would introduce the idea that some people can get to Heaven without a Saviour and that it is better for children to die, so they will be saved for eternity, than to grow up and possibly lose eternity through a wrong choice.

[145] Heppenstall, The Man Who is God, p.107.

There is a tendency on the part of some Adventists today to go back to the understanding of our early pioneers regarding original sin, in order to justify their opposition to our present understanding which they consider to be Calvinistic. However, any understanding of theological truths must take into consideration the total scriptural context as well as the inspired counsel of E. G. White.

While some believe that sin is only a wilful or negligent violation of God's will, our study of Scripture has shown that sin is also a state into which we are born (original corruption). This sinful state will remain with us until the end, though by God's grace we can overcome every temptation to sin.

A correct understanding of the nature of sin is also vital for a balanced view on the nature of Christ. While He became truly man, "made like unto his brethren" (Heb 2:17), he did not inherit the original corruption with which we are born (Heb 4:15).

The study of original sin and corruption should lead us to a greater awareness of our need of righteousness. That we need a Saviour the day we are born, not only after we have transgressed God's law, this is the message of this study. The everlasting gospel of Jesus Christ meets our need.

> "For I am not ashamed of the gospel of Christ: for it is the power of God unto salvation to everyone that believeth; to the Jew first, and also to the Greek.
> For therein is the righteousness of God revealed from faith to faith: as it is written, the just shall live by faith." (Romans 1:16, 17).[146]

[In summation then, what hath we learned thus far? It is indisputable that the Defendant, the organized church is in complete harmony with the gospel of the Scriptures and Ellen G. White on this issue. Therefore, as promised, we will now begin to exonerate an innocent party wrongfully condemned and expose the guilty party that is in blatant apostasy and place the guilty verdict where it rightly belongs!

For the benefit and convenience of the reader we will now relist the 12 stated positions and beliefs from the Plaintiff or the independents from their original sources that were presented at the beginning of this Chapter:

1. [They reject] "We are guilty by *nature*, before *any choice* of good or evil enters the picture."[147]

2. [They reject] "Our condemnation comes *from Adam*."[148]

---

[146] Gerhard Pfandl, *Some Thoughts on Original Sin*, PDF, pgs. 1-22.
[147] Dennis Priebe, *Face-to-Face With the Real Gospel* (Boise Idaho, Pacific Press Publishing Association, 1985) 12-13.
[148] Ibid., 12-13.

3. [They reject] "We are guilty because of our *inherited depravity*."[149]

4. [They reject] "*Sin* is declared to exist in the being *prior to our own consciousness of it*."[150]

5. [They assert] "*Inheritance does not* make us *guilty*, but the choice to exercise our fallen nature produces guilt."[151]

6. [They assert] "We become sinners because of the choices that we make *after we are able to choose between right and wrong*."[152]

7. [They assert] "God's condemnation is *always* based upon man's prior knowledge."[153]

8. [They assert] "We *do not inherit* guilt or condemnation."[154]

9. [They assert] "This death, the natural death that Adam died, was the *result* of sin, rather than the *penalty* of sin."[155]

10. [They assert] "This is one of the principal areas in which the new theology may be *identified*."[156]

11. [They assert] "This notion comes from *paganism*."[157]

12. [They reject] "That man is *born*, and *even conceived*, guilty because of Adam's sin."[158]

Now the reader is given further opportunity to view and compare other Scriptures and S.O.P. quotes side by side with the 12 stated positions and beliefs from the Plaintiff or the independents. Once side by side with Scripture and S.O.P. the real gospel will stand up and show its true face for all to see. Let's begin our comparison:

What saith the Scriptures?

> "For as by <u>one</u> man's disobedience many were made[2525] sinners, so by the obedience of <u>one</u> shall many be made[2525] righteous." Rom. 5:19.

---

[149] Ibid., 12-13.
[150] Ibid., 12-13.
[151] Ibid. 56.
[152] Ibid. 66.
[153] Ibid., 30. Emphasis in the original.
[154] Ibid., 28. Emphasis in the original.
[155] Ibid., 31. Emphasis in the original.
[156] Colin D. Standish & Russell R. Standish, *Deceptions of the New Theology* (Hartland Publications, 1989). 63.
[157] Ibid., 63.
[158] Ibid., 63.

2525 kaqi,sthmi kathistemi {kath-is'-tay-mee}
Meaning: 1) to set, place, put 1a) to set one over a thing (in charge of it) 1b) to appoint one to administer an office 1c) to set down as, constitute, to declare, show to be 1d) to constitute, to render, make, cause to be 1e) to conduct or bring to a certain place 1f) to show or exhibit one's self 1f1) come forward as
Origin: from 2596 and 2476; TDNT - 3:444,387; v
Usage: AV - make 8, make ruler 6, ordain 3, be 2, appoint 1, conduct 1, set 1; 22

5681 Tense - Aorist (See 5777) Voice - Passive (See 5786) Mood - Indicative (See 5791) Count - 602

Geneva Bible Notes:
Rom 5:19 (1) For as by one man's (2) disobedience (3) many were made sinners, so by the obedience of one shall many be made righteous.

(1) The foundation of this whole comparison is this, that these two men are set as two heads or roots, so that out of the one comes sin by nature, and from the other righteousness by grace springs forth upon others.
(2) So then, sin enters not into us only by following the steps of our forefathers, but we receive corruption from him by inheritance.
(3) The word "many" is contrasted with the words "a few".

We will come back to Rom. 5:19 momentarily. In the meantime what saith the S.O.P; for she has some very definitive instruction on this very issue that harmonizes perfectly with Rom. 5:19 not yet viewed:

"Adam disobeyed and *entailed* sin upon his *posterity*."[159]

What does the verb "entailed" mean?

"en·tail"

verb, past tense: **entailed**; past participle: **entailed**

in'tāl,en'tāl/

1. Involve (something) as a necessary or inevitable part or consequence.
   "a situation that entails considerable risks"

2. LAW: settle the inheritance of (property) over a number of generations so that ownership remains within a particular group, usually one family. "her father's estate was **entailed on** a cousin"

---
[159] Ellen White, 6MR 3.

What does the noun "posterity" mean?

1.

Succeeding or future generations collectively:

Judgment of this age must be left to posterity.

2.

All descendants of one person:

His fortune was gradually dissipated by his posterity.

Now that we are all on the same page, Inspiration has declared that it was "Sin" that Adam entailed upon all his descendants. Priebe and Standish are diametrically opposed to Inspiration. Please compare the list of all 12 stated positions and beliefs from the Plaintiff, independents alongside every reference submitted and the reader will see the blatant discrepancies for oneself. Again:

> "Adam sinned and the children of Adam share his *guilt* and its consequences..."[160]

Priebe and Standish are again diametrically opposed to Inspiration. Again:

> "...children received from Adam an *inheritance* of disobedience, of *guilt* and death."[161]

Priebe and Standish are again diametrically opposed to Inspiration. Again:

> "The *inheritance* of *children* is that of *sin*."[162]

Priebe and Standish are again diametrically opposed to Inspiration. Again:

> "By *nature* the heart is *evil*"[163]

Yet priebe tells us that:

> See No. 5. "*Inheritance does not* make us *guilty*, but the choice to exercise our fallen nature produces guilt."[164]

But Priebe does not stop there:

---

[160] Ellen White, *Signs of the Times*, May 19, 1890.
[161] Ellen White, 13MR 14.
[162] Ellen White, *Child Guidance*, 475.
[163] Ellen White, *Desire of Ages*, 172.
[164] Dennis Priebe, *Face-to-Face With the Real Gospel* (Boise Idaho, Pacific Press Publishing Association, 1985), 56.

> "However, if the primary meaning of sin is sinful character, then we become sinners because of the choices that we make *after we are able to choose between right and wrong.*"[165]

This statement is nothing short of incredible! Since Priebe believes we become sinners by choice and children, up to the age of 12, perhaps, but nevertheless, not until they "*are able to choose between right and wrong*" are they then under condemnation, guilt and sin! Those that advocate such a private supposition of human origin have never produced any Bible or S.O.P. for their view because there is *none*! See No. 6. This means a child from birth to the age of accountability (around 12 yrs. of age) does not need a Saviour! Are we to believe children need no Saviour? Unbelievable! "Jesus saith unto him, I am the way, the truth, and the life: <u>no man cometh unto the Father, but by me.</u>" John 14:6. *No exceptions*!

As Bro. Pfandl has shown us previously and Ellen White will confirm below momentarily this guilt or inherited stain we received from Adam refers to our fallen nature, sinful passions, our tendencies or propensities to sin, (not Adams personal sin or sins) because from birth, we have become a partaker of the Satanic nature serving Satan. Again, note the progression:

> "The fall of Adam was a terrible thing, and the consequences of his sin so fraught with *evil* that language *cannot portray it*. By his disobedience of the divine law, the world was thrown into disorder and rebellion. Because of his disobedience, *man was under the penalty of breaking the law, doomed to death.*"[166]

> "When man transgressed the divine law, *his nature became evil,* and he was *in harmony,* and *not at variance, with Satan.* There exists *naturally no enmity* [hatred] between *sinful man* and the *originator of sin*. Both *became evil* through apostasy."[167]

> "While Adam was *created sinless,* in the likeness of God, Seth, like Cain, *inherited the fallen nature* of his parents."[168]

> "Because of the transgression of Adam, Satan claimed the whole family,"[169]

> "Fallen man is Satan's lawful captive."[170]

> "Satan's effort to deceive our first parents was successful. He gained control of man's power of action. Through the senses he influenced the mind. Thus it has been from the beginning of the world. Instead of remaining under God's

---

[165] Ibid. 66.
[166] Ellen White, *Signs of the Times*, Jan. 8, 1894.
[167] Ellen White, *The Great Controversy*, 505.
[168] Ellen White, *Patriarchs and Prophets*, 80.
[169] Ellen White, *Manuscript* 16, 1893.
[170] Ellen White, *Testimonies*, 1:341.

influence in order that he might reflect the moral image of his Creator, man placed himself under the control of Satan's influence and was made selfish."[171]

"Should they [Adam and Eve] once yield to temptation, their *nature* would become so *depraved* that in themselves they would have *no power and no disposition to resist Satan.*"[172]

Priebe is again diametrically opposed to Inspiration; see No. 3. Again:

"As a result of Adam's disobedience, every human being is a transgressor of the law, and is sold under sin. Unless man *repents and is converted,* [John 3:3, 7] *he is under bondage of the law, serving Satan,* falling into the deceptions of the enemy, bearing witness against the precepts of Jehovah. Only by perfect obedience to the requirements of God's holy law can man be justified. Let those *whose natures have been perverted by <u>sin</u>*, ever keep their eyes fixed on Christ, the author and the finisher of their faith."[173]

Priebe and Standish are again diametrically opposed to Inspiration. The term Inspiration just used, "sold under sin" is from none other than Rom. 7:14: "For we know that the law is spiritual but I am carnal, *sold under sin*." What Inspiration is saying is that as a result of Adam's disobedience, every human being is a transgressor of the law and is "sold under sin." Why are we transgressors of the law? Because of our own disobedience? No. Our own disobedience is the consequence of our being transgressors of the law by Adam's disobedience. We do not become sinners because we commit sin! We commit sin because we are sinners on account of Adam's sin. "By the disobedience of one, the many were made," what? "Sinners." Rom. 5:19 "All have sinned and come short of the glory of God." Rom. 3:23. But why do they all sin? Because they, like we, are all sinners by nature. This is also further confirmed by the following:

"When man sinned, all heaven was filled with sorrow; for through yielding to temptation, *man became the enemy of God, a partaker of the Satanic nature*. The image of God in which he had been created was marred and distorted. The character of man was out of harmony with the character of God; for through <u>sin</u> man became <u>carnal</u>, *and the carnal heart is enmity against God, is not subject to the law of God, neither indeed can be.*"[174]

Priebe and Standish are again diametrically opposed to Inspiration. The next two quotes are from Priebe:

---

[171] Ellen White, *Manuscript* 55, 1902.
[172] Ellen White, *Patriarchs and Prophets*, 53.
[173] Ellen White, 8*MR* 98.
[174] Ellen White, *Signs of the Times*, February 13, 1893.

> "If we are to believe that sin is by choice, we must make a crucial distinction between evil and guilt. Guilt demands prior knowledge and willful rebellion. I am suggesting that God's condemnation is *always* based upon man's prior knowledge."[175]

> ". . . We do not inherit guilt or condemnation. We do inherit everything that Adam could pass on. We inherit all the learnings, all of the tendencies, all of the desires, and we are born in a way that God did not really intend for man to be born. But this definition says that personal sin comes through choice; sin, itself, is not inherited. Guilt, then, is not by nature; but when we choose to rebel against the light and known duty, *then* we become guilty. We must choose to make Adam's decision, the decision to rebel against God, and *then* we are guilty."[176]

Here we find Priebe again in direct conflict with Scripture and Ellen White resorting to human reasoning above clearly defined scripture and Inspiration:

> "Human *nature* is depraved and is *justly condemned* by a holy God."[177]

Priebe is again diametrically opposed to Inspiration; see No. 7.

Now it is time to fully dismantle Priebe's private supposition that we become sinners by choice rather than at birth as the Scriptures (Rom. 5:19) and Inspiration teach. Priebe and the independents teach that we do not become sinners until the age of accountability when we are then held accountable to our choices we make (approximately at the age of 12). This first blatant but obvious error is that children do not need a Savior even though Jesus has said: ". . . I am the way, the truth, and the life: no man cometh unto the Father, but by me." John 14:6. *No exceptions*! Now I turn over the platform to Stephen Wallace as he fully unmasks this heretical supposition:

> "Man weighed against God's holy law is found wanting. We are enlightened by the precepts of the law but no man can by them be justified. *Weighed and found wanting is our inscription by nature.*"[178]

> "There's good news that follows. Listen to it. Weighed and found wanting is our inscription by nature but Christ is our Mediator and accepting Him as our Savior, we may claim the promise, being justified by faith, we have peace with God through our Lord Jesus Christ. That's the gospel. But you'll never

---

[175] Dennis Priebe, *Face-to-Face With the Real Gospel* (Boise Idaho, Pacific Press Publishing Association, 1985), 30. Emphasis in the original.
[176] Ibid. 28. Emphasis in the original.
[177] Ellen White, *Review and Herald*, September 17, 1895.
[178] Ellen White, *Review & Herald*, March 8, 1906.

appreciate it and embrace it until you recognize with me that we all are weighed in the balance and found wanting by nature.

Signs of the Times, May 19, 1890: "Adam sinned and the children of Adam share his guilt and its consequences." We wrestled with that truth in an earlier study. What about this guilt of Adam that his children bear? "Adam sinned and the children of Adam share his guilt and its consequences. But" --here's the precious good news -- "Jesus bore the guilt of Adam, and all the children of Adam that will flee to Christ, the second Adam, may escape the penalty of transgression." The children of Adam bear his guilt. By natural birth, they are under condemnation on account of the sin of Adam. Do they have any choice in that matter? No. Is that fair? Sin is never fair. But praise God, they have a choice as to whether or not to continue to bear that guilt. They can choose to come to Jesus and let Him take it from them and bear it Himself. They can choose to be born again.

And brothers and sisters please recognize with me an important point. If we complain about being condemned and sentenced to death on account of Adam's sin--don't lose me--we also have to complain about being justified and promised eternal life on account of Christ's obedience. Did you follow me? Romans 5:19: "By the disobedience of one the many were made sinners." Not so, we say. Oh, but be careful. Don't be too quick. The second half says, "Even so, by the obedience of one, the many will be made" what? Righteous. Do you want to cry out, Not fair? No, you don't, do you? But please recognize the principle. These are unique individuals and they have the unique capacity being the two heads of the human race, to have legal, direct influence on the whole race. Adam as the legal representative brought condemnation upon the whole race, and the whole race is born under that condemnation and sentenced to death. Now their own sinfulness simply ratifies the fact that they are born in the fallen race, and their own sin simply verifies their own sinfulness. But what is it that is the cause of their condemnation? Adam's sin.

When we're born again--follow me, please--what is the cause of our justification? Christ's righteousness. Is it caused by something we are in ourselves? No, that new heart that we receive simply evidences the fact that we are indeed now members of the new race. And our own obedience simply ratifies the presence of the new heart. But the justification is based upon what? The obedience of the Second Adam. Do you see that truth? Don't be so quick to resent the imputation of Adam's guilt to you because, if you do, you have to resent the imputation of Christ's righteousness to you. It's on the same legal basis, precisely, because those two bear the same relationship to us. Legally, one by natural birth; the other, by rebirth.

Desire of Ages, page 598: "Those who trust in him he never disappoints. He has borne every test, he has endured the pressure of Adam's guilt and the guilt of his posterity, and he has come off more than conqueror of the powers of evil. He has borne the burdens cast upon him by every repenting sinner. In Christ, the guilty heart has found relief. He is the sure foundation. All who make him their dependence rest in perfect security."

Oh, brothers and sisters, when you confess your sinfulness of nature, as the apostles did--Acts of the Apostles, 561--men who would rather die than knowingly transgress God's law. They still did what? They confessed the sinfulness of their nature. When you confess the sinfulness of your nature, you can rest in total confidence that there is no condemnation now because He bore the sinfulness of that nature, and the condemnation for it was exhausted on His head. And why and how could He bear it? Because He didn't have it in Himself.

What does God's word say? "For he made him who knew no sin for us that we might become" what? "The righteousness of God" where? "In him." II Cor. 5:21. Oh, brothers and sisters, that was the reason He became sin for us, that we might become the righteousness of God in Him. To do both. To be our Substitute in death and to be our Substitute in life. To be our Substitute in dying to pay our debt. To be our Substitute in living a perfect life to meet the infinite standard in our behalf. In both these aspects, He had to be absolutely sinless in His humanity to accomplish His mission.

> Remember, the law requires that we have not only absolute sinlessness but that we have what? Infinite righteousness. We are hopeless unless we have One that has both absolute sinlessness and infinite righteousness. I hope that we have clearly established that in Christ we do have One who has absolute sinlessness. We must assure ourselves that in Christ we also have One who has infinite righteousness."[179]

[As we have witnessed consistently, Priebe's and the Standish brothers entire structure and private interpretation for "sin by choice" in regards to our first birth in this setting along with their private "distinction between evil and guilt" has just been fully dismantled.

Scripture and Ellen White has answered all those 12 accusations from the independents harmoniously but the answers we have been given are 180^0 diametrically opposed to the teachings of Dennis Priebe, the Standish brothers and the independents, but, fully supportive of the organized church's position!

If something is *justly condemned* by God almighty, and *a partaker of the Satanic nature* would it be permitted to pass into heaven? Of course not! What was it that we witnessed that was condemned by God? Our sinful human *natures*! Why? Because this was *not* the nature God created in man! Did this teaching come from paganism? No! See No. 11. Are we wrong to call this "Sin"? No! See No. 4. This is precisely why Jesus told Nicodemus in John 3:3, 7 that unless *all* of humanity repents and is born again we will *never see* the kingdom of God, no exceptions. Why, because further into our study we will see and understand from scripture and Inspiration that Christians are reborn, not made, with a new nature! In the Sermon on the Mount, Jesus is speaking to His followers, disciples and no doubt many are listing to him for the first time that have not yet made a decision for or against Him when Jesus declared to them, "ye then, *being evil*. . .":

> "If ye then, <u>being evil</u>, know how to give good gifts unto your children, how much more shall your Father which is in heaven give good things to them that ask him"? Matt. 7:11.

When did the human race become Evil?

> "When man [Adam] transgressed the divine law, *his nature became evil*, and he was *in harmony*, and *not at variance, with Satan*. There exists *naturally no*

---

[179] Stephen Wallace, "*Our Sinless Yet Sympathetic Savior*", revivalseminars.org. See also: americanchristianministries.org..

enmity [hatred] between *sinful man* and the *originator of sin*. Both became *evil* through apostasy."[180]

"While Adam was *created sinless,* in the likeness of God, Seth, like Cain, *inherited the fallen nature* of his parents."[181]

This is why by "nature" we are called the "children of wrath" because from birth (yes conception Ps. 51:5) we are dead in trespasses and sins, yes evil, with a depraved nature that is said to be "carnal," justly condemned by a holy God:

> Eph 2:1 "And you *hath he quickened,* who were dead in trespasses and sins;
> Eph 2:2 Wherein in time past ye walked according to the course of this world, according to the prince of the power of the air, the spirit that now worketh in the children of disobedience:
> Eph 2:3 Among whom also we all had our conversation in times past in the lusts of our flesh, fulfilling the desires of the flesh and of the mind; and were by nature the children of wrath, even as others.
> Eph 2:4 But God, who is rich in mercy, for his great love wherewith he loved us,
> Eph 2:5 Even when we were dead in sins, hath quickened us together with Christ, (by grace ye are saved;)"

No wonder John said this of us:

> "If we say that we have no sin, we deceive ourselves, and the truth is not in us." 1 John 1:8

The truth of the matter is that we do have sin, "in us" because "in us" our natures by inheritance are evil. We will now let John contrast the nature of the man, Christ Jesus, the second Adam:

> "And ye know that he was manifested to take away our sins; and in him is no sin." 1 John 3:5.

Not only do we find that Christ had no sin, 1 Peter 2:22, but John goes further and says He had no sin "in Him." His human nature was spotless, without sin!

Priebe also disputes (See No. 9.) the Biblical fact that all persons are subject to death, the *penalty* for *sin*:

---

[180] Ellen White, *The Great Controversy*, 505.
[181] Ellen White, *Patriarchs and Prophets*, 80.

> "For the wages of *sin* is *death*; but the gift of God *is* eternal life through Jesus Christ our Lord." Rom 6:23.

In this judicial setting we have shown throughout this discourse that Scripture and Ellen White have harmonized perfectly and stand squarely on the side of the organized church without the need to apologize for anything to the independents or to the church family at large thus far. And we have also proved without discrimination that not one of all 12 of the so stated positions and beliefs from the independents has been able to withstand the test of investigation.

Priebe does make a statement of which we all can agree upon pertaining to our study in the next chapter, pertaining to, the Nature of Christ:

> "So it does make a crucial difference whether we believe that sin is by nature or by choice, because that will determine the conclusions we will draw regarding the humanity of Jesus Christ."[182]

Since our study from the Scriptures and Inspiration has proven that we sin because we are sinners simply because our natures are evil and justly condemned by God due to the fact of Adams sin. Therefore, humanity naturally inherited Adam's sinful nature or guilt transferred at conception that *consisted* of Adam's sinful passions, tendencies and propensities to sin, to every man, woman and child ever born into this world since creation. As we have witnessed, none of us have or had a choice about our first birth whatsoever, Rom. 5:19 makes that abundantly clear but we do have a choice about our second birth as Scripture will soon establish in another chapter! Also, Bro. Pfandl has rightly stated in his article and exposed the inferred predispositions that the organized church's gospel teaches cheap grace or salvation in known sin:

> "While some believe that sin is only a wilful or negligent violation of God's will, our study of Scripture has shown that sin is also a state into which we are born (original corruption). This sinful state will remain with us until the end, *though by God's grace we can overcome every temptation to sin.*"[183]

Brother Pfandl closes this segment with the following, knowing full well that the church has been wrongfully labeled, New Theology and falsely condemned from the independents for decades, thus he concludes this aspect of our study with:

> There is nothing new in the teaching of the "New Theology" concerning the nature of man. 100 years ago Ellen White taught what is taught by the "New Theology" today."[184]

---

[182] Priebe, *Face-to-Face With the Real Gospel*, 43.
[183] Gerhard Pfandl, *Some Thoughts on Original Sin*, PDF, pgs. 34.
[184] Ibid. *PDF* 8.

2

The Nature of Christ

[As stated in chapter 1 we will follow the protocol in allowing the Defendant, the organized church to present her case after we have formed and present to the reader a list, designating the core stated beliefs and accusations charged against the organized church that is said to be in apostasy according to the Plaintiff, the independents.

1. [They reject] "No evidence exists to suggest that Jesus inherited only the physical results of the fall, such as hunger, weakness, thirst, and mortality, but . . ."[185]

2. [They reject] Continuing, . . . "that He did not inherit dispositional traits. These areas cannot be separated."[186]

3. [They assert] "There is no evidence that the chain of heredity was broken. The inheritance of Jesus was the same as our inheritance."[187]

4. [They assert] "The evidence from the Bible and the spirit of prophesy indicates that His inheritance was the same as our inheritance."[188]

5. [They assert] "It was important that Christ take both the form and nature of *fallen* man.[189]

6. [They assert] "Surely within our inward nature which has a bent to evil. He knows *by experience* what that is."[190]

7. [They assert] "Many have wondered why we develop these propensities while Christ did not develop them."[191]

8. [They assert] "If Jesus' life is to have any meaning as an *example* for us, then it is crucial that He inherit just what I inherit."[192]

---

[185] Dennis Priebe, *Face-to-Face With the Real Gospel* (Boise Idaho, Pacific Press Publishing Association, 1985), 50.
[186] Ibid. 50.
[187] Ibid. 50.
[188] Ibid. 50-1.
[189] Ibid. 51.
[190] Ibid. 52.
[191] Ibid. 54.
[192] Ibid. 55.

9. [They assert] "If Jesus' perfect obedience was predicted upon the fact that He had an unfallen nature, then He had an advantage I can never possess."[193]

10. [They assert] "Jesus Christ had to come down to the level at which He found man after the fall, not just to the level at which He originally created man."[194]

11. [They assert] "Satan declared that it was impossible for the sons and daughters of Adam to keep the law of God, and thus charged upon God a lack of wisdom and love. If they could not keep the law, then there was fault with the Lawgiver." –Signs of the Times, January 16, 1896."[195]

12. [They assert] "Are not our problems basically self and pride and the desire that come from our fallen nature? Do we not fall most often because of the inner desires that lead us astray? If Jesus did not have any of these, could it really be true that He was tempted in all points as we are?"[196]

13. [They assert] "Why did Jesus say, "I seek not mine own will" (John 5:30), . . But if His own will and His own inclination were tending toward the negative, then it would make sense for Him to ask that His Fathers will be done."[197]

14. [They assert] "If He did not have man's nature, He could not be our example."[198]

15. [They assert] "He knew what it was like to want to go wrong. He knew what it was like to feel the temptation to rebel against God, and that temptation arose from within His nature."[199]

16. [They assert] "Jesus in man's nature lived a life that Satan said could not be lived."[200]

17. [They assert] "Jesus….could only keep the commandments of God in the same way that humanity can keep them." –Ibid. How can we keep them? Certainly not in Adam's nature. We can only keep them in that nature which we now have- fallen nature. And Jesus kept the commandments of God in the same way we are to keep them. Jesus overcame as we are to overcome."[201]

18. [They assert] "The *new theology is* a worldwide problem. It has been used by Satan in an endeavor to derail God's remnant church. We have confidence in the testimony of Ellen White that he will not succeed, but, sadly, a huge number of God's people will be lost as a result of the acceptance of this unscriptural theology."[202]

---

[193] Ibid. 55.
[194] Ibid. 56-7.
[195] Ibid. 57-8.
[196] Ibid. 59.
[197] Ibid. 59.
[198] Ibid. 60.
[199] Ibid. 60.
[200] Ibid. 61.
[201] Ibid. 61-62.
[202] Colin D. Standish & Russell R. Standish, *Deceptions of the New Theology* (Hartland Publications, 1989). 28.

19. [They assert] "There are over 40 statements in which the issue of the human nature of Christ is specifically addressed by Sister White. Always she refers to the human nature of Christ as "fallen" or "sinful," thus confirming the words of Scripture. Never once does she use the term "unfallen" or "sinless" in relation to Christ's human nature."[203]

20. [They assert] "Perhaps the most poignant expression of Sister White upon this matter states that Christ *took* our sinful nature. He took upon His sinless nature our sinful nature, that He might know how to succor those that are tempted *(Medical Ministry,* p. 181). Some have attempted to support the view that Jesus simply took the physical form alone, but that cannot be sustained by the evidence in Sister White's writings (reread *Spiritual Gifts,* vol. 4, p. 115). To separate Christ's physical nature from His mental and moral nature would take us to the Greek pagan concept of the distinction between an evil body and a good soul. No right thinking Seventh-day Adventist dare accept that dualistic view of man. It is a satanic deception. If Christ had a fallen physical nature, and He did, then His entire nature was fallen."[204]

[Now that the reader has an honest visual as to what the Plaintiff, the independents believe from their own published sources on the nature of Christ, the reader will easily recognize the different path from one to the other as we now proceed by submitting a concise understanding and teaching of the organized church's view of the nature of Christ at large:

The Nature of Christ

Gerhard Pfandl Ph. D.

"Some people claim that the church changed its teaching on the nature of Christ in 1957, when the book ***Questions on Doctrine*** was published. While it is true that many of our books prior to 1957 taught that Jesus had a sinful human nature, this does not mean that ***Questions on Doctrine*** taught something new.

The church in the 1950s, when challenged by non-Adventist theologians, studied the question of the nature of Christ and discovered that Scripture and E.G. White give a somewhat different answer to the one found in many of our books.

On the one hand, Jesus' physical human nature was the nature of humanity after the fall (Rom. 8:3; Heb. 2:16, 17). Ellen White said, "He took upon his sinless nature the fallen nature of man"

---

[203] Ibid. 51.
[204] Ibid. 53.

(*Medical Ministry*, p.181). That is, Jesus had a deteriorated human nature, a nature that did not have all the strength, vitality and capacity that Adam had at his creation.

On the other hand, Jesus' spiritual nature was the sinless nature of Adam before the fall, i.e., He had no evil propensities (with which we are born), no inclinations to sin (with which we are born) and no tendencies to sin (which we all have).

Concerning our situation, Ellen G. White wrote:

> "The result of eating from the tree of knowledge of good and evil is manifest in every man's experience. There is in his nature a bent to evil, a force which, unaided, he cannot resist" (*Education*, p.29).

> "The first Adam was created a pure, sinless being. . . . Because of sin his posterity was born with inherited propensities of disobedience" (*SDA Bible Commentary*, vol.5, p.1128).

Furthermore, she says,

> "In order to understand this matter aright, we must remember that our hearts are naturally depraved, and we are unable of ourselves to pursue a right course" (*Counsels to Teachers*, p.544).

This is why all men, including infants, need a saviour. If Jesus had been just like all the other children, he would have needed a saviour too.

In Luke 1:35 the angel speaking to Mary says, ". . . that holy thing which shall be born of thee shall be called the Son of God." And Jesus Himself in John 14:30 says, ". . . the ruler of this world is coming, and he has nothing in Me." There was nothing in Jesus that responded in any way to Satan's temptations. He was "holy, harmless, undefiled, separate from sinners" (Heb. 7:26).

Our situation is completely different:

> "Sin is a tremendous evil. Through sin the whole human organism is deranged, the mind is perverted, the imagination is corrupt. Sin has degraded the faculties of the soul. Temptations from without find an answering chord within the heart, and the feet turn imperceptibly toward evil." *Ministry of Healing*, p.451

Jesus did not have a perverted mind or a corrupt imagination. He did not have an answering chord within His heart which responded to evil.

Ellen White in many places confirms this:

> "We should have no misgivings in regard to the perfect sinlessness of the human nature of Christ." *Signs of the Times* June 9, 1898.

> "The human nature of Christ is likened to ours, and suffering was more keenly felt by Him; for *His spiritual nature was free from every taint of sin.*" *Signs of the Times* June 9, 1898.

> "Christ came to the earth, taking humanity and *standing as man's representative*, to show in the controversy with Satan that man, *as God created him*, connected with the Father and the Son, could obey every divine requirement." *Selected Messages*, vol.1, p.253.

> "Be careful, exceedingly careful, as to how you dwell upon the human nature of Christ. *Do not set Him before the people as a man with the propensities of sin...* "Never, in any way, leave the slightest impression upon human minds that a taint of, or inclination to, corruption rested upon Christ, or that He in any way yielded to corruption.* He was tempted in all points like as man is tempted, yet He is called "that holy thing". It is a mystery that is left unexplained to mortals that Christ could be tempted in all points like as we are, and yet be without sin. The incarnation of Christ has ever been, and will ever remain, a mystery. That which is revealed, is for us and for our children, *but let every human being be warned from the ground of making Christ altogether human, such an one as ourselves; for it cannot be.*" SDA Bible Commentary, vol.5, p.1128.

Since all our theology must be based on Scripture, let us also note the following texts: 1. Peter 2:22, "Who committed no sin, nor was deceit found in His mouth", and 1. John 3:5, "And you know that He was manifested to take away our sins, and in Him there is no sin."

Please note, Peter says "He committed no sin", but John goes further and declares that "there was no sin in Him", i.e., His nature was sinless. Therefore, He could be the perfect lamb which takes away the sins of the world (Jn. 1:29), a mediator who knew no sin, but was made to be sin for us, that we might become the righteousness of God in Him (2. Cor. 5:21).

In the book *Deceptions of the New Theology* by C. and R. Standish it is claimed that:

"There are over 40 statements in which the issue of the human nature of Christ is specifically addressed by Sister White. Always she refers to the human nature of Christ as "fallen" or "sinful", thus confirming the words of Scripture. Never once does she use the term "unfallen" or "sinless" in relation to Christ's human nature." (p.51).

It seems that the authors missed her statement in *Signs of the Times*, June 9, 1898, where she says, "We should have no misgivings in regard to the perfect sinlessness of the human nature of Christ." Repeatedly she speaks of His "sinless humanity", e.g.:

"It was the purity and sinlessness of Christ's humanity that stirred up such satanic hatred" (*Manuscript Release*, vol.16, p.118), or,

"Christ unites in His person the fullness and perfection of the Godhead and the fullness and perfection of sinless humanity" (*Manuscript Release*, vol.18, p.331).

One will search in vain for expressions like "sinful nature of Christ", "fallen human nature of Christ", or "fallen nature of Christ" in the writings of Ellen White. What she does say repeatedly is that Christ took our "fallen" or "sinful" nature upon Himself (e.g., *Medical Ministry*, p.181; Manuscript 80, 1903).

At times she quotes Romans 8:3, e.g., "Christ, the second Adam, came in `the likeness of sinful flesh'" (Manuscript 99, 1903). This is in harmony with the view that Christ had the sinful physical nature of Adam after the fall, but the sinless spiritual nature of Adam before the fall.

Again, the book *Deceptions of the New Theology* claims:

"To separate Christ's physical nature from His mental and moral nature would take us both to the Greek pagan concept of the distinction between an evil body and a good soul. No right thinking Seventh-day Adventist dare accept that dualistic view of man. It is a satanic deception. If Christ had a fallen physical nature, and He did, then His entire nature was fallen." (p.53).

However, this is not what we find in the writing of E.G. White. In *Signs of the Times*, Dec. 9, 1897 she wrote, "The human nature of Christ is likened to ours, and suffering was more keenly felt by Him; *for His spiritual nature was free from every taint of sin*." She clearly distinguished between his physical and spiritual nature.

To distinguish between these two aspects in man's nature only becomes wrong when we say that each can exist separately from each other, as is the case in the belief that the soul is immortal.

After all, the Bible clearly states that man consists of "spirit, soul and body" (2. Thess. 5:23); and E.G. White wrote that "the nature of man is threefold" (Child Guidance, p.39), and that every follower of Christ should "dedicate all his powers of mind and soul and body to Him who has paid the ransom money for our souls" (Selected Messages, vol.2, p.124).

> "When man sinned, all heaven was filled with sorrow; for through yielding to temptation, man became the enemy of God, *a partaker of the Satanic nature*. The image of God in which he had been created was marred and distorted. The character of man was out of harmony with the character of God; for through sin man became carnal, and the carnal heart is enmity against God, is not subject to the law of God, neither indeed can be." ST, February 13, 1893).

There is nothing new in the teaching of the "New Theology" concerning the nature of Christ. 100 years ago Ellen White taught what the "New Theology" is teaching today."[205]

[In summation then, what hath we learned thus far? It is indisputable that the Defendant, the organized church, once again is in complete harmony with the Scriptures and Ellen G. White. I can only commend Brother Pfandl for an excellent presentation with so little words. With such a concise presentation there will be no need to relist the Plaintiff's beliefs and accusations. Therefore we will move directly into our comparison following the same procedure as outlined in Chapter 1. What saith the Scriptures:

> "For both he that sanctifieth and they who are sanctified <u>are</u> all of one:
> for which cause he is not ashamed to call them brethren," Heb. 2:11

According to Scripture, Paul is teaching that the humanity of Christ is likened *only* to those who are born again, and *then* they "are *all* of one". No, Christ humanity is not likened to the unregenerate man out on the street, neither is Christ humanity likened to the man who is justified, neither is Christ humanity likened to the man that is being sanctified but only to the man who *is* sanctified is what the Bible teaches. And *then* they are said to be all of one. Davis[206] presents an irrefutable defense from the Scriptures for this view if there are those who desire to

---

[205] Gerhard Pfandl, *What Is New In The New Theology*, PDF 3-6.
[206] Thomas A. Davis, *Was Jesus Really Like Us?* (Ukiah, CA: Orion Publishing, 2013).

look into this issue further but the text speaks for itself. Peter declares that Christ had no sin, 1 Peter 2:22, but John goes further and says Christ had no sin "in Him." His nature was sinless!

> "And ye know that he was manifested to take away our sins; and <u>in him</u> is <u>no sin</u>." 1 John 3:5.

His human nature was spotless, without sin! Yet we are told from Priebe and the others that promote his view that Jesus had a sinful fallen nature just like the unregenerate man on the street corner with the same bent to evil. Yet in the same breath we are told by Priebe and the independents that Jesus never sinned. I am sorry but this is intellectually offensive at best.

What saith the S.O.P. about Christ human nature? We begin a little differently this time with a short detour before we begin our comparison side by side with the Plaintiff, the independents and Inspiration. By allowing Priebe to present the very same quote that the organized church uses to sustain their position on the nature of Christ. In this way the reader can compare its use or abuse from both parties:

> "If Jesus' perfect obedience was predicted upon the fact that He had an unfallen nature, then He had an advantage I can never possess. However, if Jesus' obedience was based on the Holy Spirit's control of His life, then I can also choose that control of my life, and I can come to live a life of total obedience. I can have that "advantage".
>
> The following statement may be a good summary of this point. "Christ did not possess the same sinful, corrupt, fallen disloyalty we possess, for then He could not be a perfect offering."- Manuscript, 94, 1893. It is the disloyalty that is the problem. Inheritance does not make us guilty, but the choice to exercise our fallen nature produces guilt."[207]

While there is a serious problem with the first sentence of the first paragraph which is another attempt to make Christ altogether human, such as one as ourselves (See No. 9) that Ellen White says cannot be, that we will prove to be just that momentarily. It is Priebe's last sentence that we wish to focus on at this time:

> "It is the *disloyalty* that is the problem. *Inheritance does not make us guilty, but the choice to exercise our fallen nature produces guilt.*"[208]

---

[207] Dennis Priebe, *Face-to-Face With the Real Gospel* (Boise Idaho, Pacific Press Publishing Association, 1985), 55-56.
[208] Ibid. 56.

Priebe's supposition has once again been completely dismantled because as we have previously shown in chapter 1, *disloyalty* is *not* "the" problem according to Scripture and Inspiration. But *Inheritance* "is" the problem for Priebe, but not, for Ellen White:

> "...children received from Adam an *inheritance* of disobedience, of *guilt* and *death*."[209]

> "The *inheritance* of *children* is that of *sin*."[210]

Here is the same quote in full context that is clearly designating Christ sinless human nature that was *not deified* by the blending together of the two natures:

> "Through being partakers of the divine nature we may stand pure and holy and undefiled. The Godhead was not made human, and the human was not *deified* by the blending together of the two natures. *Christ did not possess the same sinful, corrupt, fallen disloyalty we possess*, for then He could not be a perfect offering."[211]

The meaning is now crystal clear and it needs no commentary.

Here is a method of research that raises a real concern. Anyone reading the quote below from Priebe[212] in *Selected Messages*, 1:408, would conclude it to be from Ellen White, correct?

> "If He did not have man's nature, He could not be our example. If He was not a partaker of our nature, He could not have been tempted as man has been. If it were not possible for Him to yield to temptation, He could not be our helper."[213]

Wrong, here is the quote in full context from the same source:

> "Letters have been coming in to me, affirming that Christ could not have had the same nature as man, for if He had, He would have fallen under similar temptations. *If He did not have man's nature, He could not be our example. If He was not a partaker of our nature, He could not have been tempted as man*

---

[209] Ellen White, 13MR, 14. [Emphasis mine]
[210] Ellen White, *Child Guidance*, 475. [Emphasis mine]
[211] Ellen White, *Manuscript 94, 1893* – MR, 6:112. [Emphasis mine]
[212] Dennis Priebe, *Face-to-Face With the Real Gospel* (Boise Idaho, Pacific Press Publishing Association, 1985), 60.
[213] Ellen White, *Selected Messages,* 1: 408. [Emphasis mine]

has been. If it were not possible for Him to yield to temptation, He could not be our helper."[214]

Without argument she is quoting the *letters* that have been coming into her! She is not sanctioning what Priebe has implemented at all! Besides, this would be a complete contradiction to all her other statements. Proof, just three paragraphs later from the same source she unequivocally states *her position* that harmonizes perfectly with all her other statements that we will soon disclose:

"Satan did not gain the victory over Christ. He did *not* put his *foot* upon the *soul* of the Redeemer. He did *not* touch the *head* though he bruised the heel."[215]

Affirming Christ purity and His sinless human nature! Please read the chapter, *How to Meet a Controverted Point* in *Selected Messages*, 1:406-416 for there is much needed insights and detection of deception regarding this very topic. Assume nothing my friend:

"There are those who pick out from the Word of God, and also from the Testimonies, detached paragraphs or sentences that may be interpreted to suit their ideas, and they dwell upon these, and build themselves up in their own positions, when God is not leading them. *Here is your danger.*"[216]

Before we present Inspirations definitive statements on the Nature of Christ we must all be on the same page regarding this explicit counsel that has been largely ignored by the independents with dreadful consequences. We shall now begin our comparison with the writings of Ellen White alongside their statements and accusations from the Plaintiff, the independents:

"*Be careful, exceedingly careful as to how you dwell upon the human nature of Christ. Do not set Him before the people as a man with the propensities of sin.* He is the second Adam. The first Adam was created a pure, sinless being, without a taint of sin upon him; he was in the image of God. He could fall, and he did fall through transgressing. *Because of sin his posterity was born with inherent propensities of disobedience.* But Jesus Christ was the only begotten Son of God. He took upon Himself human nature, and was tempted in all points as human nature is tempted. He could have sinned; He could have fallen, *but not for one moment was there in Him an evil propensity.* He was

---

[214] Ellen White, *Selected Messages,* 1:408. [Emphasis mine]
[215] Ellen White, *Selected Messages,* 1:409. [Emphasis mine]
[216] Ellen White, *Selected Messages,* 1:179. [Emphasis mine]

assailed with temptations in the wilderness, as Adam was assailed with temptations in Eden. Bro. ____, avoid every question in relation to the humanity of Christ which is liable to be misunderstood. Truth lies close to the track of presumption. In treating upon the humanity of Christ, you need to guard strenuously every assertion, lest your words be taken to mean more than they imply, and thus you lose or dim the clear perceptions of His humanity as combined with divinity. His birth was a miracle of God; for, said the angel, "Behold, thou shalt conceive in thy womb, and bring forth a son, and shalt call his name JESUS. He shall be great, and shall be called the Son of the Highest: and the Lord God shall give unto him the throne of his father David: and he shall reign over the house of Jacob for ever; and of his kingdom there shall be no end. Then said Mary unto the angel, How shall this be, seeing I know not a man? And the angel answered and said unto her, The Holy Ghost shall come upon thee, and the power of the Highest shall overshadow thee: therefore also that holy thing which shall be born of thee shall be called the Son of God."

These words do not refer to any human being, except to the Son of the infinite God. *Never, in any way, leave the slightest impression upon human minds that a taint of, or inclination to, corruption rested upon Christ, or that He in any way yielded to corruption. He was tempted in all points like as man is tempted, yet He is called "that holy thing."* It is a mystery that is left unexplained to mortals that Christ could be tempted in all points like as we are, and yet be without sin. The incarnation of Christ has ever been, and will ever remain a mystery. That which is revealed, is for us and for our children, *but let every human being be warned from the ground of making Christ altogether human, such an one as ourselves; for it cannot be.* The exact time when humanity blended with divinity, it is not necessary for us to know. We are to keep our feet on the Rock Christ Jesus, as God revealed in humanity

I perceive that there is danger in approaching subjects which dwell on the humanity of the Son of the infinite God. He did humble Himself when He saw He was in fashion as a man, that He might understand the force of all temptations wherewith man is beset.

The first Adam fell; the second Adam held fast to God and His Word under the most trying circumstances, and His faith in His Father's goodness, mercy, and love did not waver for one moment." [217]

As will be seen throughout this discourse, much of her explicit *italicized* instruction has been met with a total disregard from Priebe, Standish brothers, 1888 Message Study Committee and

---

[217] Ellen White, *Letter* 8, 1895; *SDABC*, 5:1128-9. [Emphasis mine]

the independents and has resulted in opening the door wide open to Satan's counterfeit gospel. It is this fanaticism and open rebellion that plagues the church yet today!

Next, we will be concentrating on a single quote from the Standish brothers that will be presented in three different stages for clarity purposes. In the first stage we will show the first false charge that will not withstand investigation:

> "There has been a-none-too-subtle attempt to undermine the Bible truth on the human nature of Christ by indicating that this emphasis of *Jones and Waggoner was a result of progressive apostasy in what they believed. That this is not true is evidenced by the fact that there is no extant letter from the servant of the Lord rebuking them or counseling them in respect of this teaching.*"[218]

1. That *this is true* that what Jones and Waggoner believed was a result of progressive apostasy by walking away from Scripture and Inspiration that Priebe, the Standish brothers and the independents have so chosen to follow man rather than Scripture and Ellen White. Priebe, the Standish brothers and the independents have built their entire structure upon the men, A. T. Jones and E.J. Waggoner and here is the proof:

> "Then Satan took Jesus upon an exceeding high mountain, and showed him all the kingdoms of the world, and the glory of them, too – the glory, the honor, the dignity, - he showed him all that. *And there at that moment there was stirred up all the ambition that ever appeared in Napoleon, or Caesar, or Alexander, or all of them put together.* But from Jesus still the answer is: 'It is written, Thou shalt worship the Lord thy God, and Him only shalt thou serve. . . *Now the flesh of Jesus Christ was our flesh, and in it was all that is in our flesh,-all the tendencies to sin that are in our flesh were in his flesh, drawing upon him to get him to consent to sin.*"[219]

> "Well, then, in his [Christ] human nature, when he was upon the earth, was he in any wise different from what you are in your human nature to-night? (A few in the congregation responded, "NO") I wish we had heard everybody in the house say, "NO" with a load voice."[220]

Waggoner says:

> **"Likeness of Sinful Flesh**. – There is a common idea that this means that Christ simulated sinful flesh; that he did not take upon himself actual sinful

---

[218] Colin D. Standish & Russell R. Standish, Deceptions of the New Theology (Hartland Publications, 1989). 47. See also the article, Dennis Priebe, *Original Sin, Forgiveness, And Obedience*, 7-9. [Emphasis mine]
[219] A.T. Jones, *The Third Angels Message*, 1895 General Conference Bulletin, No. 17. 87-88 (327). [Emphasis mine]
[220] Ibid. 67, (233).

flesh, but only what appeared to be such. But the Scriptures do not teach such a thing."[221]

Jones and Waggoner are clearly teaching that Christ had a sinful nature such as you and I have, yet this chapter will prove that Jones, Waggoner and anyone else to be completely out of step with Scripture and Inspiration. We will come back to this first quote in due time but first we continue to read further into the quote from the Standish brothers concerning the second false charge:

2. "That *this is not true* is evidenced by the fact that there *is no extant letter from the servant of the Lord rebuking them or counseling them in respect of this teaching*."[222]

However, Ellen White *did* respond to the many inquiries made to her on Jan. 29, 1890 that we just witnessed previously pertaining to the nature of Christ:

> "*Letters have been coming in to me*, affirming that Christ could not have had the same nature as man, for if He had, He would have fallen under similar temptations. *If He did not have man's nature, He could not be our example. If He was not a partaker of our nature, He could not have been tempted as man has been. If it were not possible for Him to yield to temptation, He could not be our helper.* It was a solemn reality that Christ came to fight the battles as man, in man's behalf. His temptation and victory tell us that humanity must copy the Pattern; man must become a partaker of the divine nature."[223]

Without argument, as we have just viewed previously, she is quoting the *letters* that have been coming into her! Then just three paragraphs later she responds to the inquiries and she unequivocally states *her position* that harmonizes perfectly with all her other statements that we will soon disclose:

> "Satan did not gain the victory over Christ. He did *not* put his *foot* upon the *soul* of the Redeemer. He did *not* touch the *head* though he bruised the heel."[224]

Ironically in the year of 1888 she penned these words in *The Review and Herald* for all to see in stark contrast to the position of Jones and Waggoner on the nature of Christ as she was growing and receiving in knowledge and in light:

---

[221] E.J. Waggoner, *Waggoner on Romans*, (Berrien Springs, MI; Glad Tidings Publishers, 1997), 128. Originally published, Signs of the Times, Oct. 1895 – Sept. 1896.
[222] Colin D. Standish & Russell R. Standish, Deceptions of the New Theology (Hartland Publications, 1989). 47.
[223] Ellen White, *Selected Messages,* 1: 408.
[224] Ellen White, *Selected Messages,* 1:409.

> "Christ was not insensible to ignominy and disgrace. He felt it all most bitterly. He felt it as much more deeply and acutely than we can feel suffering, as *His nature was more exalted and pure, and holy than that of the <u>sinful</u> race for whom He suffered.*"[225]

Affirming Christ purity and His sinless human nature! Now we proceed to the third accusation:

3. The reader will find by the end of this chapter that the italicized statement by the Standish brothers will not even remotely withstand investigation:

> "There has been a-none-too-subtle attempt to undermine the Bible truth on the human nature of Christ by indicating that this emphasis of Jones and Waggoner was a result of progressive apostasy in what they believed. That this is not true is evidenced by the fact that there is no extant letter from the servant of the Lord rebuking them or counseling them in respect of this teaching. On the other hand, we have letter after letter written by Sister White in an attempt to help them in other areas of their presentations when she recognized that they were losing the beauty of the message they had presented. *More importantly, the writings of Sister White herself are full of unequivocal statements supporting the central truth of the fallen human nature of Jesus Christ. . .*"[226]

Ellen White expressed some most exceptional details of the role and nature of the second Adam. A gem, which has been hidden and misrepresented by the traditions of men:

> "After the fall of man, Satan declared that human beings were proved...." [Were proved. Past tense.] "To be incapable of keeping the law of God, and he sought to carry the universe with him in this belief. Satan's words appeared to be true and Christ came to unmask the deceiver."[227]

Priebe says:
> "Jesus in man's nature lived a life that Satan said could not be lived."[228]

After Priebe stated the above he concludes with the following:

> "In our conclusions, we make many mistakes because of our erroneous views of the human nature of our Lord. When we give His human nature a

---

[225] Ellen White, *The Review and Herald*, September 11, 1888. (Italics supplied.)
[226] Colin D. Standish & Russell R. Standish, *Deceptions of the New Theology* (Hartland Publications, 1989). 47-48.
[227] Ellen White, *Selected Messages*, 1:252.
[228] Dennis Priebe, *Face-to-Face*, 61.

power that is not possible for man to have in his conflicts with Satan, we destroy the completeness of His humanity." – Ellen G. White Comments, S.D.A. Bible Commentary, vol. 7, p. 929. We simply do not have the power of Adam's nature available to us. The warning is clear that by giving to Jesus' human nature a power that we cannot have, we destroy the completeness of His humanity. "The Lord now demands that every son and daughter of Adam… serve Him in human nature which we now have…. Jesus….could only keep the commandments of God in the same way that humanity can keep them." –Ibid. How can we keep them? Certainly not in Adam's nature. We can only keep them in that nature which we now have- fallen nature. And Jesus kept the commandments of God in the same way we are to keep them. Jesus overcame as we are to overcome."[229]

Priebe is once again diametrically opposed to Ellen White and the ramifications here are huge that we will take back up in chapter 6. Inspiration says that Christ, as the second Adam overcame Satan "*as God created him*" in Adam's pre-fall nature. Priebe says that Christ overcame Satan in Adam's post fall nature. Who is right?

> "Christ is called the *Second Adam*. In purity and holiness, connected with God and beloved by God, *he began where the first Adam began.* Willingly he passed over the ground where Adam fell and redeemed Adam's failure."[230]

Christ came to disprove the lie that man *as God created him* could perfectly obey. In order to do that, in order to pass over the same ground where Adam stumbled and fell, where would he logically have to begin? Where Adam began, before he fell! In order to unmask the deceiver, how did He have to come? As a man, yes, but as a man separated from God, or as a man in perfect union with God? Ellen White answers this vital question for us:

> "*Christ* came to the earth, taking *humanity* and standing as man's representative, *to show in the great controversy with Satan that man, as God*

---

[229] Ibid. 61-62.
[230] Ellen White, *Youth's Instructor*, June 2, 1898.

> _created him_, connected with the Father and the Son, _could obey every divine requirement._"[231]

Again:

> "Satan had claimed that it was impossible for man to obey God's commandments; and in our own strength it is true that we cannot obey them. But _Christ came in the form of humanity_, and by _His perfect obedience He proved_ that humanity and divinity combined can obey every one of God's precepts."[232]

> "Christ came to give moral power to man; to elevate, ennoble, and strengthen him. He came to prove the falsity of Satan's charge that God had made a law which man could not keep. _While possessing man's nature, Christ kept the Ten Commandments. Thus He proved to the inhabitants of the unfallen worlds and to human beings that it is possible for man perfectly to obey the law_. He _vindicated_ God's justice in demanding obedience to His law. Those who accept Christ as their Saviour, becoming partakers of the divine nature, are enabled to follow His example of obedience to every divine precept."[233]

Christ came to prove what? To show in the great controversy, not that _man as he was separated from God and alienated from God by nature could perfectly obey every requirement_, but that what? Man as God "_created him_", connected with the Father and the Son, could obey every divine requirement!

Without further delay we hereby present Inspirations definitive statements on the nature of Christ as promised that many may be unfamiliar with. These unequivocal statements further and fully support Scripture and the organized churches' view of Christ sinless spiritual nature and will forevermore lay to rest the unfounded accusations by the Plaintiff, the independents. In the following quotes and illustrations please compare the complete harmony of the previous Scriptures submitted and how Pfandl so elegantly illustrated the threefold union of humanity from the scriptures and Ellen White's writings that the Standish brothers, Priebe, Weiland and

---

[231] Ellen White, _SDABC_, 7: 926.
[232] Ellen White, _Christ Object Lessons_, 314.
[233] Ellen White, _Signs of the Times_, May 14, 1902.

Short of the 1888 Message Study Committee and the independents reject in order to hold onto their unsustained premise of Christ having a sinful nature:

> "He was to take His position at the head of humanity by taking the *nature but not the sinfulness of man.*"[234]

> "Man weighed against God's holy law is found wanting. We are enlightened by the precepts of the law but no man can by them be justified. *Weighed and found wanting is our inscription by nature.*"[235]

Here is a legitimate argument and I am turning over the platform to Pastor Stephen Wallace to answer this one for the benefit of the reader. Wallace establishes how Christ legally first became our substitute for he answers this so elegantly:

> "Man weighed against God's holy law is found wanting. We are enlightened by the precepts of the law but no man can by them be justified. *Weighed and found wanting is our inscription by nature.*"[236]
>
> "There's good news that follows. Listen to it. Weighed and found wanting is our inscription by nature but Christ is our Mediator and accepting Him as our Savior, we may claim the promise, being justified by faith, we have peace with God through our Lord Jesus Christ. That's the gospel. But you'll never appreciate it and embrace it until you recognize with me that we all are weighed in the balance and found wanting by nature.
>
> Signs of the Times, May 19, 1890: "Adam sinned and the children of Adam share his guilt and its consequences." We wrestled with that truth in an earlier study. What about this guilt of Adam that his children bear? "Adam sinned and the children of Adam share his guilt and its consequences. But" --here's the precious good news -- "Jesus bore the guilt of Adam, and all the children of Adam that will flee to Christ, the second Adam, may escape the penalty of transgression." The children of Adam bear his guilt. By natural birth, they are under condemnation on account of the sin of Adam. Do they have any choice in that matter? No. Is that fair? Sin is never fair. But praise God, they have a choice as to whether or not to continue to bear that guilt. They can choose to come to Jesus and let Him take it from them and bear it Himself. They can choose to be born again.

---

[234] Ellen White, *Signs of the Times*, May 29, 1901)
[235] Ellen White, *Review & Herald,* March 8, 1906.
[236] Ellen White, *Review & Herald,* March 8, 1906.

And brothers and sisters please recognize with me an important point. If we complain about being condemned and sentenced to death on account of Adam's sin--don't lose me--we also have to complain about being justified and promised eternal life on account of Christ's obedience. Did you follow me? Romans 5:19: "By the disobedience of one the many were made sinners." Not so, we say. Oh, but be careful. Don't be too quick. The second half says, "Even so, by the obedience of one, the many will be made" what? Righteous. Do you want to cry out, Not fair? No, you don't, do you? But please recognize the principle. These are unique individuals and they have the unique capacity being the two heads of the human race, to have legal, direct influence on the whole race. Adam as the legal representative brought condemnation upon the whole race, and the whole race is born under that condemnation and sentenced to death. Now their own sinfulness simply ratifies the fact that they are born in the fallen race, and their own sin simply verifies their own sinfulness. But what is it that is the cause of their condemnation? Adam's sin.

When we're born again--follow me, please--what is the cause of our justification? Christ's righteousness. Is it caused by something we are in ourselves? No, that new heart that we receive simply evidences the fact that we are indeed now members of the new race. And our own obedience simply ratifies the presence of the new heart. But the justification is based upon what? The obedience of the Second Adam. Do you see that truth? Don't be so quick to resent the imputation of Adam's guilt to you because, if you do, you have to resent the imputation of Christ's righteousness to you. It's on the same legal basis, precisely, because those two bear the same relationship to us. Legally, one by natural birth; the other, by rebirth.

Desire of Ages, page 598: "Those who trust in him he never disappoints. He has borne every test, he has endured the pressure of Adam's guilt and the guilt of his posterity, and he has come off more than conqueror of the powers of evil. He has borne the burdens cast upon him by every repenting sinner. In Christ, the guilty heart has found relief. He is the sure foundation. All who make him their dependence rest in perfect security."

Oh, brothers and sisters, when you confess your sinfulness of nature, as the apostles did--Acts of the Apostles, 561--men who would rather die than knowingly transgress God's law. They still did what? They confessed the sinfulness of their nature. When you confess the sinfulness of your nature, you can rest in total confidence that there is no condemnation now because He bore the sinfulness of that nature, and the condemnation for it was exhausted on His head. And why and how could He bear it? Because He didn't have it in Himself.

What does God's word say? "For he made him who knew no sin for us that we might become" what? "The righteousness of God" where? "In him." II Cor. 5:21. Oh, brothers and sisters, that was the reason He became sin for us, that we might become the righteousness of God in Him. To do both. To be our Substitute in death and to be our Substitute in life. To be our Substitute in dying to pay our debt. To be our Substitute in living a perfect life to meet the infinite standard in our behalf. In both these aspects, He had to be absolutely sinless in His humanity to accomplish His mission.

Remember, the law requires that we have not only absolute sinlessness but that we have what? Infinite righteousness. We are hopeless unless we have One that has both absolute sinlessness and infinite righteousness. I hope that we have clearly established that in Christ we do have One who has absolute sinlessness. We must assure ourselves that in Christ we also have One who has infinite righteousness."[237]

With special thanks to Pastor Stephen Wallace for his excellent insights, Continuing on:

"*He was born without a taint of sin*, but came into the world in like manner as the human family. He did not have a mere semblance of a body, but He took human nature, participating in the life of humanity."[238]

"There should not be the faintest misgivings in regard to the *perfect freedom from sinfulness in the human nature of Christ*."[239]

---

[237] Stephen Wallace, "*Our Sinless Yet Sympathetic Savior*", revivalseminars.org. See also: americanchristianministries.org.
[238] Ellen White, 10*MR*, 173.

"Adam and Eve were given a probation in which to return to their allegiance; and in this plan of benevolence *all their posterity were embraced*. After the Fall, Christ became Adam's instructor. He acted in God's stead toward humanity, saving the race from immediate death. He took upon Him the work of mediator between God and man. In the fullness of time He was to be revealed in human form. He was to take His position at the head of humanity by taking the *nature* but *not the sinfulness of man*.[240]

"The love that Christ manifested cannot be comprehended by mortal man. It is a mystery too deep for the human mind to fathom. *Christ did in reality unite the offending nature of man with his own sinless nature*, because by this act of condescension he would be enabled to pour out his blessings in behalf of the fallen race. Thus he has made it possible for us to partake of his nature. By making himself an offering for sin, he opened a way whereby human beings might be made one with him. He placed himself in man's position, becoming capable of suffering. The whole of his earthly life was a preparation for the altar."[241]

These quotes and the previous quotes submitted have without dispute shown that the organized church's position withstands investigation.

Next we must address some serious misrepresentations of Christ and private interpretations by Priebe and the Standish brothers along with the independents that totally misrepresent the character of Christ before the world. When men run off course doctrinally they always leave a theological paper trail that will fully expose their errors. Priebe is no exception:

"Why did Jesus say, 'I seek not mine own will' (John 5:30), and 'I come down from heaven, not to do mine own will' (John 7:38)? Why would it be necessary to say this if His own will was faultless and pure, and holy? But if His own will and His own inclinations were tending toward the negative, then it would make sense for Him to ask that His Father's will be done."[242]

Please realize that Priebe is here saying that Jesus' will was *not* "faultless, pure and holy" and also that "His own will and His own inclinations were tending toward the negative." He is also interpreting John 5 & 6 to be saying that Jesus' "will" was different than His Father's. There are

---

[239] Ellen White, 16*MR*, 117.
[240] Ellen White, *Signs of the Times*, May 29, 1901.
[241] Ellen White, *Review & Herald*, July 17, 1900.
[242] Dennis Priebe, *Face-to-Face*, 59.

two parts to this that we need to examine: His "will" and His "inclination". Priebe says:

> "His own will was tending toward the negative."[243]

Let's compare this to two Spirit of Prophecy quotes:

> "The time of the Passover was drawing near, and again Jesus turned toward Jerusalem. In His heart was the peace of *perfect oneness with the Father's will*, and with eager steps He pressed on toward the place of sacrifice."[244]

". . . Perfect oneness with the Father's *will*". Can Priebe's statements and this quote be made to harmonize? The last quote may be the best one for this comparison, because it is from the chapter in Desire of Ages, which is a commentary on John 5, which Priebe uses to say that Jesus' will was contrary to His Father's and that "His own will was tending toward the negative." In Desire of Ages she says:

> "Jesus repelled the charge of blasphemy. My authority, He said, for doing the work of which you accuse Me, is that I am the Son of God, one with Him in nature, in *will*, and in purpose."[245]

In the very discourse where Jesus is claiming His oneness with God it says:

> "Therefore the Jews sought the more to kill him, because he not only had broken the Sabbath, but said also that God was his Father, making himself equal with God." John 5:18.

And where Ellen White says He is "one with Him in *will*", Priebe is saying "His will was tending toward the negative", and contrary to His Father's. Again, in Desire of Ages she says:

> "The humble Nazarene asserts His real nobility. He rises above humanity, throws off the guise of sin and shame, and stands revealed, the Honored of the angels, the Son of God, One with the Creator of the universe. His hearers are spellbound. No man has ever spoken words like His, or borne himself with such a kingly majesty. His utterances are clear and plain, fully declaring His mission, and the duty of the world."[246]

And as an answer to the often asked questions, "Why did Jesus say 'I seek not mine own will'?" First, He was trying to make them understand that everything He did was from God the Father – Whom they claimed to acknowledge as their supreme Ruler – Jesus, they didn't acknowledge, and that in rejecting Him, they were truly rejecting God. "He that honoureth not

---

[243] Dennis Priebe, *Face-to-Face*, 59.
[244] Ellen White, *Desire of Ages*, 547.
[245] Ibid. 208.
[246] Ibid. 210.

the Son honoureth not the Father which hath sent Him." John 5:23. A similar statement is found in one of the very next chapters of John's Gospel, where He says, "My doctrine is not mine, but his that sent me." John 7:16. Again He was trying to make them understand that in rejecting His "doctrine", they were in reality, rejecting God's doctrine. No one would ever say that Jesus was here saying His "doctrine" was different from His Fathers'. Secondly, Jesus was showing an example of submission and *surrender* to God, just as He was baptized as an example. Please read, Desire of Ages pgs. 208-9. She gives a very strong illustration of this. And in the midst it says, "He [Jesus] said, '*I delight* to do *thy will....*" Ps. 40:8.

The divide comes about because Priebe is building upon a false premise by giving Christ a sinful fallen nature rather than the 4000 years of fallen physical liabilities that Christ took upon Himself. "For four thousand years the race had been decreasing in physical strength, in mental power, and in moral worth; and Christ took upon Him the infirmities of degenerate humanity."[247] And as we have witnessed, Scripture and Inspiration in no wise support Priebe's view.

Now the other part of Priebe's quote that concerns His "inclinations". But first, Ellen White:

> *"Never, in any way, leave the slightest impression upon human minds that a taint of, or inclination to, corruption rested upon Christ, or that He in any way yielded to corruption.* He was tempted in all points like as man is tempted, yet He is called "that holy thing." . . . *but let every human being be warned from the ground of making Christ altogether human, such an one as ourselves; for it cannot be. . . I perceive that there is danger in approaching subjects which dwell on the humanity of the Son of the infinite God. . . .* for the prince of this world cometh, and hath *nothing in me"--nothing to respond to temptation. On not one occasion was there a response to his manifold temptations. Not once did Christ step on Satan's ground, to give him any advantage. Satan found nothing in Him to encourage his advances."*[248]

Please read this partial quote over and over and let every word have its proper bearing, and then compare both quotes very carefully:

> *"Never, in any way, leave the slightest impression upon human minds that a taint of, or inclination to, corruption rested upon Christ, or that He in any way yielded to corruption."*[249]

> Now Priebe again: "His own inclination was tending toward the negative."[250]

---

[247] Ellen White, Desire of Ages, 117.
[248] Ellen White, *SDABC*, 5:1128-9.
[249] Ibid. 1128-9.

There is no way that these quotes can be made to harmonize. This is precisely why Inspiration warned us about when taking the humanity of Christ too far when she said:

> *"I perceive that there is danger in approaching subjects which dwell on the humanity of the Son of the infinite God."*[251]

This will be seen to have a direct application when we examine Priebe's book on pg. 55. And then trying to fit Christ in the very same precise mold as ourselves:

> "If Jesus life is to have any meaning as an example for us, then it is crucial that He inherit just what I inherit."[252]

Here Priebe again clearly elevates human reasoning above Scripture. Priebe, Standish brothers and the independents completely disregards Ellen White's explicit counsel:

> *". . . making Christ altogether human, such an one as ourselves; for it cannot be."*[253]

And the consequences that have followed this rejection of God's word continue to speak and bear fruit for the last 60 yr.'s and Oh what a crop and divide it has produced!

The next issue we want to look at is on pg. 60. Priebe says:

> "He knew what it was like to want to go wrong. He knew what it was like to feel the temptation to rebel against God, and that temptation arose within His nature."[254]

There are two points in this quote that we need to examine. First, "He knew what it was like to *want* to go wrong". Please realize that he is saying Jesus knew from *experience*. Unbelievable! Again, let us compare a few of Ellen White quotes with Priebe's statement:

> "...as we are clothed with the righteousness of Christ we have a power and a strength that is imparted unto us, and we will not *want* to sin."[255]

"...we will not *want* to sin". Again, there is no way these two quotes can be made to harmonize. Here are a few more to consider:

> "Never before had there been a being upon the earth who hated sin with so perfect a hatred as did Christ."[256]

---

[250] Dennis Priebe, *Face-to-Face*, 59.
[251] Ellen White, *SDABC*, 5:1128-9.
[252] Dennis Priebe, *Face-to-Face*, 55.
[253] Ellen White, *SDABC*, 5:1128-9.
[254] Dennis Priebe, *Face-to-Face*, 60.
[255] Ellen White, *1888 Materials*, 2:538.

"...Never lived there another who so hated evil."[257]

Try to think of anything you have a "perfect" hatred for and then ask yourself if you "want" to do it! Inspiration says:

"...the refined sensibilities of His holy nature rendered contact with evil unspeakably painful to Him."[258]

Can you imagine "wanting" to do something that in just witnessing it you find it "unspeakably painful"?

"...as the sinless one His "nature" recoiled from evil."[259]

These two authors are clearly coming from two different sources. One author proclaims a post fall nature; the other author proclaims a pre fall nature. Who are you going to follow? The second part of that quote by Priebe we need to examine says:

"He knew what it was like to feel the temptation to rebel against God, *and that temptation, arose from within His nature.*"[260]

In contrast to Inspiration:

"Temptation is enticement to sin, and this does not proceed from God, but from *Satan* and from the *evil of our own hearts*."[261]

I find Priebe's quote extremely disturbing in the light of this quote. Now coming from a different aspect is this quote:

"The completeness of Christian character is attained when the impulse to help and bless others springs constantly from within."[262]

Once again I find a serious conflict between what Ellen White says and on pg. 59 that Priebe says:

"Are not our problems basically self and pride and the desire that come from our fallen nature? Do we not fall most often because of the inner desire

---

[256] Ellen White, *Selected Messages,* 1: 254..
[257] Ellen White, *Education*, 79.
[258] Ellen White, *SDABC*, 7:927.
[259] Ellen White, *Testimonies*, 2:202.
[260] Dennis Priebe, *Face-to-Face*, 60.
[261] Ellen White, *Mount of Blessing*, 116.
[262] Ellen white, *Acts of the Apostles*, 551.

that lead us astray? If Jesus did not have any of these, could it really be true that He was tempted in all points as we are?"[263]

This quote is absolutely incredible! Notice that Priebe chose the specific words that he did – *self* and *pride*. Let us compare his statement with the following quotes by Ellen White:

> "So utterly was Christ emptied of *self* that He made no plans for Himself."[264]

> "The drunkard is despised and is told that his sin will exclude him from heaven; while *pride*, selfishness, and covetousness too often go unrebuked. But these are sins that are especially offense to God; for they are contrary to the benevolence of His character, to that unselfish love which is the very atmosphere of the unfallen universe."[265]

> "The divine love ruling in the heart *exterminates pride* and *selfishness*."[266]

> "Human nature is ever struggling for expression, ready for contest; but he who learns of Christ is *emptied* of *self*, of *pride*, of love of supremacy, and there is silence in the soul."[267]

> "*Pride*, ambition, deceit, hatred, selfishness, must be cleansed from the heart."[268]

> "It was the *pride* and ambition cherished in the heart of Satan that banished him from heaven. These evils are deeply rooted in our fallen nature, and if not removed they will overshadow every good and noble quality and bring forth envy and strife as their baleful fruits."[269]

Again, two different authors using two different sources. There is one more very important point which must be examined. It concerns what Christ inherited by nature according to Priebe:

> "If Jesus' life is to have any meaning as an example for us, then it is crucial that He inherit just what I inherit."[270]

---

[263] Dennis Priebe, *Face-to-Face*, 59.
[264] Ellen White, *Desire of Ages*, 208.
[265] Ellen White, *Steps to Christ*, 30.
[266] Ellen White, *Testimonies*, 5:168.
[267] Ellen White, *Mount of Blessing*, 15.
[268] Ellen White, *Testimonies*, 5:175.
[269] Ellen White, *Testimonies*, 5:242.
[270] Dennis Priebe, *Face-to-Face*, 55.

Priebe says:

> "We do inherit *badness*, weakness, and *corruption* from Adam."[271]

Again, Priebe says:

> "...it is, crucial that He inherit just what I inherit."[272]

Ellen White says:

> "...Because of sin his [Adam's] posterity was *born* with *propensities of disobedience*. But Jesus Christ was the only begotten Son of God. . . not for one moment was there *in Him an evil propensity*."[273]

Ellen White clearly teaches *we inherit* evil propensities, in the same paragraph she contrasts Christ with us and she says *He did not inherit evil propensities*."

Priebe says:

> "The *crucial* point is that a *sinful propensity is permitted to develop from our inherited bent to evil*. Jesus never developed such sinful propensities."[274]

Priebe again:

> "If Jesus' life is to have any meaning as an example for us, then it is *crucial* that He *inherit just what I inherit*."[275]

Please reread those last two quotes very closely. Priebe is clearly and openly teaching that Jesus Christ *had a bent to evil*. In contrast, Ellen White is clearly and openly teaching that Jesus Christ *did not have a bent to evil*. Please give this point some very serious thought and study. How you stand on it is *absolutely critical* if you are to stay on the straight and narrow or take the fork in the road! Unbelievable!

As promised, we return to a statement of A.T. Jones:

> "Then Satan took Jesus upon an exceeding high mountain, and showed him all the kingdoms of the world, and the glory of them, too – the glory, the honor, the dignity, - he showed him all that. *And there at that moment there was stirred up all the <u>ambition</u> that ever appeared in Napoleon, or Caesar, or Alexander, or all of them put together*. But from Jesus still the answer is: 'It is written, Thou shalt worship the Lord thy God, and Him only shalt thou serve. .

---

[271] Ibid. 27.
[272] Ibid. 55.
[273] Ellen White, *SDABC*, 1128.
[274] Dennis Priebe, *Face-to-Face*, 54.
[275] Ibid. 55.

. Now the flesh of Jesus Christ was our flesh, and in it was all that is in our flesh,-all the tendencies to sin that are in our flesh were in his flesh, drawing upon him to get him to consent to sin."[276]

Here are a few quotes from Inspiration about "ambition".

"With the gentle touch of grace the Savior banishes from the soul unrest and unholy *ambition*..."[277]

"Pride, *ambition*, deceit, hatred, selfishness, must be cleansed from the heart. With many these evil traits are partially subdued, but not thoroughly uprooted from the heart."[278]

"It was the *pride* and *ambition* cherished in the heart of Satan that banished him from heaven. These evils are deeply rooted in our fallen nature, and if not removed they will over shadow every good and noble quality and bring forth envy and strife as their baleful fruits."[279]

"The prince of this world cometh,' said Jesus, 'and hath nothing in Me." John 14:30."[280]

There was in Him *nothing that responded* to Satan's sophistry.

Jones says:

". . .There at that moment there was *stirred up* all the ambition that ever appeared in ..."[281]

According to Jones there was something in Him that responded, but He kept it from coming out. Now consider this quote very carefully:

"The law of God takes note of the jealousy, envy, hatred, malignity, revenge, lust and *ambition* that surge through the soul, but have not found expression in outward action, because the opportunity, not the will, has been wanting. And these *sinful emotions* will be brought into the account in the day when 'God shall bring every work into judgment, with every secret thing, whether it be good, or whether it be evil.'" Eccl 12:14.[282]

---

[276] A.T. Jones, *The Third Angels Message*, 1895 General Conference Bulletin, No. 17. 87-88 (327-8).
[277] Ellen White, *Prophet and Kings*, 60.
[278] Ellen White, *Testimonies*, 5:175.
[279] Ellen White, *Testimonies*, 5:242.
[280] Ellen White, *Desire of Ages*, 123.
[281] Jones, *GCB*, No. 17. 87-88 (327-8).
[282] Ellen White, *Selected Messages*, 1: 217.

This is exactly where Jones is putting Christ. Jesus did not subdue this "sinful emotion". There was none in Him. (John 14:30.). On the contrary, *He was* infinite humility:

> "What He taught, He lived. 'I have given you an example,' He said to His disciples; 'that ye should do as I have done.' 'I have kept My Father's commandments.' John 13:15; 15:10. Thus in His life, Christ's words had perfect illustration and support. *And more than this*; what He taught, *He was*. His words were the expression, not only of His own life experience, but of His own character. Not only did He teach the truth, but *He was* the truth. It was this that gave His teaching power."[283]

As we have witnessed earlier, Priebe says *Pride*, Jones says *Ambition*. These are the very characteristics of Satan himself:

> "It was the *pride* and *ambition* cherished in the heart of Satan that banished him from heaven."[284]

Please consider these next two quotes very carefully, for this is a very serious charge I am making:

> "With his own evil characteristics he sought to invest the loving Creator. Thus he deceived angels. Thus he deceived men."[285]

> "Satan had charged upon God the attribute he himself possessed. Now in Christ he saw God revealed in His true character."[286]

Satan has simply skirted his attack from the Father to the Son,

> "Who was a perfect representation of the Father."[287]

> "Amid impurity, Christ maintained His purity. *Satan could not stain or corrupt it*. His character revealed a *perfect hatred for sin*. It was His holiness that stirred against Him all the passion of a profligate world; for by His perfect life He threw upon the world a perpetual reproach, and made manifest the contrast between transgression and the pure, spotless righteousness of One that knew no sin. This *heavenly purity annoyed the apostate foe as nothing else could do*, and he followed Christ day by day, using in his work the people that claimed to have superior purity and knowledge of God, putting into their

---

[283] Ellen White, *Education*, 78-9.
[284] Ellen White, *Testimonies*, 5:242.
[285] Ellen White, *Desire of Ages*, 22.
[286] Ellen White, *Selected Messages*, 1: 254.
[287] Ellen White, *Selected Messages*, 1: 254.

hearts a spirit of hatred against Christ, and tempting His disciples to betray and forsake Him."[288]

What have we learned and confirmed? Let's go down the list:

1. [They reject] "No evidence exists to suggest that Jesus inherited <u>only</u> the physical results of the fall, such as hunger, weakness, thirst, and mortality, but . . "[289]

This accusation has been proven to be utterly false.

2. [They reject, Continuing], . . "that He did not inherit dispositional traits. These areas cannot be separated."[290]

It has adequately been shown that Christ "dispositional traits" meaning His inclinations or tendencies were the same as ours has been proven to be utterly false.

3. [They assert] "There is no evidence that the chain of heredity was broken. The inheritance of Jesus was the same as our inheritance."[291]

In the Desire of Ages 117, Inspiration says He took, "four thousand years" . . . of the "infirmities of degenerate humanity" but nothing of *inheritance* as claimed by Priebe. As we have previously witnessed, Christ did take four thousand years of degenerate humanity upon Himself in that he was hungered and needed rest like ourselves but he never had or took upon Himself a sinful fallen nature. However, there was a very distinct variation in His birth to that of ours. The Holy Ghost *overshadowed* Mary (if you will) and therefore supernaturally fathered Jesus! Hence the human reasoning behind the rejected counsel still shines thru: *"but let every human being be warned from the ground of making Christ altogether human, such an one as ourselves; for it cannot be."*[292]

---

[288] Ellen White, *Signs of the Times* May 10, 1899.
[289] Dennis Priebe, *Face-to-Face With the Real Gospel* (Boise Idaho, Pacific Press Publishing Association, 1985), 50.
[290] Ibid. 50.
[291] Ibid. 50.
[292] Ellen White, *Letter* 8, 1895; *SDABC*, 5:1128-9.

4. [They assert] "The evidence from the Bible and the spirit of prophesy indicates that His inheritance was the same as our inheritance."²⁹³

"...children received from Adam an *inheritance* of disobedience, of *guilt* and *death*."²⁹⁴

"The *inheritance* of *children* is that of *sin*."²⁹⁵

Really? Again, we see where Satan can take fallen humanity when we wilfully ignore Heavens counsel!

5. [They assert] "It was important that Christ take both the form and nature of *fallen* man.²⁹⁶

Again, this accusation has been proven to be utterly false. He did indeed take the form and fallen physical liabilities of degenerate humanity but He did not take the "nature" of sinful fallen humanity.

6. [They assert] "Surely within our inward nature which has a bent to evil. He knows *by experience* what that is."²⁹⁷

Again, this blatant accusation has been proven to be utterly false.

7. [They assert] "Many have wondered why we develop these propensities while Christ did not develop them."²⁹⁸

---

²⁹³ Dennis Priebe, *Face-to-Face.*.51.
²⁹⁴ Ellen White, 13MR, 14.
²⁹⁵ Ellen White, *Child Guidance*, 475.
²⁹⁶ Dennis Priebe, *Face-to-Face*. 51.
²⁹⁷ Ibid. 52.
²⁹⁸ Ibid. 54.

We turn over the floor to Priebe to let you see how he answers his own question and the sources he provides for his interpretation:

> "*Many have wondered why we have developed these propensities while Christ did not develop them.* It must be *admitted* that this is the period of Christs life *(from birth to the age of accountability)* about which we have *very little information in the inspired writings.* Therefore any conclusions must remain *somewhat tentative. One suggestion* is that the parents of Jesus took special care to guide the developing mind of the infant Jesus so that sinful propensities did not develop in Jesus. *Another suggestion* is that the ability to discern between right and wrong was present very early in the child Jesus and was exercised to prevent sinful propensities from developing. *Another suggestion* is that Christ was not intended to be an example to mankind as an infant; therefore events during His infancy are not relevant to issues in the great controversy. *The solution that I favour* is that because of the supernatural birth of Christ through the Holy Spirit, He was born much as we are reborn. Because the power of the Holy Spirit was directing His life from birth, He did not develop the sinful habit patterns or propensities which we develop from birth."[299]

No Bible. No Spirit of Prophecy = No Doctrine!

8. [They assert] "If Jesus' life is to have any meaning as an *example* for us, then it is crucial that He inherit just what I inherit."[300]

This has been shown that Priebe again places human reasoning above divine revelation.

9. [They assert] "If Jesus' perfect obedience was predicated upon the fact that He had an unfallen nature, then He had an advantage I can never possess."[301]

This accusation has been proven to be utterly false, see No. 12 below.

---

[299] Dennis Priebe, *Face-to-Face*, 54-55.
[300] Ibid. 55.
[301] Ibid. 55.

10. [They assert] "Jesus Christ had to come down to the level at which He found man after the fall, not just to the level at which He originally created man."³⁰²

Again, this accusation has been proven to be utterly false. Please reread Heb. 2:11.

11. [They assert] "Satan declared that it was impossible for the sons and daughters of Adam to keep the law of God, and thus charged upon God a lack of wisdom and love. If <u>they</u> could not keep the law, then there was fault with the Lawgiver." –Signs of the Times, January 16, 1896."³⁰³

Here is another example of research by Priebe that raises a real concern! This isolated statement implies a contradiction along with a biased meaning to what we have presented previously from Ellen White's own published statements. But the deception is easily unmasked when we read just a little further:

"Satan declared that it was impossible for the sons and daughters of Adam to keep the law of God, and thus charged upon God a lack of wisdom and love. If they could not keep the law, then there was fault with the Lawgiver. Men who are under the control of Satan repeat these accusations against God, in asserting that men cannot keep the law of God. *Jesus humbled himself, clothing his divinity with humanity, in order that he might stand as the head and representative of the human family, and by both precept and example condemn sin in the flesh, <u>and give the lie to Satan's charges</u>*. He was subjected to the fiercest temptations that human nature can know, yet he sinned not; for sin is the transgression of the law. By faith he laid hold upon divinity, even as humanity may lay hold upon infinite power through him. Altho tempted upon all points even as men are tempted, he sinned not. *He did not surrender his allegiance to God, as did Adam.*" ³⁰⁴

---

³⁰² Ibid. 56-7.
³⁰³ Ibid. 57-8.
³⁰⁴ Ellen White, *Signs of the Times*, January 16, 1896.

This we had witnessed that it was Christ in a sinless pre-fall nature like Adam that had met and had proven the accusation of Satan to be false just as we have read it here. With the rest of the story!

12. [They assert] "Are not our problems basically self and pride and the desire that come from our fallen nature? Do we not fall most often because of the inner desires that lead us astray? If Jesus did not have <u>any of these</u>, could it really be true that He was tempted in all points as we are?"[305]

Here is a legitimate argument and I am turning over the platform to Pastor Frank Phillips to answer this one for the benefit of the reader. Phillips answers this accusation and permanently lays the issue in the grave when he asks the question, "Was Jesus Tempted Just Like We Are?" And then he answers his own question so elegantly. Page numbering is in brackets [ ] and emphases are in the original:

[102] "For we have not an high priest which cannot be touched with the feelings of our infirmities; but was in all points tempted like as we are, yet without sin." Hebrews 4:15. This verse of Scripture has been, and still is, the basis for a great deal of unhealthy discussion regarding the human nature of Christ. There are some who claim Jesus had to be tempted in the identical manner as every human being has been tempted in order to meet the requirements of this text. This conclusion is arrived at without taking into account all that God has revealed to His church on the subject. If Jesus was tempted to steal, lie, swear, be impure in thought or deed, he resisted that temptation in one of two ways: (1) by resisting the inclination to yield or (2) by realizing that He was helpless and turning the problem over to His Father. In either case He would have had to have a propensity, or inclination, for Satan to appeal to. Yet, Jesus said, "Hereafter I will not talk much with you: for the prince of this world cometh, and hath found nothing in me." John 14:30. This was very close to the end of Jesus' life on earth. Satan had probed into every corner of Christ's life and could find nothing to build any temptation upon.

> "Not even by a thought could Christ be brought to yield to the power of his subtle temptations. Satan finds in human hearts some point where he can [103] gain a foothold—some sinful desire is cherished by means of which his temptations assert their power."[306]

Remember, it was as a human being that Jesus met these temptations.

---

[305] Ibid. 59.
[306] Ellen White, *The Review and Herald*, November 8, 1887.

"Not a single thought or feeling responded to temptation."[307]

Notice, there was no response by either thought or feeling which must precede a temptation.

"Every sin, every discord, every defiling lust that transgression had brought, was torture to His spirit."[308]

"Never, in any way, leave the slightest impression upon human minds that a taint of, or *inclination* to, corruption rested upon Christ, or that He in any way yielded to corruption."[309]

"As the sinless One, His nature recoiled from evil."[310]

Our text being considered says,

" . . . [He] was tempted in all points like as we are . . . " and this is true. In order to find the answer to the "how" question, let us look at another quotation about our Lord. "It was a difficult task for the Prince of life to carry out the plan which He had undertaken for the salvation of man, in clothing His divinity with humanity. He had received honor in the heavenly courts, and was familiar with absolute power. It was *as difficult* for Him to keep the *level of humanity* as for man to rise above the low level of their depraved natures, and be *partakers of the divine nature.*"[311]

"To keep *His glory veiled* as the child of a fallen race, this was the most severe discipline to which the Prince of life could subject Himself."[312]

This is where we all have our difficulties. It is a problem for us to let the divine nature of Christ be reflected in us. Let us analyze what this quotation is telling us. It was extremely difficult for Christ to clothe His *divinity with humanity*. Why?

"Jesus revealed *no qualities*, and *exercised no powers*, that *men may not have through faith in Him. His perfect humanity is that which all His followers may* [104] *possess, if they will be in subjection to God as He was.*"[313]

Jesus said, "I can of mine own self do nothing . . . " John 5:30. It is quite clear that when Christ:

---

[307] Ellen White, *Testimonies*, vol. 5, p. 422.
[308] Ellen White, *The Desire of Ages*, p. 111.
[309] Ellen White, *The SDA Bible Commentary*, Vol. 5, pp. 1128, 1129, *Letter 8, 1895*. (Italics supplied.)
[310] Ellen White, *Testimonies*, vol. 2, p. 202.
[311] Ellen White, *The SDA Bible Commentary*, Vol. 7, p. 930, *The Review and Herald*, April 1, 1875 (Italics supplied.)
[312] Ellen White, *The SDA Bible Commentary*, vol. 5, p. 1081, *Letter 19, 1901*. (Italics supplied.)
[313] Ellen White, *The Desire of Ages*, p. 664. (Italics supplied.)

"laid aside His royal robe and kingly crown,"[314]

He took upon Him the nature of man *"as God created him."*

> "Christ came to the earth, taking humanity and standing as man's representative, to show in the controversy with Satan that man, *as God created him,* connected with the Father and the Son could obey every divine requirement."[315]

> *"He began where the first Adam began."[316]*

Christ, as the second Adam, must succeed where the first Adam failed, using only the same power the first Adam had available to him.

> "When Adam was assailed by the tempter in Eden he was without the taint of sin . . . Christ, in the wilderness of temptation, stood in Adam's place to bear the test he failed to endure."[317]

There is no evidence in the Word of God that sinful nature can ever be obedient to God! The message of God to man is that he *inherently* has a sinful carnal nature which is unredeemable.

"The inheritance of children is that of sin. Sin has separated them from God. Jesus gave His life that He might unite the broken links to God. As related to the first Adam, men receive from him nothing but guilt and the sentence of death."[318]

"Because the carnal mind is enmity (hatred) against God: *for it is not subject to the law of God, neither indeed can be."* Romans 8:7. (Italics supplied.) Christ never tried to show to anyone that *sinful nature* could become *sinless nature*. His message was always, " . . . Ye must be born again." John 3:7. " . . . Except a corn of wheat fall into the ground and die, it abideth alone . . . " John 12:24. " . . . Are ye able to drink of the cup that I shall drink of, and to be baptized with the baptism that I am baptized with? . . ." Matthew 20:22. [105] If Christ had sinless nature how could He be tempted like I am? What is temptation?

> "Temptation is resisted when man is powerfully influenced to do a wrong action and, knowing that he can do it, resists, by faith, with a firm hold upon divine power."[319]

---

[314] Ellen White, *The Review and Herald*, June 15, 1905.
[315] Ellen White, *Signs of the Times*, June 9, 1898. (Italics supplied.)
[316] Ellen White, *The Youth's Instructor*, June 2, 1898. (Italics supplied.)
[317] Ellen White, *The Review and Herald*, July 28, 1874.
[318] Ellen White, *Child Guidance*, p. 475.
[319] Ellen White, *The SDA Bible Commentary*, vol. 5, p. 1082, *The Youth's Instructor*, July 20, 1899.

Temptation only exists when there is a "powerful influence to do a wrong action." "But every man is tempted when he is drawn away of his own lust, and enticed" James 1:14. How could Christ be tempted to do an evil thing when

> "The refined sensibilities of His holy nature rendered contact with evil unspeakably painful to Him"?[320]

Christ hated sin with a perfect hatred. ["Thou hast loved righteousness, and hated iniquity;" Heb. 1:9.] His Spirit, indwelling man, is the only power that brings man to hate sin, which every born-again Christian must learn to do. Christ, in order to be tempted as we are, must have had a strong desire to do a wrong act, but resisted by trusting in His Father. How could Satan find something that would fit these criteria? Satan learned, even when Christ was a child that it was useless to try to tempt Him to retaliate. Even when abused, to be irritated angered, or to do any *bad thing* was unthinkable to Him.

> "Of the bitterness that falls to the lot of humanity, there was no part that Christ did not taste. There were those who tried to cast contempt upon Him because of His birth, and even in His childhood He had to meet their scornful looks and evil whisperings. If He had responded by an impatient word or look, if He had conceded to His brothers by even one wrong act, He would have failed of being a perfect example. Thus He would have failed of carrying out the plan for our redemption."[321]

Satan knows how difficult it is for man to live here as a born-again Christian, keeping his natural sinful nature crucified. He knows that it takes a daily dying to self (1 Corinthians 15:31)—even a continuous crucifixion of habits from that old, but natural, nature. 2 Corinthians 4:10-12. Therefore, he [106] switched his approach to Christ, tempting Him to reveal *His natural nature*, which He had laid aside when He came to this earth. To reveal His natural divine nature would have ruined the plan of salvation, for Christ must use only that which is available to man. Never had there been born a sinless human being until Christ was born of Mary. Never has there been born one since. Satan's experience in dealing with *sinful* babies, children, youth or adults was of no value when dealing with *sinless* human nature. He tried in every way possible to force Christ to reveal His *natural divine nature*. Realizing that Christ's greatest problem while here on earth was to be *accepted as the Messiah* (the anointed One), Satan would use *this natural desire* and try through temptations to get Him to take Himself out of His Father's hands and respond by using His own divine nature that He had laid aside. From His childhood to Calvary this one goal was never given up by Satan. His temptations become more powerful until at the cross the challenge was hurled at Him for hours, "If you are the Christ come down and we will believe." Christ, knowing that He could respond at any time and compel His tormentors to acknowledge Him as Lord and King, refused. He trusted His present and future life to His Father's hands.

---

[320] Ellen White, *The SDA Bible Commentary*, vol. 7A, p. 451, *The Review and Herald*, November 8, 1887.
[321] Ellen White, *The Desire of Ages*, p. 88.

"Thus when Christ was treated with contempt, there came to Him *a strong temptation* to manifest His divine character. By a word, by a look, He could compel His persecutors to confess that He was Lord above kings and rulers, priests and temple. But it was *His difficult task* to keep to the position He had chosen as one with humanity."[322]

What a temptation! No human could ever be tempted like He was! How was He tempted as we are? The born-again Christian must die to *his old natural nature*, which is *sinful*. "They that are Christ's have crucified the flesh with the affections [107] and lusts." Galatians 5:24. This is stated over and over in God's Word.

Selfishness is declared to be the root of all evil.[323]

In the judgement all sins come under the heading of selfishness.[324]

"What is the sign of a new heart? A changed life. There is a daily, hourly dying to selfishness and pride."[325]

It would have shown *selfishness* for Christ to act at any time *on His own desires*. Let your mind probe to its greatest depths and you will find that all sin is selfishness! It is for this reason that when Satan tempts the born-again Christian to do a wrong thing, the old nature, which he has crucified, still seems to urge him to do it. How can this be when the old nature is crucified? Here is where Satan's method of working is revealed. Satan takes advantage of the fact that the born-again Christian, who has a new *nature* given to him at justification, does not receive a new *character* in the same way. A character still has to be developed. This was true with Adam and it is still true with all of the human family. God created Adam perfect in every way, but he had to develop a perfect character, which he failed to do. This is where Christ succeeded and Adam failed. Christ then credits to the born-again Christian's account His own sinless character. This is *placed* to the *account* of the Christian who accepts this as a fact and then allows Christ to begin the work of sanctification, which is God *changing* his *character* so that it will reflect the *character* that is *legally credited* to him in justification. What does this have to do with how Satan tempts us? Let us take a look at what character really is.

"The character is revealed, not by occasional good deeds and occasional misdeeds, but by the tendency of the habitual words and acts."[326]

---

[322] Ellen White, *The Desire of Ages*, p. 700. (Italics supplied.)
[323] Ellen White, *Child Guidance*, p. 294.
[324] Ellen White, *Testimony Treasures*, vol. 1, p. 518.
[325] Ellen White, *The Youth's Instructor*, September 26, 1901.
[326] Ellen White, *Steps to Christ*, pp. 57, 58.

Habits, then, make up our *character*. So, when we live with a sinful nature controlling us, the *habits* that we form reflect that *sinful nature*. Habits or character cannot be given instantaneously; that is why

"There is no such thing as instantaneous sanctification."[327]

[108] With the *old habits* still alive in the newborn Christian, even though they are being worked on by Christ, we can see how Satan sets the trap. He knows that he has no power to bring back to life the *old nature*, and Christ *will not* bring it back, so Satan's only hope is through the habits. He sets that trap, which may be through people or circumstances, so the natural response is a *habitual* response. Then he blames us for responding, and uses our habitual response as proof that the *old nature* is not dead after all. He hopes in this way to force us into discouragement and to get us to *give up and turn away from Christ*, thinking that the whole plan is not working. It is thus that we resurrect the *old nature*. Only then can Satan take *control* again. Can you see that Satan is tempting the Christian in exactly the same way he tempted Christ? In both cases he is trying to force the tempted ones to reveal their *natural natures*. The difference is that our *natural nature* is wicked, so we do not want to reveal it. Christ's *natural nature* was *divine*, so He *desired* to reveal it. But *both* must rely on *surrender to divine control—Christ to His Father and us to Christ*. Christ's surrender led Him to Calvary and apparent defeat from every human viewpoint. Our surrender leads us to eternal life and peace with God. *Selfishness*, the root, is the target. But there is one vast difference between Christ's temptation and ours. If we fail, " . . . we have an advocate with the Father, Jesus Christ the righteous." 1 John 2:1. If Jesus had failed, *all* would have been lost! The *entire* plan of redemption would have failed and Satan would have triumphed. Yes, " . . . [He] was tempted in all points like as we are, yet without sin." Hebrews 4:5.[328]

13. [They assert] "Why did Jesus say, "I seek not mine own will" (John 5:30), . . But if His own will and His own inclination were tending toward the <u>negative</u>, then it would make sense for Him to ask that His Fathers will be done."[329]

Again, this blatant accusation has been proven to be utterly false.

14. [They assert] "If He did not have <u>man's nature</u>, He could not be our example."[330]

---

[327] Ellen White, *The Sanctified Life*, p. 10.
[328] Frank B. Phillips, *His Robe Or Mine*, 102-108.
[329] Ibid. 59.
[330] Ibid. 60.

Again, this accusation has been proven to be utterly false but we will cement this fact in chapter 6.

15. [They assert] "He knew what it was like to want to go wrong. He knew what it was like to feel the temptation to rebel against God, and that temptation arose from within His nature."[331]

Again, this absurd accusation has been proven to be utterly false.

16. [They assert] "Jesus in man's nature lived a life that Satan said could not be lived."[332]

This misrepresentation of statement by Priebe was shown from Inspiration that said that Christ, the second Adam overcame Satan "as God created him" in Adam's pre-fall nature. This was promised to be addressed further in chapter 6.

17. [They assert] "Jesus....could only keep the commandments of God in the same way that humanity can keep them." –Ibid. How can we keep them? Certainly not in Adam's nature. We can only keep them in that nature which we now have- fallen nature. And Jesus kept the commandments of God in the same way we are to keep them. Jesus overcame as we are to overcome."[333]

Again, this blatant accusation has been proven to be utterly false.

18. [They assert] "The *new theology is* a worldwide problem. It has been used by Satan in an endeavor to derail God's remnant church. We have confidence in the testimony of Ellen White that he will not succeed, but, sadly, a huge number of God's people will be lost as a result of the acceptance of this unscriptural theology."[334]

Is the so called *new theology* a worldwide problem? If not, then where did the *real* worldwide problem originate from?

---

[331] Ibid. 60.
[332] Ibid. 61.
[333] Ibid. 61-62.
[334] Colin D. Standish & Russell R. Standish, *Deceptions of the New Theology* (Hartland Publications, 1989). 28.

19. [They assert] "There are over 40 statements in which the issue of the human nature of Christ is specifically addressed by Sister White. Always she refers to the human nature of Christ as "fallen" or "sinful," thus confirming the words of Scripture. <u>Never once does she use the term "unfallen" or "sinless" in relation to Christ's human nature</u>."[335]

Brother Pfandl has shown this statement to be utterly false.

20. [They assert] "Perhaps the most <u>poignant expression</u> of Sister White upon this matter states that Christ *took* our sinful nature. He took upon His sinless nature our sinful nature, that He might know how to succor those that are tempted *(Medical Ministry,* p. 181). Some have attempted to support the view that Jesus simply took the <u>physical form alone</u>, but that cannot be sustained by the evidence in Sister White's writings (reread *Spiritual Gifts,* vol. 4, p. 115). <u>To separate Christ's physical nature from His mental and moral nature would take us to the Greek pagan concept of the distinction between an evil body and a good soul. No right thinking Seventh-day Adventist dare accept that dualistic view of man. It is a satanic deception</u>. If Christ had a fallen physical nature, and He did, then His entire nature was fallen."[336]

Again, Brother Pfandl has shown this statement to be utterly false.

To further unmask Satan's gospel and cement the fact that the Bible and Ellen White *never* portray Christ as having a sinful nature and to further permanently lay this issue to rest as promised, we submit the definitive closing remarks from Pastor Frank Phillips. Page numbering is in brackets [ ] and emphases are in the original:

[123] "The human nature of Christ means everything to us and the subject deserves more than just ordinary investigation.

> "When we approach this subject, we would do well to heed the words spoken by Christ to Moses at the burning bush, 'Put off thy shoes from off thy feet, for the place where on thou standest is holy ground.' We should come to this study with the humility of a learner, with a contrite heart. And the study of the incarnation of Christ is a fruitful field, which will repay the searcher who digs deep for hidden truth."[337]

In Hebrews 2:16 we read, "For verily he took not on him the nature of angels; but he took on him the seed of Abraham." A quick analysis of this verse might lead one to rationalize that if Christ took the seed of Abraham, He could not have been the second Adam. However, the whole human family has their roots in Adam, not angels. Paul, whom I believe wrote both Romans and

---

[335] Ibid. 51. [Emphasis mine]
[336] Ibid. 53. [Emphasis mine]
[337] Ellen White, *The Youth's Instructor,* October 13, 1898.

Hebrews, gives us another reason why Christ was the second Adam. Romans 9:6 says, ". . . they are not all Israel, which are of Israel." Verse seven says, " . . . In Isaac shall thy seed be called." Abraham's children, or seed, were to be of promise. In verse eight we read, " . . . the children of the flesh, these are not the children of God: but the children of the promise are counted for the seed." Christ was the Child of promise, [124] the Son of God. He would, of necessity, be the seed of Abraham as He was born not of the will of the flesh. John 1:13. There are only two origins for man, by the will of the flesh or directly from God. Adam was direct from God as was the second Adam, Jesus Christ.

> "Christ did not make believe take human nature; He did verily take it. He did in reality possess human nature. As the children are partakers of flesh and blood, He also, Himself, likewise took part of the same. He was the son of Mary; He was the seed of David according to human descent."[338]

Yes, Jesus was truly a human being just as much as was Adam, whom He had created. Spiritually, He was the seed of Abraham and, fleshly, the seed of David. In Romans 8:3 Paul even gets a bit more specific,

" . . . God sending his own Son in the *likeness* of sinful flesh . . ."

The inspired commentary on this verse says,

> "As the image made in the *likeness* of the destroying serpents was lifted up for their healing, so One made 'in the *likeness* of sinful flesh' was to be their Redeemer."[339]

The people of Israel knew the brazen serpent was not one of the fiery serpents, but it was made in the *likeness* of them. Jesus was made in the *likeness* of His brethren. Man was made in the likeness of God, but he was not God. To be born of the flesh, according to Jesus when He talked to Nicodemus, was what made it absolutely necessary to have a new birth. John 3:1-6. Obviously, there is something wrong with man's first birth.

> "Christ is called the second Adam. In purity and holiness, connected with God and beloved by God, *He began where the first Adam began.* Willingly He passed over the ground where Adam fell, and redeemed Adam's failure."[340]

God *must* be vindicated for creating man with a *sinless human nature,* for it was in this nature that man was overcome. The question was: Did God make a mistake in creating man, or was man responsible [125] for his fallen condition? Never has God attempted to claim that *fallen,*

---

[338] Ellen White, *The Review and Herald,* April 5, 1906.
[339] Ellen White, *The Desire of Ages,* pp. 174, 175. (Italics supplied.)
[340] Ellen White, *The SDA Bible Commentary,* vol 7A, p. 650, *The Youth's Instructor,* June 2, 1898.

sinful human nature can be victorious over Satan. If that were possible, all man would need would be an example to follow, not a Saviour who on Calvary's cross

> ". . . was earning the right to become the advocate of men in the Father's presence."[341]

Jesus must redeem Adam's failure, then raise all men who would accept His plan of salvation by *imputing His righteousness* to them and giving them a *new nature* that God could work with, for the new nature does not hate God. This is what the new birth is all about.

> "While He was free from the taint of sin, the r*efined sensibilities of His holy nature* rendered contact with evil unspeakably painful to Him."[342]

If Christ's nature were holy, obviously, it could not have been sinful. This could be speaking only of His human nature for its *sensibilities were refined.* In order for Christ to begin where Adam began He would, of necessity, have to have the same human nature as Adam had when He began his life here on earth.

> "Christ came to earth, taking humanity and standing as man's representative, to show in the controversy with Satan that man, *as God created him,* connected with the Father and the Son could obey every divine requirement."[343]

He had to be tested in the "as God created him" nature that Adam was created in. The first Adam failed the testing, but the second Adam succeeded and "His holy nature" was refined. The refining and testing process was a part of the character building that He must accomplish on man's behalf. His death then earned Him the right to impute this character to those who would believe and accept Him as Lord and Saviour. If Jesus had a sinful nature by inheritance, how could He develop a perfect character? Paul makes it very clear that " . . . the carnal mind is enmity against God: for it is not subject to the law of God, neither indeed can be." Romans 8:7.

> "The brain is the capital of the body."[344]

We must now discover if the brain, or mind, is also the nature [126] of man. There is much misunderstanding in this area. A clear, penetrating statement from inspiration should help us.

> "Pure religion has to do with the will. The will is the governing power in the nature of man, bringing all the other faculties under its sway. The will is not the taste or the inclination, but it is the deciding power, which works in the children of men unto obedience to God or unto disobedience."[345]

---

[341] Ellen White, *The Desire of Ages*, p. 745.
[342] Ellen White, *The SDA Bible Commentary*, vol. 7A, p. 655, *The Review and Herald*, November 8, 1887.
[343] Ellen White, *The SDA Bible Commentary*, vol. 7A, p. 650, *The Signs of the Times*, June 9, 1898.
[344] Ellen White, *Messages to Young People*, p. 236.
[345] Ellen White, *Messages to Young People*, p. 151.

There can be no doubt that decisions are made in the brain which is the capital of the body. We have learned that the will is the governing power, or deciding power, that works in man to obedience or disobedience. We have also learned that this will is the governing power *in the nature of man.* If we accept the governing power, or deciding power, to be the same as the brain, or mind, which is the capital of the body, we have our answer. The brain is also the residence of the nature of man. Since the heart and mind are the same, it follows that when we receive a new heart, we receive a new mind, nature and will. As to the carnal mind Paul says, "For to be carnally minded is death; but to be spiritually minded is life and peace." Romans 8:6. Could this be the reason that David cried out in Psalm 51:10, "Create in me a clean heart, O God; and renew a right spirit within me," and Paul also counseled the Philippians, "Let this mind be in you, which was also in Christ Jesus." Philippians 2:5. Yes, Jesus did have an advantage over sinful man, but not over the born-again Christian.

> "Through the victory of Christ the same advantages that He had are provided for man; for he may be a partaker of a power out of and above himself, even a partaker of the divine nature, by which he may overcome the corruption that is in the world through lust."[346]

[127] The nature determines the character that will be developed. A sinful or carnal nature produces a sinful or carnal character. It can produce nothing else.

> "The idea that it is necessary only to develop the good that exists in man *by nature,* is a fatal deception."[347]

Now we can readily see why the new birth is essential in the experience of every man. However, Jesus needed no new birth for He was "that holy thing" or the Son of God from the beginning. Luke 1:35. *We become* sons or daughters of God through the *new birth.* We had nothing to do with our first birth, but we have everything to do with our second birth. "That which is born of the flesh is flesh; and that which is born of the Spirit is spirit." John 3:6 Character acceptable to God can only be developed in sinless nature. Jesus, the second Adam, was born with this sinless nature. We must be born *into* this sinless nature. If the carnal mind, or nature, is ". . . not subject to the law of God . . ." Romans 8:7, and the law of God is a transcript of His character, we have a real problem if we insist that Christ inherited a sinful nature. When Christ took upon Himself the sins of the world it did not make Him a sinner, for He did this vicariously. He took our sinful nature the same way. All the weakness and hereditary effects, physical and mental, He took so that while:

> "Sinless and exalted by nature, He consented to take the habiliments of humanity, to become one with the fallen race."[348]

---

[346] Ellen White, *The Signs of the Times*, January 16, 1896.
[347] Ellen White, *Steps to Christ*, pp. 18, 19. (Italics supplied.)
[348] Ellen White, *The Signs of the Times*, April 25, 1892.

Habiliments, Webster defines as "characteristic apparatus." We could say identifiable characteristics. Why is this important for us to understand? God's plan of salvation requires man to have a perfect character, and he does not have this to offer.

> "It was possible for Adam, before the fall, to form a righteous character by obedience to God's law. But he failed to do this, and because of his sin our natures are fallen and we cannot make ourselves [128] righteous. Since we are sinful, unholy, we cannot perfectly obey the holy law. We have no righteousness of our own with which to meet the claims of the law of God. But Christ has made a way of escape for us . . . He lived a sinless life. He died for us, and now He offers to take our sins and give us His righteousness . . . Christ's character stands in place of your character, and you are accepted before God just as if you had not sinned."[349]

This is the work of justification which is a free gift to all who will accept God's plan. None of this would have been possible if Christ had inherited a sinful nature. But, thank God, it did happen and thus we know that:

> ". . . with an antagonism to evil such as can exist *only in a nature spotlessly pure,* Christ manifested toward the sinner a love which infinite goodness alone could conceive."[350]

> "The humanity of Christ reached to the very depths of *human wretchedness,* and identified itself with the *weaknesses* and *necessities* of fallen man, while His *divine nature grasped the Eternal.* His work in bearing the guilt of man's transgression was not to give him license to continue to violate the law of God, which made man a debtor to the law, which debt Christ was Himself paying by His own suffering. The trials and sufferings of Christ were to impress man with a sense of his great sin in breaking the law of God, and to bring him to repentance and obedience to that law, and through obedience to acceptance with God. *His righteousness He would impute to man,* and thus raise him in moral value with God, so that his efforts to keep the divine law would be acceptable. Christ's work was to *reconcile man to God through His human nature, and God to man through His divine nature.*"[351]

[129] Notice: It was through *Christ's humanity* that man was to be reconciled to God. Romans 8:7 tells us, " . . . the carnal mind [nature] is enmity against God: for it is not subject to the law of God, neither indeed can be." *Reconciliation through sinful human nature is obviously impossible.* The problem is that man has always tried to solve his sin problem by *bringing Christ*

---

[349] Ellen White, *Steps to Christ*, p. 62.
[350] Ellen White, *Patriarchs and Prophets*, p. 140. (Italics supplied.)
[351] Ellen White, *Selected Messages, book 1*, pp. 272, 273. (Italics supplied.)

down to man's own sinful nature, rather than allowing *Christ to bring man up from his fallen, sinful nature through His imputed righteousness to stand before God with a new nature* that God can work with. The new nature does not hate God. However, man's new nature must also be refined, and this is the work sanctification accomplishes. We can scarcely believe what the sinful nature has done to man.

> "The result of eating of the tree of knowledge of good and evil is manifest in every man's experience. There is in his nature a bent to evil, a force which, unaided, he cannot resist. To withstand this force, to attain that ideal which in his inmost soul he accepts as alone worthy, he can find no help but in one power. That power is Christ."[352]

> *"The inheritance of children is that of sin.* Sin has separated them from God. Jesus gave His life that He might unite the broken links to God. *As related to the first Adam, men receive from him nothing but guilt and the sentence of death."*[353]

In order for Christ to unite the broken links (which includes the whole human family), He must have an entirely *different nature than we are born with.*

> "Man could not atone for man. *His sinful, fallen condition* would constitute him an imperfect offering, an atoning sacrifice of less value than *Adam before his fall.* God made man perfect and upright, [130] and after his transgression there could be no sacrifice acceptable to God for him, unless the offering made *should in value be superior to man as he was in his state of perfection and innocency."*[354]

The *sinful, fallen condition is sinful, fallen nature.* This is that which is passed on from generation to generation. It is this *inherited condition* that would have constituted Jesus an imperfect offering, had He *inherited sinful nature.* Every offering selected must be without blemish of any kind.

> "In the days of ancient Israel the sacrifices brought to the high priest were cut open to the backbone to see if they were *sound at heart."*[355]

Jesus Christ must be pure without spot or blemish. 1 Peter 1:19. Webster defines a blemish as "an imperfection that mars or damages *immaculateness."* It is, then, quite clear how *sinful, fallen condition, if inherited by Jesus,* would have constituted Him an imperfect offering. Hence, the

---

[352] Ellen White, *Education*, p. 29.
[353] Ellen White, *Child Guidance*, p. 475. (Italics supplied.)
[354] Ellen White, *The SDA Bible Commentary*, vol. 7A, p. 665, *The Spirit of Prophecy*, vol. 2 (1877 ed.) pp. 9,10. (Italics supplied.)
[355] Ellen White, *The SDA Bible Commentary*, vol. 1, p. 1110, *Manuscript* 42, 1901. (Italics supplied.)

offering would have to be rejected by the Father. However, *He was accepted, the atonement was perfect—without spot or blemish.*

> "The incarnation of Christ has ever been, and will ever remain a mystery. That which is revealed, is for us and for our children, but let every human being be warned from the ground of making Christ *altogether human, such a one as ourselves; for it cannot be.*"[356]

We must learn that *sinful nature* cannot be *controlled, modified* or *improved* in any way. Both the Old Testament and the New Testament teach this. Isaiah 64:6 "But we are all as an unclean thing, and all our righteousness are as filthy rags . . . " Job 14:4 "Who can bring a clean thing out of an unclean? not one." Psalms 51:10 "Create in me a clean heart, O God; and renew a right spirit within me." [131] Ezekiel 36:26-7 "A new heart also will I give you, and a new spirit will I put within you: and I will take away the stony heart out of your flesh, and I will give you a heart of flesh." John 12:24 "Verily, verily, I say unto you, Except a corn of wheat fall into the ground and die, it abideth alone: but if it die, it bringeth forth much fruit." 2 Corinthians 5:17 "Therefore if any man be in Christ, he is a new creature: old things are passed away; behold, all things are become new." Galatians 5:24 "And they that are Christ's have crucified the flesh with the affections and lusts."

> "The Christian's life is not a modification or improvement of the old, but a *transformation of nature.* There is a *death to self and sin,* and *a new life altogether.* This change can be brought about only by the effectual working of the Holy Spirit."[357]

If we picture Christ with a *sinful nature* He would have had to undergo this same transformation. But the devil could find not even an inclination (propensity) upon which to build his temptations when tempting Christ. *This would not have been the case if Christ had inherited sinful nature.*

> "When Christ bowed His head and died, He bore the pillars of Satan's kingdom with Him to the earth. *He vanquished Satan in the same nature over which in Eden Satan obtained the victory.* The enemy was overcome by Christ in His human nature."[358]

In His human nature Christ overcame Satan. *This, sinful human nature cannot do.* It (the sinful nature) must die and be replaced, and man must be a partaker of Christ's divine nature before he can live a victorious life.

---

[356] Ellen White, *The SDA Bible Commentary*, vol. 5, p. 1129, *Letter 8, 1895.* (Italics supplied.)
[357] Ellen White, *The Desire of Ages*, p. 172. (Italics supplied.)
[358] Ellen White, *The SDA Bible Commentary*, vol. 7A, p. 651, *The Youth's Instructor*, April 25, 1901.

> "Be careful, exceedingly careful as to how you dwell upon the human nature of Christ. Do not set [132] Him before the people as a man with the propensities [inclinations] of sin. He is the second Adam. *The first Adam was created a pure, sinless being, without a taint of sin upon him; he was in the image of God.* He could fall, and he did fall through transgression. Because of sin his posterity was *born with inherent propensities of disobedience.* But Jesus Christ was the only begotten [unique] Son of God. He took upon Himself human nature, and was tempted in all points as human nature is tempted. He could have sinned; He could have fallen, but not for one moment was there in Him an evil propensity."[359]

Christ is the only child ever born with sinless human nature. In this sense He is truly unique. Notice: Man *inherited his sinful nature.* Christ *took upon Him human nature.*

> "God desires to heal us, to set us free. But, since this requires an entire transformation, *a renewing of our whole nature,* we must yield ourselves wholly to Him."[360]

Since this is His requirement, we can understand why:

> "*As Jesus was in human nature, so God means His followers to be.*"[361]

Does God mean for His follower to be hampered with fallen, sinful nature? *What, then, was Christ's relation to our sinful human nature?*

> "*He took upon His sinless nature* our *sinful nature,* that He might know how to succor those that are tempted."[362]

There is a difference between that which Christ took upon Himself, *through inheritance*, and *what He voluntarily took* in order to win man back to God. He humbled Himself until there was no lower place to which He could descend. He became *experientially acquainted* with the weakest of the weak. All our *infirmities, handicaps of whatever nature, He was willing to bear.* But, we must remember Christ always retained *His perfect hatred for sin.* If Christ had [133] inherited a sinful nature there would have been an *unbearable dichotomy* between His *two natures*, rather than *perfect peace.* Is that what God desires His children to have?

> "Christ could have done nothing during His earthly ministry in saving fallen man if the divine had not been blended with the human. The limited capacity of man cannot define this wonderful mystery— the blending of the two natures, the divine and the human. It can never be explained. Man must

---

[359] Ellen White, *The SDA Bible Commentary*, vol. 5, p. 1128, *Letter 8, 1895*. (Italics supplied.)
[360] Ellen White, *Steps to Christ*, p. 43. (Italics supplied.)
[361] Ellen White, *Testimonies*, vol. 8, p. 289. (Italics supplied.)
[362] Ellen White, *Medical Ministry*, p. 181. (Italics supplied.)

wonder and be silent. And yet man is privileged to be a partaker of the divine nature, and in this way he can to some degree enter into the mystery."[363]

Through the new birth man is freed from his old nature by death and receives a new nature by birth. It is only in this new nature that we can be a partaker of the divine nature. From the cradle to the grave there was always that perfect harmony between Christ's two natures. *Anything that man has used as an excuse for sin*, Jesus was willing to bear—*abuse, loneliness, poverty, being misunderstood, family rejection, physical abuse and pain, mental torture, apparent failure in life's goals, betrayal, worked against by those closest to Him, even apparently forsaken by God Himself.* Is it any wonder that we have this counsel from God,

> *"We should have no misgivings in regard to the perfect sinlessness of the human nature of Christ."*[364]

> "The exact time when humanity blended with divinity, it is not necessary for us to know."[365]

May I suggest something that might throw a bit of light on the subject?

> "Satan with all his synagogue—for Satan claims to be religious—determined that Christ should not carry out the counsels of heaven. After Christ was baptized, He bowed on the banks of the Jordan; and *never before had heaven listened to such a prayer as* [134] *came from His divine lips. Christ took our nature upon Himself.* The glory of God, in the form of a dove of burnished gold, rested upon Him, and from the infinite glory was heard these words, 'This is My beloved Son, in whom I am well pleased.'"[366]

It is no wonder that heaven had never heard such a prayer as came from His divine lips. If Christ at this time took the last step in humbling Himself, just imagine what that prayer must have been—*an earnest plea to the Father to now let the guilt of every sin man has committed be charged against Him.* Angels and all heavenly beings must have been shocked beyond their capacity to understand why unworthy, ungrateful, sinful man should be offered salvation *by Christ actually taking man's guilt*. It must have been almost impossible for them to comprehend. Adam became a sinner when he chose to believe Satan instead of God. His *nature was changed* from a *sinless* to a *sinful nature*. Christ *chose* to *take upon Himself* the guilt of the world which included *man's sinful nature*. The cleansing process must reach *beyond the deeds of man even to the source—the nature or mind of man. It is thus that Christ can give us a new mind, heart or*

---

[363] Ellen White, *The SDA Bible Commentary*, vol. 7, p. 904, *Letter 5, 1889.*
[364] Ellen White, *The SDA Bible Commentary*, vol. 5, p. 1131, *The Signs of the Times*, June 9, 1898. (Italics supplied.)
[365] Ellen White, *The SDA Bible Commentary*, vol. 5, p. 1129, *Letter 8, 1895.*
[366] Ellen White, *Temperance*, p. 284. (Italics supplied.)

nature. This process accomplishes *man's complete restoration* and at the same time *does not contaminate the Restorer,* for the *guilt was not His own but ours—hence vicarious and by His own choice.* Oh, the wonder of God's plan of redemption. When Christ entered the wilderness of temptation He bore the heavy burden of guilt for the sins of the world. This was a burden too great for any being less than God. Christ was fully divine and fully human, a mystery we cannot fathom. If Christ had a sinful human nature as an *inherited part of Him, He could not have been the express image of His Father.* Webster defines sinful as "full of sin." He, Himself, said, ". . . *He that hath seen me hath seen the Father . . ."* John 14:9. (Italics supplied.) [135] *Inherited sinful human nature can, to a limited degree, be held in control. But, is this the freedom that Christ offers the believer?* How can we be delivered both from the *power* and the *penalty* of sin? *"If the Son therefore shall make you free, ye shall be free indeed."* John 8:36. (Italics supplied.) If Christ's *perfect life of obedience* was achieved through *perfect control of His sinful nature,* then His example for us is to control *our natural sinful natures.* The Bible, however, declares *that nature* to be *incorrigible* and that *it must die, and we must be born again.* God's desire is expressed in this quotation:

> "He would have us comprehend something of His love in giving His Son to die that He might counteract evil, *remove the defiling stains of sin from the workmanship of God,* and reinstate the lost, elevating and ennobling the soul to its *original purity through Christ's imputed righteousness."*[367]

This imputing of His righteousness is the work He is doing now for all who truly believe. He is preparing men and women, through justification, by willingly taking the responsibility for the sins recorded against them and changing their record to read *"just as if we had never sinned."* It would have accomplished nothing for Christ to have accepted sinful nature and even lived without sinning outwardly. The law of God convicts of sin, not only in the *act,* but in the *thought.*

> "The law of God, as presented in the Scriptures, is broad in its requirements. Every principle is holy, just, and good. The law lays men under obligation to God; it reaches to the thoughts and feelings; and it will produce conviction of sin in every one who is sensible of having transgressed its requirements. *If the law extended to the outward conduct only, men would not be guilty in their wrong thoughts, desires, and designs.* But the law requires that [136] the *soul itself be pure and the mind holy, that the thoughts and feelings may be in accordance with the standard of love and righteousness."*[368]

The *sinful nature* constitutes the *disease of sin,* the sins are but the *symptoms* of *the disease.* ". . . The whole head is sick, and the whole heart faint." Isaiah 1:5. If Christ had lived a perfect life while possessing *inherited sinful nature,* He would still be *infected with the disease* and *He*

---

[367] Ellen White, *The Review and Herald*, November 8, 1892. (Italics supplied.)
[368] Ellen White, *Selected Messages*, book 1, p. 211. (Italics supplied.)

would have had to have a Saviour for Himself. If His nature was what kept Him from having *sinful desires*, it could not have been *sinful nature*. If He *had sinful desires* but resisted them, it would have *contaminated Him, for in the thought* is the seed of sin. How can we deal with Hebrews 4:15? "For we have not an high priest which cannot be touched with the feeling of our infirmities; but was in all points tempted like as we are, yet without sin." In order to think our way through this problem it is necessary for us to set aside our preconceived ideas and try to see sin as God sees it. *Selfishness, or self-idolatry, is the foundation of all sin.* (See Testimony Treasures, vol. 1, p. 518 and The Great Controversy, p. 294.) *At this altar every human being has worshiped.* He either *worships himself* or *hates himself*. Jesus said, "He that loveth his life shall lose it; and he that hateth his life in this world shall keep it unto life eternal." John 12:25. This is the same message Jesus gave to Nicodemus in John 3:6, "That which is born of the flesh is flesh; and that which is born of the Spirit is spirit." How was Christ tempted as we are, yet without sin? If selfishness is the root of all sin, then *different sins* are but *variations of the plant from which they grow*. It would be true that the more *carefully self was camouflaged within the temptation, the stronger would be the temptation*. Now we know that ". . . God cannot be tempted with evil . . ." James 1:13. Christ, while on earth was wholly God and wholly man. Because Christ's human nature was sinless, [137] as was Adam's nature when he was created, and Christ's divine nature was God's nature, there was *complete harmony between His two natures—His human and divine.*

> "Christ ever retained the utmost hatred for sin . . ."[369]

He hated sin with a perfect hatred.

> "In the unregenerate heart there is love of sin and a disposition to cherish and excuse it. In the renewed heart there is hatred of sin and a determined resistance against it."[370]

> "Through an appreciation of the character of Christ, through communion with God, sin will become hateful to us."[371]

> "He [God] proposes to remove from man the offensive thing that He hates, but man must cooperate with God in the work. Sin must be given up, hated, and the righteousness of Christ must be accepted by faith. Thus will the divine co-operate with the human."[372]

How can God develop in man hatred for sin when man has a nature that hates God instead of sin? Romans 8:7. It is only accomplished by Paul's counsel in the same letter in chapter 12:2,

---

[369] Ellen White, *The SDA Bible Commentary*, vol. 7, p. 904, *The Signs of the Times*, January 20, 1898.
[370] Ellen White, *The Great Controversy*, p. 508.
[371] Ellen White, *The Desire of Ages*, p. 668.
[372] Ellen White, *Testimonies*, vol. 5, p. 632.

"And be not conformed to this world: but be ye *transformed by the renewing of your mind,* that ye may prove what is that good, and acceptable, and perfect, will of God." (Italics supplied.) Then we will " . . . abhor that which is evil; cleave to that which is good." Romans 12:9. We should be able to establish the fact that *Satan could not tempt Christ to do something He hated.* This hatred for sin was always natural with Christ. It is not natural with the human family. We are miles apart; how can we be tempted in the same way? We must remember that it was on this point that the most powerful being who was ever created fell. Selfishness manifested itself in pride, jealousy, deceitfulness and open rebel [138] lion. Our first parents were victims of the same temptation. Eve was tempted to question why God withheld the fruit of the tree of knowledge of good and evil. This became very strong when she thought the serpent had gained his capacity to speak by eating of this fruit. "Why should I not have such wonderful fruit?" This is selfishness of the most common kind. Adam determined to share her fate, thinking his act was one of true love. He dared to hope that things could come out somehow, as long as he got what he wanted. This was pure selfishness! Remember, all of this activity was entered into while the individuals possessed *sinless natures.* It was the same with every *fallen angel.* This must be the method Satan used on Christ, as well as on man. How could he get Christ to reveal selfishness that would not look like selfishness? The answer lies in the following inspired quotations:

> "It was a difficult task for the Prince of life to carry out the plan which He had undertaken for the salvation of man, in clothing His divinity with humanity. He had received honor in the heavenly courts and was familiar with absolute power. It was as difficult for Him to keep the level of humanity as for men to rise above the low level of their depraved natures, and be partakers of the divine nature."[373]

> "To keep His glory veiled as the child of a fallen race, this was the most severe discipline to which the Prince of life could subject Himself."[374]

The divine nature He had set aside was *sinless,* perfect and familiar with absolute power. It was extremely difficult for Christ, while on earth, to keep His *natural divine nature* from showing through His new human *sinless nature.* This nature had been weakened by four thousand years of sin. When we are born again and Christ gives us a new sinless nature, it is extremely difficult for us to keep our crucified and buried *natural nature* which was *sinful, vile* [139] and *filled with pride* from showing through *our born-again new nature.* Satan's continuous temptations hurled at Christ throughout His human life were to *tempt Him to reveal that divine nature.* "If you are the Christ, prove it." These were the words spoken by humans, as well as by Satan, to Jesus. Never was Christ free from this temptation. His own family and closest disciples often urged Him along this line. Rulers, priests and leaders were used by Satan to try to force Him to *take Himself out of His Father's hands and use His own power.* Jesus must, though

---

[373] Ellen White, *The SDA Bible Commentary,* vol. 7, p. 930, *The Review and Herald,* April 1, 1875.
[374] Ellen White, *The SDA Bible Commentary,* vol. 5, p. 1081, *Letter* 19, 1901.

familiar with absolute power, remain true to His chosen position, *"I can of mine own self do nothing . . . "* John 5:30. (Italics supplied.) Satan is constantly tempting every born-again Christian, *even though he has a new nature that is compatible with God,* to reveal the *old nature that he has crucified.* He tempts us through the products of the old nature that controlled us for so long before we were born again. These products are our *bad habits and hereditary tendencies.* He knows them well, for he was the one who developed them in us. He fans the old nature into flame through circumstances and situations of his own making. He knows that *he cannot* resurrect our old crucified nature, and Christ *would never resurrect it. We are the only ones who can be tempted to do this.* It is through the old habits that we have not yet surrendered to Christ that Satan does his most efficient work as he tries to force us to reveal our old nature. If he can get us to yield to the habits of the old self-life often enough, he knows we will be more inclined to *discouragement and will give up.* It is when *we are in this condition that we take ourselves out of Christ's control* and often, *in rebellion, turn away from God.* This, no doubt, is why Christ *would not be discouraged.* Christ was constantly tempted to do even the good things that He did by *using His own power*—as we are constantly [140] tempted to take ourselves away from Christ and "do our own thing," whether good or bad. Total surrender was Jesus' only safety, and so it is for us. He was, indeed, tempted in all points like as we are. Every temptation is, and always has been, a temptation to *demonstrate selfishness* in one degree or another. *Selfishness always separates from God. This is Satan's goal.* If Christ had used His own power by His own choice He would not have been a perfect example for us to follow, thus the plan of salvation would have failed, for He would not have demonstrated perfect trust in His Father.

> "Jesus revealed no qualities, and exercised no powers, that men may not have through faith in Him. His perfect humanity is that which all His followers may possess, if they will be in subjection to God as He was."[375]

Perfect trust is what righteousness by faith is all about! In order to inspire in man that perfect trust, God's plan of salvation establishes a relationship between the human family and divinity that will never end:

> "To assure us of His immutable counsel of peace, God gave His only-begotten Son to become one of the human family, forever to retain His human nature."[376]

> "The Son of God now at the Father's right hand, still pleads as man's Intercessor. *He still retains His human nature,* is still the Saviour of mankind."[377]

---

[375] Ellen White, *The Desire of Ages*, p. 664.
[376] Ellen White, *The Desire of Ages*, p. 25.
[377] Ellen White, *The Signs of the Times*, July 15, 1908. (Italics supplied.)

" . . . He gave His only-begotten Son to come to earth, to take the nature of man, not only for the brief years of life, but to retain His nature in the heavenly courts, an *everlasting pledge* of the faithfulness of God."[378]

"In passing from the scenes of His humiliation, Jesus has *lost none of His humanity . . .* He never forgets that He is our representative, that He bears *our nature.*"[379]

"That Christ should *take human nature,* and by a life of humiliation *elevate man* in the scale of moral [141] worth with God: He should carry His adopted nature to the throne of God, and there present His children to the Father, to have conferred upon them an honor exceeding that conferred upon the angels,—this is the marvel of the heavenly universe, the mystery into which angels desire to look."[380]

"Christ's work was to *reconcile man to God through His human nature,* and *God to man through His divine nature.*"[381] "God desires to heal us, to set us free. But since this requires *an entire transformation, a renewing of our whole nature,* we must yield ourselves wholly to Him."[382]

"In heaven it is said by the ministering angels: The ministry which we have been commissioned to perform we have done. We pressed back the army of evil angels. We sent brightness and light into the souls of men, quickening their memory of the love of God expressed in Jesus. Their hearts were deeply moved by a sense of the sin that crucified the Son of God. They were convicted. They saw the steps to be taken in conversion; they felt the power of the gospel; their hearts were made tender as they saw the sweetness of the love of God. They beheld the beauty of the character of Christ. But with the many it was all in vain. *They would not surrender their own habits and character."*[383]

"Through the victory of Christ the *same advantages that He had are provided for man;* for he may be a partaker of a power out of and above himself, even a partaker of the divine nature, by which he may overcome the corruption that is in the world through lust."[384] [142]

---

[378] Ellen White, *Selected Messages,* book 1, p. 258. (Italics supplied.)
[379] Ellen White, *Testimonies to Ministers,* p. 19. (Italics supplied.)
[380] Ellen White, *Sons and Daughters of God,* p. 22. (Italics supplied.)
[381] Ellen White, *The Review and Herald,* August 4, 1874. (Italics supplied.)
[382] Ellen White, *Steps to Christ,* p. 43. (Italics supplied.)
[383] Ellen White, *Christ's Object Lessons,* p. 318. (Italics supplied.)
[384] Ellen White, *Signs of the Times,* January 16, 1896. (Italics supplied.)

> "*All the natural goodness of man is worthless in God's sight.* He does not take pleasure in any man who *retains his old nature*, and is *not so renewed* in knowledge and grace that he is a new man in Christ."[385]

> "He would have us comprehend something of His love in giving His Son to die that He might counteract evil, remove the defiling stains of sin from the workmanship of God, and *re-instate the lost, elevating and ennobling the soul to its original purity through Christ's imputed righteousness.*"[386]

This is the work to be accomplished in every born-again Christian through God's unspeakable gift of justification through faith.

The question that must be answered is: If Christ had a sinful human nature, is He to retain that nature throughout eternity? If not, then He had to be freed from that sinful nature sometime. When did this occur?—certainly not at Calvary! He was a perfect offering—not a flaw of any kind was in Him. If Christ had entertained an evil thought even once, He could have accomplished nothing more than any other human priest. Every human priest, by birth, had been contaminated with sinful human nature. Therefore, he must first make an offering for himself each year (Hebrews 9:7) before he could serve as a type of Christ. We can then rest assured that at the cross:

> "He [Christ] *vanquished Satan in the same nature over which in Eden Satan obtained the victory.*"[387]

That nature was, obviously, sinless human nature for that is the way Adam was created. He (Adam) was also defeated in his sinless human nature. If Christ, at the cross, had the same human nature Adam had when he was created, He could not have sinful nature at the same time. A house divided against itself cannot stand. His sinless human nature did not, however, relieve His suffering at the cross or throughout His lifetime. He did take [143] His sinless human nature with Him into heaven and will bear it forever, united and identified with humanity eternally.

> "Christ was not insensible to ignominy and disgrace. He felt it all most bitterly. He felt it as much more deeply and acutely than we can feel suffering, as *His nature was more exalted and pure, and holy than that of the sinful race for whom He suffered.*"[388]

. . . How thankful we should be that our Saviour has identified Himself with the human family by retaining our human nature forever."[389]

---

[385] Ellen White, *God's Amazing Grace*, p. 66, *The Review and Herald*, August 24, 1897. (Italics supplied.)
[386] Ellen White, *The Review and Herald*, November 8, 1892. (Italics supplied.)
[387] Ellen White, *The SDA Bible Commentary*, vol 5, p. 1108, *Questions on Doctrines*, p. 651, *The Youth's Instructor*, April 25, 1901.
[388] Ellen White, *The Review and Herald*, September 11, 1888. (Italics supplied.)
[389] Frank B. Phillips, *His Robe Or Mine*, 123-145.

In closing Brother Pfandl can testify to the fact along with the reader that the false accusations leveled against the organized church from the Independents have not withstood investigation:

> "There is nothing new in the teaching of the "New Theology" concerning the nature of Christ. 100 years ago Ellen White taught what the "New Theology" is teaching today."[390]

---

[390] Gerhard Pfandl, *What Is New In The New Theology*, PDF 6.

3

The Atonement

The Plaintiff (independents) has also accused the organized church of apostasy regarding the Atonement. However, this is an accusation that rest entirely upon shallow thinking as Brother Pfandl will demonstrate again by presenting the organized church's view and stand upon this vital topic from Scripture and the writings of Ellen White:

"The Atonement

Gerhard Pfandl Ph.D.

"The book *Deceptions of the New Theology* claims:

> "It is held by Evangelicals and "New Theology" supporters alike that the atonement was completed at the cross. In weakness we have often yielded on this point when, indeed, there are compelling biblical reasons to support the Seventh-day Adventist position. Using one isolated statement from Sister White against a large number that clearly state that the atonement of Jesus is completed in the heavenly sanctuary, many have made statements to the effect that "Christ is now ministering the benefits of His atonement in the heavenly sanctuary." But this is an incomplete representation of the doctrine of the atonement. Christ's sacrifice was, indeed, the central event in the atonement, but so also is His high priestly ministry. The atoning sacrifice of Christ is completed by the ministration of His precious blood in the heavenly sanctuary."[391]

---

[391] Colin D. Standish & Russell R. Standish, *Deceptions of the New Theology* (Hartland Publications, 1989). 90-91.

The issue of whether the atonement was completed at the cross or not, is largely a matter of definition. In theological circles the term "atonement" has assumed a technical meaning and is generally used to describe the redeeming effect of Christ's incarnation, sufferings, and death on the cross. In this sense E.G. White uses it in the following statements:

Gospel Workers, p.325

"The sacrifice of Christ as an atonement for sin is the great truth around which all other truths cluster."

Review and Herald, Sept. 24, 1901

"He planted the cross between heaven and earth, and when the Father beheld the sacrifice of his Son, He bowed before it in recognition of its perfection. "It is enough", he said, "the Atonement is complete."

Signs of the Times, Aug. 16, 1899

"No language could convey the rejoicing of heaven or God's expression of satisfaction and delight in His only begotten Son as He saw the completion of the atonement."

Testimonies, vol.5, p.190

"The ransom paid by Christ - the atonement on the cross - is ever before them."

Thus, those who teach that a complete atonement was made on the cross view the term in its technical meaning as the all-sufficient atoning sacrifice of Christ offered for our salvation on Calvary.

This is the meaning of Hebrews 9:12, "Not with the blood of goats and calves, but with His own blood He entered the Most Holy place once for all, having obtained eternal redemption", and 10:10, "By that will we have been sanctified through the offering of the body of Jesus Christ once for all." It is described as a "sacrifice of atonement" in Romans 3:25 (NIV) and as a "ransom" in 1. Timothy 2:6.

However, the word atonement has also a wider connotation. In Scripture this is referred to as "reconciliation", which includes the effect the atonement has on His creation. Thus, Paul writes to the Colossians, "For it pleased the Father that in Him all the fullness should dwell, and by Him to reconcile all things to Himself, by Him, whether things on earth or things in heaven, having made peace through the blood of His cross" (1:19,20).

And to the Corinthians he says, "We implore you on Christ's behalf, be reconciled to God" (2. Cor. 5:20). This wider meaning includes the application of the benefits of the atonement made on the cross to the individual sinner. This is provided for in the priestly ministry of Jesus in the heavenly sanctuary.

In this sense E.G. White uses it in the following quotations:

Early Writings 260

"The great Sacrifice had been offered and had been accepted, and the Holy Spirit which descended on the day of Pentecost carried the minds of the disciples from the earthly sanctuary to the heavenly, where *Jesus had entered by His own blood, to shed upon His disciples the benefits of His atonement."*

Fundamentals of Education 370

"Our Saviour is in the sanctuary pleading in our behalf. He is our interceding High Priest, making an atoning sacrifice for us, *pleading in our behalf the efficacy of His blood."*

Testimonies to Ministers 37

"Jesus is our great High Priest in heaven. And what is He doing? - *He is making intercession and atonement for His people who believe in Him."*

Thus, Ellen White can speak of a "final atonement" on the Day of Atonement (*Great Controversy*, p.485; *Patriarchs and Prophets*, pp.352, 355). She used the word "atonement" both ways - in its technical sense as an all-sufficient, complete, once-for-all sacrifice on Calvary, and in its wider sense which includes the application of the benefits of the sacrificial atonement Christ made on the cross.

Again, there is nothing new in the teaching of the "New Theology" concerning the atonement. 100 years ago Ellen White taught what is taught by the "New Theology" today. Indeed, it is a distortion of the truth to declare such teaching as "New Theology".

As far as the Sanctuary Message and the Spirit of Prophecy are concerned, the church at large has never wavered from its commitment to these truths. While there may well be individuals within the church who have doubts or reservations or an incomplete understanding concerning these truths, the church's position has not changed as is evidenced by chapters 17 and 23 in the book *Seventh-day Adventists Believe* ...

THE SPIRIT OF CRITICISM - AN ISSUE OF CONCERN

The spirit of criticism exhibited by some of the critical ministries is deplorable. Church members and critics alike do well to take note of the counsel given this church long ago:

Testimonies, vol.5, p.294

"The worst enemies we have are those who are trying to destroy the influence of the watchman upon the walls of Zion. . . Be careful lest you be found aiding the enemy of God and man by spreading false reports and by criticism and decided opposition."

Evangelism, p.634

"Remember that he who takes the position of a criticiser, greatly weakens his own hands. God has not made it the duty of men and women to find fault with their fellow workers."

Testimonies, vol.8, p.83

"The time spent in criticising the motives and works of Christ's servants might be better spent in prayer. Often if those who find fault knew the truth in regard to those with whom they find fault, they would have an altogether different opinion of them."

Evangelism, p.102

"The Lord never blesses him who criticises and accuses his brethren, for this is SATAN'S work."

CONCLUSION

In this study we have seen that the claims by some of the critical independent ministries that the church in the 1950s changed its theology are not justified. What is called "New Theology" is really not new; it is thoroughly biblical. Moreover, it is the theology which Ellen White proclaimed 100 years ago. Critics of the church need to take a closer look at these teachings before claiming that they are evidence of apostasy in the church."[392]

[Indeed, the jury is in; the verdict is out, and the organized church is Not Guilty of the crimes she has been falsely accused of for decades concerning the Atonement! Case closed! This concludes the fine work from Brother Pfandl for the organized church's view of the everlasting gospel.

In chapter 4 we shall continue to expose the false gospel of the independents and exhibit a hands on approach to the genuine mechanics of the real gospel so the reader can tangibly grasp and experience this for oneself and meet the requirements delineated by Heaven in order to retain our justification and receive of the latter rain.]

---

[392] Gerhard Pfandl, What Is New In The New Theology, PDF 7-11.

4

The Man of Romans 7
Converted or Unconverted?

In Chapters 4 we are excited to begin to show the reader why all this documentation in the previous chapters was so important because it defines the *only* acceptable path by Heaven to Heaven for the redemption of fallen humanity. As the reader has and will in this chapter as well witness for oneself, another complete disregard to the counsel of Paul and Inspiration by the independents:

> "Knowing that a man is not justified by the works of the law, but by the faith of Jesus Christ, even we have believed in Jesus Christ, that we might be justified by the faith of Christ, and not by the works of the law: for by the works of the law shall no flesh be justified." Gal. 2:16.

This will be fully demonstrated in this chapter but first we must address and expose another major deception of the gospel as presented by the leadership of the independents. As stated before, our procedure will begin with the Plaintiff's (independents) statements of belief and their source authority, A.T. Jones and E.J. Waggoner. We had previously established that Jones and Waggoner's teachings were a result of progressive apostasy in that they believed Jesus had a sinful nature. The reader is now going to witness that their apostasy did not stop there! Waggoner declares the man of Romans 7 is:

> "Convicted, but Not Converted . . . conviction is not converted."[393]

Jones likewise advocates the same belief for the man of Romans 7:

> ". . . Now just another thought there. He hates the evil and declares he will never do it; and yet against his will, and against all his being for that matter, it is done. But what is it, and who is it, that actually does it? [Congregation: "Sin that dwelleth in him"] And who rules that? [Congregation: "Satan"] Who is the master of that man? [Congregation: "Satan"][394]

---

[393] E.J. Waggoner, *Waggoner on Romans*, (Berrien Springs, MI; Glad Tidings Publishers, 1997), 123. Originally published, Signs of the Times, Oct. 1895 – Sept. 1896.
[394] A.T. Jones, *The Third Angels Message*, 1893 General Conference Bulletin, No. 12. 259.

"Convicted, but Not Converted" is the position of Jones and Waggoner. This is the prominent view of all the independents and their leadership and their study generally stops with quotes from Jones and Waggoner that we witnessed in a previous chapter quoted here again for the benefit of the reader:

> "There has been a-none-too-subtle attempt to undermine the Bible truth on the human nature of Christ by indicating that this emphasis of *Jones and Waggoner was a result of progressive apostasy* in what they believed. That *this is not true* is evidenced by the fact that there *is no extant letter from the servant of the Lord rebuking them or counseling them in respect of this teaching*."[395]

We saw that *this was true* that what Jones and Waggoner believed that Christ had the same sinful nature as ourselves with the same bent to evil as ourselves and this is indeed a result of progressive apostasy by walking away from the Scriptures and Inspiration that Priebe, the Standish brothers and the independents have so chosen to do. The ramifications for this unscriptural belief will become exceedingly clear to the reader by the conclusion of this chapter. This next quote is from the Standish brothers that are simply echoing Jones and Waggoner that the man of Romans 7 is the unconverted man:

> "It was because of this concept that Augustine saw the man depicted in Romans 7: 14-24 as a fully converted man. Unlike previous understandings which saw the man of Romans 7 as an earnest individual struggling and failing in human weakness, Augustine saw him as in a saved relationship with God. He ignored the plain testimony of Paul in relation to this passage:"[396]

We now turn to Ellen White for her voice and position on the matter and the reader will now see she repeatedly states and specifies in no uncertain terms that the man of Romans 7 is none other than the *converted man* and yes; she is in perfect harmony with the Scriptures that we will momentarily submit and prove our point. In this *Review and Herald* quote Ellen White spells out the Scriptural account clear back in the year 1870, long before Jones and Waggoner ever came on the stage of action. I am amazed at the love and patience of God Almighty when he continually sends us warning after warning, entreaty after entreaty and instruction after instruction when it still falls on deaf ears and closed eyes:

> "But those who would delight to have the law done away, would delight in sin. Their carnal hearts are not in unison with that law which the apostle declares to be holy, just, and good. Paul inquires, "Is the law sin? God forbid. Nay, I had not known sin, but by the law; for I had not known lust, except the

---

[395] Colin D. Standish & Russell R. Standish, *Deceptions of the New Theology* (Hartland Publications, 1989). 47. [Emphasis mine].
[396] Ibid. 12.

law had said referring to one of the ten commandments, Thou shalt not covet." Saul did not commence a raid against the law in order to justify a life of sin; but when his mind was enlightened in regard to the claims of the law of God, he saw himself a sinner, a transgressor of the law. His sins were brought before him, and what was the result? Did he commence a tirade against the law which showed him that he was a transgressor? Is it in his heart to crucify that law? Oh no! he crucified the carnal mind which rises in enmity against the law of God. "Sin revived," says Paul, "and I," not the law, "died." Oh! when will professed Christians awake to see the brink of the precipice they are standing upon in refusing to acknowledge the claims of the law of God?

The transgressor of God's law may pass on for a time without exposure; but, sooner or later, he will find himself overtaken, exposed, and condemned. Whoever dares to violate the law of God will experience for himself that "the way of the transgressor is hard." The opposition and willing ignorance in regard to the law of God, is the reason so few feel that they are under moral obligation. They despise the law which was the instrument that slew Paul. They cannot say with him, I die; but they earnestly strive to live, while they cry, Death to the law!

This is virtually their testimony. The commandment came, sin revived; the law died, and the carnal mind lived. This is the order with the transgressor. Their spiritual powers are benumbed. Eternal things are not discerned. Their works are carnal, and their example is corrupting."[397]

In fact, she even wrote a personal letter to A.T. Jones pertaining to this very issue in hope to correct his error, but to no avail:

"The Lord would have every teacher of truth behold Him, <u>until</u> he is <u>changed</u> into the <u>same image</u>. Then <u>he will delight in the law after the inward man</u>."[398]

---

[397] Ellen White, *Review & Herald*, March 8, 1870.
[398] Ellen White, *Letter* 84, 1899, p. 5. (To A. T. Jones, April 28, 1899.) 7MR 149.

Please carefully read the following quotes by Inspiration along with Romans chapter 7 and just try to insert the phrase, "The unconverted man". One will immediately realize he is trying to insert a square peg into a round hole. Ask yourself; does the natural man on the street corner "Delight in the law of God after the inward man" Rom. 7:22? Of course not, the answer is obvious. These quotations are all self-explanatory and require no commentary. All emphasis is mine:

> "Those who are *converted*, experience peace and assurance forever. In place of being *slaves*, they are made *free* through Jesus Christ. Brought into the liberty of *obedient children, they can say, "I delight in the law of God after the inward man."*
>
> *We see and are compelled to acknowledge human depravity*, but we do not need to *stop at this conclusion*, for through faith in Christ life and immortality are brought to light. "Behold the Lamb of God, which taketh away the sin of the world!"[399]

Again:

> "I beseech you to make an unreserved surrender to God, and to make it now, just now. *When you make this surrender you will have an experience entirely different from the experience that you have had for many years. Then you will be able to say with the apostle Paul*, "I count all things but loss for the excellency of the knowledge of Christ" (Eph. 3:8). "*I delight in the law of God after the inward man*" (Romans 7:22)."[400]

Again:

> "Sanctification is not the work of a moment, an hour, a day, but of a lifetime. It is not gained by a happy flight of feeling, but is the result of constantly dying to sin, and constantly living for Christ. Wrongs cannot be righted nor reformations wrought in the character by feeble, intermittent efforts. It is only by long, persevering effort, sore discipline, and stern conflict, that we shall overcome. We know not one day how strong will be our conflict the next. So long as Satan reigns, we shall have self to subdue, besetting sins to overcome; so long as life shall last, there will be no stopping place, no point which we can reach and say, I have fully attained. Sanctification is the result of lifelong obedience.
>
> None of the apostles and prophets ever claimed to be without sin. Men who have lived the nearest to God, men who would sacrifice life itself rather than

---

[399] Ellen White, *Sings of the Times*, November 5, 1894.
[400] Ellen White, 11MR 312.

knowingly commit a wrong act, men whom God has honored with divine light and power, have confessed the sinfulness of their nature. They have put no confidence in the flesh, have claimed no righteousness of their own, but have trusted wholly in the righteousness of Christ.

So will it be with all who behold Christ. The nearer we come to Jesus, and the more clearly we discern the purity of His character, the more clearly shall we see the exceeding sinfulness of sin, and the less shall we feel like exalting ourselves. There will be a continual reaching out of the soul after God, a continual, earnest, heartbreaking confession of sin and humbling of the heart before Him. *At every advance step in our Christian experience our repentance will deepen. We shall know that our sufficiency is in Christ alone and shall make the apostle's confession our own:* "I know that in me (that is, in my flesh,) dwelleth no good thing." "God forbid that I should glory, save in the cross of our Lord Jesus Christ, by whom the world is crucified unto me, and I unto the world." Romans 7:18; Galatians 6:14. Let the recording angels write the history of the holy struggles and conflicts of the people of God; let them record their prayers and tears; but let not God be dishonored by the declaration from human lips, "I am sinless; I am holy." Sanctified lips will never give utterance to such presumptuous words.

The apostle Paul had been caught up to the third heaven and had seen and heard things that could not be uttered, and yet his unassuming statement is: "Not as though I had already attained, either were already perfect: but I follow after." Philippians 3:12. Let the angels of heaven write of Paul's victories in fighting the good fight of faith. Let heaven rejoice in his steadfast tread heavenward, and that, keeping the prize in view, he counts every other consideration dross. Angels rejoice to tell his triumphs, but Paul makes no boast of his attainments. The attitude of Paul is the attitude that every follower of Christ should take as he urges his way onward in the strife for the immortal crown.

. . . . True sanctification means perfect love, perfect obedience, perfect conformity to the will of God. We are to be sanctified to God through obedience to the truth. Our conscience must be purged from dead works to serve the living God. *We are not yet perfect*; but it is our privilege to cut away from the entanglements of self and sin, and advance to perfection. *Great possibilities, high and holy attainments, are placed within the reach of all.*

. . . . As your soul yearns after God, you will *find more and still more of the unsearchable riches of His grace.* As you contemplate these riches you will come into possession of them and will reveal the merits of the Saviour's sacrifice, the protection of His righteousness, the fullness of His wisdom, and

His power *to present you before the Father "without spot, and blameless." 2 Peter 3:14."*[401]

Again:

"None of the apostles or prophets ever claimed to be without sin. Men who have lived nearest to God, men who would sacrifice life itself rather than knowingly commit a wrong act, men whom God had honored with divine light and power, have confessed the sinfulness of their own nature. They have put no confidence in the flesh, have claimed no righteousness of their own, but have trusted wholly in the righteousness of Christ. So will it be with all who behold Christ.

At every advance step in Christian experience our repentance will deepen. It is to those whom the Lord has forgiven, to those whom He acknowledges as His people, that He says, "Then shall ye remember your own evil ways, and your doings that were not good, and shall loathe yourselves in your own sight." Eze. 36:31. Again He says, "I will establish My covenant with thee, and thou shalt know that I am the Lord; that thou mayest remember, and be confounded, and never open thy mouth any more because of thy shame, when I am pacified toward thee for all that thou hast done, saith the Lord God." Eze. 16:62, 63. Then our lips will not be opened in self-glorification. *We shall know that our sufficiency is in Christ alone. We shall make the apostle's confession our own.* "I know that in me (that is, in my flesh) dwelleth no good thing." Rom. 7:18. "God forbid that I should glory, save in the cross of our Lord Jesus Christ, by whom the world is crucified unto me, and I unto the world." Gal. 6:14.

In harmony with this experience is the command, *"Work out your own salvation with fear and trembling. For it is God which worketh in you both to will and to do of His good pleasure. Phil. 2:12, 13."*[402]

Again:

"Chap. 209 - **A Daily Experience in Conversion**

"For which cause we faint not; but though our outward man perish, yet the inward man is renewed day by day. 2 Cor. 4:16.

Genuine conversion is needed, not once in years, but daily. This conversion brings man into a new relation with God. Old things, his natural passions and hereditary and cultivated tendencies to wrong, pass away, and he is renewed and sanctified. But this work must be continual; for as long as Satan exists, he will make an effort to carry on his work. *He who strives to serve God will*

---

[401] Ellen White, *Acts of the Apostles*, See Chapter 55.
[402] Ellen White, *Christ Object Lessons*, 160-1.

encounter a strong undercurrent of wrong. His heart needs to be barricaded by *constant* watchfulness and prayer, or else the embankment will give way; and like a millstream, the undercurrent of wrong will sweep away the safeguard. No renewed heart can be kept in a condition of sweetness without the daily application of the salt of the Word. Divine grace must be received daily, or *no man will stay converted*. . . . Test and trial will come to every soul that loves God. The Lord does not work a miracle to prevent this ordeal of trial, to shield His people from the temptations of the enemy. . . . Characters are to be developed that will decide the fitness of the human family for the heavenly home--characters that will stand through the pressure of unfavorable circumstances in private and public life, and that will, under the severest temptations, through the grace of God grow brave and true, be firm as a rock to principle, and come forth from the fiery ordeal, of more value than the golden wedge of Ophir. God will endorse, with His own superscription, as His elect, those who possess such characters. . . .

The Lord accepts no halfhearted service. He demands the whole man. Religion is to be brought into every phase of life, carried into labor of every kind. The whole being is to be under God's control. We must not think that we can take supervision of our own thoughts. They must be brought into captivity to Christ. *Self cannot manage self*; it is not sufficient for the work. . . . *God alone can make and keep us loyal*."[403]

Again:

"Christ was manifested to take away our sins, and in him was no sin. But were the law abolished, as some claim, we would have no need of a Saviour to take away sin, for "where there is no law, there is no transgression." "Therefore by the deeds of the law there shall no flesh be justified in his sight; for by the law is the knowledge of sin." "What shall we say then? Is the law sin? God forbid. Nay, I had not known sin, but by the law; for I had not known lust, except the law had said, Thou shalt not covet. But sin, taking occasion by the commandment, wrought in me all manner of concupiscence. For without the law sin was dead. For I was alive without the law once; but when the commandment came [home to the conscience], sin revived, and I died. And the commandment, which [if obeyed] was ordained to life, I found to be unto death. For sin, taking occasion by the commandment, deceived me, and by it slew me. Wherefore the law is [a yoke of bondage, against me, and something to be trampled underfoot because it points out my sins?--No.] holy, and the commandment holy, and just, and good. Was then that which is good made death unto me? God forbid. But sin, that it might appear sin, working death in

---

[403] Ellen White, *Our High Calling*, 215.

me by that which is good; that sin by the commandment might become exceeding sinful. For we know that the law is spiritual; but *I am carnal, sold under sin."*

But though we are carnal, **[Ellen White is including herself because she is a sinner by birth as well and needs a Savior just like you and me. Even after conversion we are all still carnal this side of the second coming just like Paul because we have all sinned. However, to be "carnally minded" (Rom. 8:6-7) is altogether another thing, that condition places humanity outside of a saving relationship with Christ]** we are to reckon ourselves "dead indeed unto sin, but alive unto God through Jesus Christ our Lord. . . . But God be thanked, that ye were the servants of sin, but ye have obeyed from the heart that form of doctrine, which was delivered you. Being then made free from sin, ye became the servants of righteousness. . ."[404]

The ramifications here are huge dear reader and Satan does not want you to see and understand the simplicity of the gospel spelled out by Paul in Romans chapter 7 and 8 that has been so marred by his teachings from misguided men. This is because Romans chapter 7 and 8 is the only place in the entire Bible that defines so precisely our walk of Sanctification and as to what Jesus meant when He said unto his disciples:

". . .If any *man* will come after me, let him deny himself, and take up his cross, and follow me." Matt. 16:24.

Romans chapter 7 and 8 defines just *what* the converted are to "deny" when we take up our cross in the walk of Sanctification. The reader who has been misled by the false teachings of men and Satan regarding the man of Romans 7 will be overjoyed with such a clear and concise view of the simplicity of the real gospel as presented by the Apostle Paul. Never again will the reader be in doubt as to which path *is* the straight and narrow and the part Heaven has outlined that we must follow when we take up our cross in order to retain our Justification. In bringing this understanding to the reader we submit the outstanding work of Pastor Stephen Wallace that brings this vital instruction from Heaven and its Biblical mandate to the comprehension of all:

"You know what the most subtle form of legalism is? The most subtle form of legalism is not, of course, presuming to be righteous on the basis of your own efforts to keep God's law. That's a very blatant form of legalism that almost nobody is troubled with. The most subtle form of legalism, however, is coming to the conclusion that one is righteous on the basis of what the Holy Spirit does in him. Are we righteous or justified on the basis of what the Holy

---

[404] Ellen White, *Signs of the Times*, October 1, 1894.

Spirit does in us? We are never righteous on the basis of what the Holy Spirit does in us. That which justifies us is what Jesus Christ has done for us. By the obedience of one, through many shall be made righteous Rom. 5:19. Is that clear? How could Paul state it more clearly than that. Does he say by the obedience of each spirit-filled Christian they will be made righteous? He says by the obedience of one. For only one has a righteousness that is sufficient to meet the infinite standard. All the rest of us, even empowered by the Holy Spirit are weighed in the balance and found wanting. That's why we have to have an intercessor before our obedience is even acceptable. That statement that we were studying yesterday. *Selected Messages vol. 1, 344*, she cries out after she has told us that the religious services, the prayer, the praise, the penitent confession of sin ascend as incense from true believers as incense to the heavenly sanctuary but passing through the corrupt channels of humanity, they are so defiled that unless purified by blood they can never be of value with God. Just after she has established that truth, and these are things inspired by the Holy Spirit in true believers. After she establishes the passing through the corrupt channels of humanity, they are so defiled. That unless purified by blood, she sums up that discussion by saying, "Oh that all may see that everything in obedience must be placed upon the glowing fire of the righteousness of Christ." Everything in what? Obedience. Has to be place where? On the glowing fire of the righteousness of Christ. Why? What does fire do? It purges and purifies. Do you see how we must recognize that we can never be justified on the basis of our spirit-inspired obedience. Because even that has to be purified by the fire of Christ's righteousness. Even that has to have His blood to cleanse it and His righteousness added to it before it is acceptable. And then, mind you, it is not acceptable as merit. It is not as acceptable as something that we offer towards earning our salvation. It's acceptable even then only as a gift of gratitude for the salvation that has already been purchased for us by the One who is not weighed in the balance and found wanting, Jesus Christ. But the subtle form of legalism that has just plagued us as a people, and my heart breaks when I see how many of us are rich and increased in goods and have need of nothing because the Holy Spirit is doing it all in us. Praise God for the Holy Spirit. Enabling grace is absolutely essential. But what the Holy Spirit does in us will never earn our right standing with God. It is what Jesus Christ has done for us. That's our title. What the Holy Spirit does in us is our fitness. Praise God. We've got to have a fitness. But legalism is when we turn our fitness into a title. Do you hear me. Legalism is when we come to the conclusion that our fitness entitles us to heaven. That's the most subtle form of legalism. And we have got to be protected from that. Romans chapter 7 is probably the most controversial passage in all of Scripture. It has been the passage that has caused controversy for centuries in the church and has been wrestled with and hassled with and argued over for hundreds of years. Do you know why it has been so controversial? Because it is one of the most profound truths in all of Scripture. And the devil knows that if this truth is grasped, his power is broken to get into either ditch--the ditch of antinomianism or the ditch of legalism. Because Romans 7 is the final word that keeps us out of both ditches if we will hear what that word has to say. It is such a profound and precious truth. And it is my prayer that the next series that we tackle will be on Romans 5-8, but particularly focused on Romans 7. The truth in Romans 7 is absolutely essential to rightly understand. And because it is so essential to rightly understand, the devil has worked harder to keep this obscure than any other passage. And one of the things that has kept that passage obscure is the translation. Let me give you just one example. In this passage in the King James, you see the predominance and prevalence of the verb "to do" don't you? It comes over and over again. It seems a little redundant there in the middle. Do you realize that in the Greek, that verb that is rendered consistently in the King James "I do" is actually three distinct Greek verbs: **katergazomai {G2716}, prassō {G4238}, and poieō {G4160}** (???) These are all translated "I do" in the English. Do you begin to see how some of the nuances in subtle truths that Paul is trying to communicate are completely obscured from our vision. Do you see that? Because those verbs have been completely ignored. And you cannot see the relationships between those verbs.

And he uses them in relationship to each other. Now we cannot possibly do an in-depth study in this. It will take many deep studies to really get down to the heart and core of what Romans 7 has to say. But please. Let me consider with you just quickly in passing some of the high points and help you see that we must come to the conclusions that we have been seeking to come to.

Romans 7:1, "Or do you not know, brethren, for I speak to those who know the law that the law has dominion over a man as long as he lives. For the woman who has a husband is bound by the law to her husband as long as he lives. But if the husband dies, she is released from the law of her husband. So, then, if while her husband lives she marries another man, she will be called an adulteress. But if her husband dies, she is free from the law so that she is no adulteress though she has married another man. Therefore my brethren, you also have become dead to the law through the body of Christ that you may be married to another, even to Him, who was raised from the dead that we should bear fruit to God." What fruit we bear in our lives is determined directly by what our will conceives. How is temptation yielded to? When lust hath conceived, it gives birth to sin. There is an old man in each one of us that we are born with, and the will is its wife. Now the two of them are lawfully married by natural birth. The will is totally by natural birth committed to the desires of the flesh. And she can do nothing but consent to the desires of the old man, conceive them. Therefore we bear fruit unto death by nature. The law of the husband is the law in Genesis 3:16, "To the woman I will greatly multiply your sorrow and your conception. In pain you shall bring forth children. Your desire shall be for your husband, and he shall rule over you. By nature the will is married to this old man. So the law says that she submits, and they are married until death do them part. By law she is bound to consent to conceive the desires of the old man until death. Now please hear me. If she tries to consent to have a relationship with anyone else while the old man is still living, what's that condemned as? Adultery, that is spiritual hypocrisy. That is the Christian trying to commit his will to Jesus Christ while the old man is still alive. And all that he can do in that condition is hypocrisy. And it's condemned. It's repulsive to God. He may be, or she may be, able with sufficient ego-motivation to be as Saul was by the deeds of the law blameless. He or she might be able to keep that will so apparently committed that as far as outward behaviour is concerned, we are law-abiding, good, upright, moral people. Wasn't that precisely what the Jews were? And in contrast to the nations about them, they were righteous, judged by behaviour. They could look down their self-righteous noses and look at all of that terrible behaviour, brush their robes, and thank God that they weren't like all the rest of them when inside it was consenting to the lusts of the flesh. The carnal mind is enmity against God. It does not subject itself to the law of God. It is not even able to do so. With a carnal mind, though we may be able to subject our behaviour to the law of God, can we subject our own thoughts and feelings to the law of God, our character? Absolutely not. It is an impossibility. But watch out! You can go a long ways in subjecting your behaviour, and you can deceive others and you can even deceive yourself. But you may not be what you think you are. "As a man thinketh in his heart, so is he." You are not a Christian on the basis of your behaviour. You're a Christian on the basis of having the mind of Christ. You're a Christian because you think and feel like Jesus does. Therefore, your behaviour is a genuine expression. It's not hypocrisy. But as long as you are in your natural state, and it is the natural state to be carnally minded. Ellen White says the carnal mind is the natural mind. Why? Because the woman is naturally married to the flesh. That's our natural condition. And because of that our mind can only be carnal by nature. And she will by nature be married to the flesh until death do them part. What is the only way she can cease to concede the lust of the flesh, even if only the private recesses of the thought life? By the death of the husband. Precisely. Then and only then is she free to be married to another. Romans 7:4, "Therefore, my brethren, you also have become dead to the law," what law is this--the law of the husband, the law that says you've got to be submitted to your husband. The will has got to be submitted to the one it's married to, to the one it's committed to. In this case, an unholy deadlock. By natural birth this poor wife (or will) is absolutely locked in. "Therefore, my brethren, you also have become dead to the law through the body of Christ that you may be married to another," who is that, "even to him who is raised from the dead that we should bear fruit to God." And what fruit is that? The fruit of the Spirit. Precisely. Look at verse 5, "For when we were in the flesh [when we were married to the old man, when our will was subject to the tyranny of his perverted appetites and passions] the passions of sin which were aroused by the law were at work in our members to bear fruit to death. You see this old man hates the law. He is in that sense completely in harmony with Satan. At the fall, our lower, corrupt nature was not at enmity with Satan. It was at enmity with God, and this hatred drives the old man to demand that the will yield to its desires and bear fruit to death. And when the old man is told not to do it, his hatred for God and the law only drive him to do it all the more. He is rebellious by nature. For when we were in the flesh, the passions of sin which were aroused by the law were at work in our members to bear fruit to death. Do you see the truth there? Verse 6, "But now we have been delivered from the law." Which law is this? The law of the husband, the law that says you have got to be submitted, wife, to whoever you are married to. But now we have been delivered from the law having died to what we were held by. What were we held by? The old man. That's what held us. Having died to what we were held by so that we should serve in newness of spirit and not in oldness of letter. In other words, no longer in hypocrisy but in genuine heart-felt obedience. Verse 7, "What shall we say then. Is the law sin? Certainly not. On the contrary. I would not have known sin except through the law for I would not have known covetousness unless the law had said you shall not covet. What sin is he discovering by means of this law? Inbred sin. The sin of nature. That old man which is his as a natural inheritance from his fallen parents. This what he discovers by the law. Which law is it? You shall not covet. It's unique among the ten. Why? we pointed this out in our study. It's the only one that deals exclusively in the realm of the mind. And you see it is only an understanding of this law that can protect us from hypocrisy. Saul had come to the place where he was so ego-motivated that by the deeds of the law he was blameless. But suddenly by means of this tenth commandment, he discovered that the law was spiritual, that it had to do with more than just his behaviour. It reeks down to the inner recesses of his private thought life, and it required perfect obedience there. And he discovered by means of this law that rather than being blameless he was what? He was a sinner. Look what happened. Verse 8, "But sin taking opportunity by the commandment produced in me all manner of evil desire. For apart from the law sin was dead. I was alive once without the law." He perceived himself as being God's elect and thereby entitled to life. "I was alive once without the law, but when the commandment came sin revived and I died." Paul is converted. Romans 7:9 --please note this with me. Ellen White brings this out very clearly. Paul himself died. He was converted at this point. He became a converted man. *R & H*, March 8 (1870) is one. "And the commandment which was to bring life I found to bring death. For sin taking occasion by the commandment deceived me and by it killed me. Therefore the law is holy and the commandment is holy and just and good. Please note this word **good "agathos."** {G18} (??) It occurs in the future in our study here. Has then what is good become death to me? Certainly not! "But sin that it might appear sin" now what does your King James say at this point? "Working death in me." Good. In the New King James, it says, "was producing death in me." It is in the present tense, the present reflexive. "Sin is of itself producing death in me." Present reflexive is the Greek verb there. "Sin is of itself producing death in me through what is good so that sin through the commandment might become exceedingly sinful."

Now what conclusion does he come to? Even after conversion--what does he discover--sin is producing death in him. What does he conclude then. This producing is **"katergazomai."** {G2716} This is one of the verbs that is translated "to do" in the following passage. Work out, bring about, produce. Sin is producing death in me through what is good. Why is the reason for this? Verse 14, "For we know that the law is spiritual but I am carnal sold under sin." But in the Greek that's sold under "the sin." That's in reference to Adam's sin. And again Ellen White makes this absolutely crystal clear. She has a statement that confirms that completely. Try *Manuscript* 122 (1901). You can't look that up anyway. I wish I had this material here. But you'll have to put a little bit of confidence in my assurance that this is precisely how Ellen White translate this. "Sold under the sin" is in reference to Adam's sin.

"As a result of Adam's disobedience, every human being is a transgressor of the law, and is sold under sin. Unless man repents and is converted, he is under bondage of the law, serving Satan, falling into the deceptions of the enemy, bearing witness against the precepts of Jehovah. Only by perfect obedience to the requirements of God's holy law can man be justified. **Let those whose natures have been perverted by sin, ever keep their eyes fixed on Christ, the author and the finisher of their faith."** 8MR 98.

When did the human race become carnal? In Eden. When Adam sinned, we become carnal, sold under sin by Adam. Here is a most fascinating study that proceeds. The microcosm or the outline of this study is found in Galatians 5. Paul is saying the same truth in Galatians 5 as he's saying in what proceeds now in Romans 7. But he is saying it much more in-depth in Romans 7. He is developing this truth that he states succinctly and simply in Galatians 5:16-17. "I say then walk in the spirit and you shall not fulfil the lusts of the flesh. The law is spiritual but we are carnal." You see parallels here. "Walk in the spirit and you will not fulfil the lusts of the flesh." Note what he says following:" For the flesh lusts against the spirit and the spirit against the flesh, and these are contrary to one another." What is the consequence of this contrariness, this opposition of the lusts of the flesh and the lusts of the spirit? It is not only war, but there is a hindrance, there is a limitation that is the consequence. What is the limitation? So that you do not do the things that you would. Who is it that does the willing in us? It's our will. In the born-again Christian, what happens? What has happened to the old man? When we go to the foot of the cross and we look up there and see Christ and him crucified for us, we have the privilege of counting ourselves, reckoning ourselves to be dead indeed unto sin. Let me jump back with you to Romans 6. Baptism is what allows us (actually our faith in Christ's death for us is what allows us) to reckon ourselves dead indeed unto this old man. Baptism symbolizes what our faith has accepted. This is why we baptize by immersion. The old man is buried, dead and buried, by a faith acceptance of Christ's death and burial as our own. The baptismal font is a tomb for the old man. But it is a womb for the new. We come out to be born again, born of the water and born of the spirit, to walk in newness of life. We have a new nature. This is the spiritual nature. This becomes the new husband of the will. She is now in a position to be married to another. Why? Because death has done her part from the old man. Now her will is united to the spiritual nature which is, of course, the counterpart in our being of Jesus Christ. It is through our conscience, that's the spiritual nature, that Christ communicates with us. And as the will is submitted to the conscience now, the highest faculty in man, she is able to bear fruit until life, unto righteousness. What about the old man. Does he disappear from the scene? Is he eradicated at the moment of conversion? No. We are to reckon him dead. Why does it say reckon him dead? Because it is by faith. And faith is evidence of things hoped for, the conviction of things hoped, the evidence of things not seen. Do we see the death of that old man as we look within. I don't know about you, but I don't. I see a very _____ old man that's constantly trying to get me to yield to his desires. Is that your experience. The flesh lusts against the spirit. And in the Greek that's the present, active indicative. The flesh in continually lusting against the spirit. And whose experience is this? The born again Christian's experience. So the old man is not eradicated, but he is rendered powerless to get his way in our lives; because we have the privilege of reckoning him dead and thereby refusing to be bound by the law that says that we must submit to our husband. Note how Paul says this in Romans 6:5, "For if we have been united together in the likeness of his death, certainly we also shall be in the likeness of his resurrection." That's in reference to baptism, the symbolism there. And what's our privilege of knowing? Romans 6:6, knowing this that our old man was what? Crucified with him that the body of sin might be (now watch out here--the King James says "destroyed," the New King James says "done away with") that we should no longer be slaves of sin. Now neither of those renderings is accurate to the Greek verb. In the margin of the New King James it has "that the body of sin might be rendered in operative." The New International Version puts it this way, "rendered powerless." That is the Greek verb. It is not eradicated at the point of conversion. But its power is taken away. Its reigning power is removed, not its remaining presence. When does God remove the remaining presence of sin? At glorification. But from the cross to the crown, there is earnest work to be done. There is wrestling with inbred sin. God does not deal with the remaining presence at conversion. He deals with the reigning power at conversion, and he takes away that power by giving us the privilege of reckoning ourselves dead so that we are no longer slaves of sin. Verse 7, "For he who has died has been freed from sin." Free from the tyrannies of bondage--the utter, hopeless, helpless subjection of that poor wife to the dictates of that old man. And the world is the governing power in the nature of man. So if the will is set free from the tyranny of that set nature, we are set free. Verse 8, "Now if we died with Christ, we believe that we shall also live with him knowing that Christ, having been raised from the dead, dies no more. Death no longer has dominion over him." Verse 10, "For the death that he died, he died to sin once for all. But the life he lives, he lives to God." Likewise, you also reckon yourselves to be dead indeed unto sin but alive unto God in Christ Jesus.

Ellen White says, "Though we are carnal, we are to reckon ourselves dead indeed unto sin but alive unto God in Christ Jesus." Do you see why we must reckon it. Because it is not at this point an empirical reality. It won't become such until when? Glorification. It is now only a spiritual reality. But by the way, a spiritual reality transcends an empirical experiential reality. And when our experience contradicts spiritual truths, which truth are we to believe and operate on the basis of? Spiritual truth. That's the fight of faith. We are, in spite of ourselves being carnal, to reckon ourselves dead to sin. On the basis of what we see? No. On the basis of what we hear. Faith cometh by hearing. And Jesus said, "you're dead." Jesus, I believe it in spite of what all of my senses tell me,

I believe it. _____ dead in you and I am going to act accordingly. That's faith. On the basis of that faith reckoning, what can we do? Verse 12, "Therefore," in conclusion _____ from what we have just established, "Therefore, let not sin reign in your mortal body that you should obey in its lusts. Do you see that? He doesn't say don't let it remain in your mortal body. He knows it remains until this mortal puts on immortality. But it doesn't have to reign. Praise God. We don't have to obey it in its lusts. But here's the point. Though it doesn't reign, even its remaining presence is a constant opposition factor that will hinder us in our quest to be like Christ. Now, turn back with me to Galatians 5:17, "For the flesh lusts against the spirit and the spirit against the flesh, and these are contrary to one another so that you do not do the things that you wish." Now what's that in reference to? That's in reference to both the desires of the flesh because of the opposition of the spirit and that is also in reference to the desires of the spiritual man because of the opposition of the flesh. The flesh hinders, the flesh limits because of its constant opposition the kind of obedience that we long to give God. And what does God require of us? That we love the Lord with all our heart. But there is a problem. There is a dimension of our being that does not love God, that is enmity against God, that lower corrupt nature that until the day we die or are glorified, whichever comes first, remains in rebellion against God. And so our desire to love God with all our strength, with all our soul, and with all our mind is hindered, thwarted, because of this opposition factor. Am I talking here about wilful disobedience. No. Please don't mistake me. I am not talking about wilful disobedience. The Christian must not be wilfully disobeying. I am talking about an obedience that is rendered faulty imperfect because we are not obeying with our whole being. There is still this dimension that resists. This spiritual man wants to obey God. His prayer is the prayer Jesus gave him, "Thy will be done on earth as it is in heaven." He wants to obey like the sinless beings there do. But what does he find? He finds this constant opposition, this dimension of his nature that hinders him. And so the desires of his heart place in there by God's spirit are not fulfilled. Sanctified Life 81, "But he who is truly seeking for holiness of heart and life delights in the law of God and morns only that he fall so far short of meeting its requirements." What is the cause of this shortfall? It's the opposition of the flesh. It hinders him. It trembles him. Remember the word Ellen White uses. Only in heaven will we be untrammelled by sin--this lower corrupt nature. So its remaining presence, not its reigning power, hinders and limits and causes to be imperfect our obedience. Turn back to Romans 7. Note how Paul develops these two truths. These two truths are so clearly developed. First of all, he deals with the fact that the desires of the flesh are not fulfilled because of the opposition of the spirit. Then he deals with the fact that the desires of the spirit are not fulfilled because of the opposition of the flesh. Verse 15, "For what I am doing," Now this "am doing," what do you suppose that is in the Greek verb? That is Katergazomai. When did he last use the word "Katergazomai?" In reference to lusts of every kind. What are we talking about? Are we talking about the realm of behaviour here? We're talking about the realm of the mind. Precisely. Please don't forget that Paul is zeroing in here almost exclusively on the realm, the intimate private recesses of his thought life. He has told us that he is telling us about the law that says thou shalt not covet. He is saying to us he discovered by that law coveting of every kind. And the last time that verb was used, not only in reference to coveting of every kind, but it was used in verse 13--sin was producing. Katergazomai again. Producing death. And remember, that was the present reflective. Sin is of itself producing death in me, continually. For what I am doing--this is a challenge, brothers and sister, I will do my best. You do your best to follow me. What I am doing--what is he talking about? He's talking about using that verb--he's telling us that he is talking about coveting and producing death. So what "I" is he talking about here? The carnal "I" or the spiritual "I"? The carnal "I." What I as a carnal man sold under sun, "For what I am doing, I do not allow." Do you see what he is telling us. That verb in the Greek is **ginōskō {G1097}**. Do you know what **ginōskō** is?--**"to know."** What I am doing as a carnal man--these lusts I as a spiritual man--do not conceive. To know is to conceive. He is stating categorically that he refuses to consent with the will to the lusts of the flesh. Why? Because his will is no longer married to the old man. By death, it has been separated; and now his will is married to whom? Jesus Christ. So this wife is a faithful wife, and she refuses to indulge what that lower corrupt nature, which he has to acknowledge is himself, he has to call it "I" because it is, what that lower corrupt nature is trying to do, his spirit-energized will is consistently refusing to indulge. What condition is that. He can state without qualification that which I, the lower corrupt nature, am producing--covetousness in the realm of my mind I, the spiritual man, refuse to acknowledge. That's not only conversion, not only sanctification, but Christian character perfection. What is character perfection. Character perfection is coming to the place where even in the private recesses of our thought life we would rather die than knowingly transgress God's law. Do you realize what Paul is saying here? He is saying that by God's grace his will is so totally and habitually and continually submitted to the lordship of Jesus Christ that he consistently, constantly refuses to know the lust of that old man--to conceive them. Now keep this in mind. We are talking here not about just a born-again Christian. We are talking here about one who is attained to Christian character perfection. Now that may be such a radical thought for you that you might not be able to swallow it. But follow me. For what I am doing, I, the carnal man, am doing (gardegedzomi in reference to coveting) I, the spiritual man, do not allow, do not know--conceive; for what I, the carnal man, will to do, that I, the spiritual man, do not practice. Now that's another verb, "prassō ." For what I will to do, that I do not practice. But what I hate, which man is that? No, that's the carnal--you see the parallel? He goes back and forth--each phrase--first what I am doing, I do not know. That's the first parallel. Carnal spiritual. He goes right back and forth. Then second phrase--for what I will to do that I do not practice. The second parallel--but what I hate as a carnal man, that I do. *Ministry of Healing* 542, "The life of the Apostle Paul was a constant conflict with self." He said, 'I die daily.' His will and his desires everyday conflicted with duty and the will of God. Instead of following inclination, he did God's will, however, crucifying to his nature." What did he do? He did what he hated as a carnal man. Do you see it? He did precisely what his carnal man hated. Everyday his will and his desires, the will and desires of this carnal man, conflicted with duty and the will of God. But did he get it in to it? No. He did precisely what the old man hated to do. He crucified self. Do you see that? I don't ask you to believe it or accept it, but I just to know that you are at least understanding this interpretation. Praise God, my brother, my sister, we can come to that experience. Do you believe it? We can come to the place where our will is consistently submitted to the new husband, and we are consistently refusing to cheat on Christ and have an affair with that old man, even in the private recesses of our thought life. We can. We can consistently come to the place where what we do is what he hates. Do you believe it? Oh, praise God for the new husband. Praise God for a spirit-energized will that will allow us to come to such an experience.

Verse 16, "If then"--now, here is its conclusion, "If then I"--this is the spiritual man—"If then I do"--you see we know that because the verbs are parallel. In the last--I wish you could see the Greek here. "What I hate that I do"--do there is poieō. He uses that same verb to tell us which "I" he's talking about. We know he's talking about the spiritual "I" the end of verse 15 "That I do." Then verse 16, "If then I do (poieō--same verb, that therefore is the spiritual "I" that he's talking about. "If then I do what I, carnal "I" will not to do--what is this conclusion? I agree with the law that it is good. Do you see it? In the Greek that's **symphēmi* {G4852}.** He is in **harmony** with the law, my brother, my sister. Why? Because he is refusing to do what he hates which is the desires of the old man which are in rebellion against the law. But he is doing, rather, what his spiritual man desires which are in harmony with the law. Therefore, he can conclude that I am symphēmi with the law. I am in harmony with the law. This is a born again Christian. This is one who is not only born again. This is one who has reached Christian character perfection. I am symphēmi. I am in agreement with the law that it is good. Now what can he conclude? What does he have the privilege of concluding. Because his will is totally committed to God, because he is in harmony with the law of God, he can disown responsibility for that rebellious dimension of his being. Verse 17, "Now then it is no longer I (spiritual Paul) who do"--what verb do you suppose that is? Katergazomai. This is the lusting. Bear in mind we are talking about the lusting here. We are talking about the realm of the mind. For it is no longer I who do it. It is no longer the spiritual "I" that is doing the lusting, but "sin that dwells in me." It is this inbred sin that's responsible for it. But he can disown responsibility for it, why? Because he does not indulge it. If we indulge it, can we disown it? No we cannot not. But when we refuse to indulge it, we have the privilege of disowning it, saying, "that's not me. That's my old man. That's indwelling sin. It's dead." Do you see that? Verse 18, "For I (the spiritual Paul) that in me that is in my flesh dwells no good thing." How does he know that? "For to will is present with me." This is the desire of his spiritual nature which is to keep the law of God as it is kept in heaven. "For to will is present with me but how to perform what is good I do not find." We are moving to the second part of this study. Remember in Galatians we said that because of the opposition of the spiritual nature to the carnal nature, the carnal doesn't get its way. We have just studied that. But now Paul moves to consider that because of indwelling sin, the spiritual nature doesn't get its way either in the fullest complete sense of the word. What is that? Nothing good dwells in me for to will is present with me. But how to perform what is good is not. In other words, he wills to do good but he recognizes because of indwelling sin he doesn't have the faculties to perform the good that he desires. He delights in the law of God, in other words, but he morns only that he falls so far short of meeting its requirements. It is a problem with his will though? No. Where is the problem? It's the resistance, the limitations due to the indwelling sin. Verse 19, "For the good that I will," this is the spiritual "I" only the spiritual "I" wills to do good--and by the way this good is the same word, agathos, which is in reference to the law which is holy, just, and good. In others words, he desires to do what the law requires. "For the good that I will to do, I do not do. But the evil I will not to do, that I practice. Now, what is this evil? Is this wilful transgression of God's law? This is not wilful transgression of God's law. This is imperfect obedience. But Paul's conscience is so sensitive that even his obedience he recognizes as in a very real sense--evil. Please, consider with me these definitions. "Sin is the conscience knowing and deliberate transgression of the divine law, the Father's will. "Sin is the measure of unwillingness to be divinely led and spiritually directed." "Sin is in the realm of the will." Now, that is not the word that Paul uses here. He uses the word evil. Here is a definition I want to share with you. "Evil is the unconscious or unintended transgression of the divine law, the Father's will. Evil is likewise the measure of the imperfections of obedience to the Father's will." Oh, I wish we had time to develop this and support it more thoroughly. But we don't. Evil is the unconscious or unintended transgression of the divine law, the Father's will. Evil is likewise the measure of the imperfections of obedience to the Father's will." Evil then is in the realm of unknown sin, it's in the realm of imperfect obedience, but it is not in the realm of wilful transgression. What Paul is acknowledging here is what he sees within himself is so far short of what God's law requires that he calls it evil. But what is his privilege of doing? Verse 20, "Now if I (spiritual Paul) do what I will not to do, it is no longer I who do it but sin that dwells in me." What is responsible for this short fall? Is it Paul? No. It is indwelling sin. Verse 21, "I find in a law that evil is present with me, the one who wills to do good." Verse 22, "For I delight in the law of God according to the inward man. Now, brothers and sisters, what does sound like? *Sanctified Life 81*, "He who is truly seeking for holiness of heart and life delights in the law of God but mourns only that he fall so far short of meeting its requirements. In other words--can produce only that which is really in contrast to the infinite standard, evil. Why? Because of indwelling sin. There are deficiencies that cause it not to meet the infinite standard. Oh, this is a humbling truth. Do you see how this truth absolutely, finally puts to death legalism? It is a most humbling truth. Now is Paul saying here that he cannot obey? Absolutely and most emphatically not. He does obey. He is in symphēmi with the law. He refuses to indulge the lust of the flesh. What is he here lamenting? Not his wilful disobedience but the quality of his obedience. It is faulty, it is defective. Remember *Selected Messages vol. 1, 344*, the religious services, the pray, the praise, the penitent confession of sin. A sin from true believers, true believers as incense to the heavenly sanctuary, but passing through the corrupt channels of humanity, they are so defiled--evil. In that sense, so defiled that unless purified by blood they can never be of value with God. That's what he's lamenting when he says it's evil. It's not wilful transgression. It's a miserable short fall in his obedience due to indwelling sin. So defiled. That which is so defiled is evil. But do we despair? No. Why? Because there is an intercessor who can do what with that evil? Cleanse it with his blood and add his righteousness to it and thereby make it acceptable to God." Let's read on, "The religious services, the prayer, the praise, the penitent confession of sin, a sin from true believers as incense to the heavenly sanctuary, but passing through the corrupt channels of humanity, they are so defiled that unless purified by blood they can never be of value with God." They ascend not in spotless purity. And that's our desire isn't it that we offer God something that is spotlessly pure. But, brothers and sister, I don't know about you. But I've never done anything that that's spotless and pure. And the more I look at my Lord and his spotless righteousness, the more I see that all of my righteousness is as filthy rags. In contrast my very best efforts to obey my Lord and Saviour are really so defiled that I have to call them evil. But do I despair? No. Because I am justified on the basis of who righteousness? His righteousness. And I don't despair either because I know I have an intercessor. And I know his blood is there to cleanse my obedience and I know his righteousness is there to be added to it so it's acceptable. Listen, "They ascend not in spotless purity, and unless the intercessor who is at God's right hand presents and purifies all by his righteousness, it is not acceptable to God. Why is it not acceptable to God in itself? because in itself it's defiled. In itself it's evil. Is this coming through? All incense from earthly tabernacles must be moist with the cleansing drops of the blood of Christ. Why does our obedience have to be moist with the cleansing drops of the blood of Christ? Because there is an element in that obedience that is evil. That's defiled. Do you see it? All our obedience must be moist with the cleansing drops of the blood of Christ. He holds before the Father the censor of his own merits in which there is no taint of earthy corruption. Praise God for such a righteousness. Oh, we would be without hope, But you see, brothers and sisters, I get so distressed when I hear us in our efforts to make Christ a sympathetic elder brother--give him the same corrupt channel we have. If he had that same corrupt channel, what's the condition of his obedience? So defiled that unless purified by blood, it can never be of value to God. Whose blood purified his obedience, pray tell? Whose righteousness made up for its short fall, pray tell? Do you see how if we make him one who is altogether like us we destroy his substitutionary capacity because he ceases us to be absolutely sinless, and he ceases to have an infinite righteousness, both of which we need if we are going to have any hope in Christ. What does he do? He holds before the Father the censor of his own merits which there is no taint of earthly corruption. She says he born without the taint of sin. It that a sinfulness that's due to wilful sin? Of course not. He was born without it. He was not a corrupt channel by birth. He couldn't be. If we make him a corrupt channel by birth, we destroy his substitutionary capacity. We can't. He was born without the taint of sin. He gathers into this censor the prayers, the praise, and the confessions of his people; and with these he puts his own spotless righteousness. Oh, praise God that there is a spotless righteousness. Mine is spotty. I don't know about yours. And, brothers and sisters, if you don't recognize that yours is spotty, I have news for you. You haven't yet got a look at Jesus Christ. I have to come to that conclusion. If you think for one moment that you have an obedience even done by the power of the Holy Spirit that meets the infinite standard, I have got news for you. You are terribly deceived. You are in the most Laodicean condition. You are rich and increased in goods and have need of nothing, and you do not know that you are poor and blind and miserable and naked. And I challenge you, take one look at Jesus Christ. What will be your experience? *Sanctified Life 7*, "Those who are really seeking to perfect Christian character will never indulge the thought that they are sinless. Never! Their lives may be irreproachable. Are we talking about wilful sin here at the level of behaviour that keeps us from claiming that we are sinless? No. Their lives may be irreproachable. They may be living representative of the truth which they have accepted, but the more they discipline their minds to dwell upon the character of Christ and the nearer they approach to his divine image, the more clearly will they discern its spotless perfection and the more deeply will they feel their own defects. And if that isn't your experience, I beg of you, for the sake of your own soul and for the sake of Jesus that he might not have died for you in vain, look to Jesus quick. Take just one glimpse of his glory, and you will never more say by the deeds of the law blameless. You will say, rather, "Chief of sinners." He gathers into this censor the prayers, the praise, the confessions of his people. And with these he puts his own spotless righteous. When it's been purified by blood and had righteousness added to it, our prayers, our religious services, our obedience inspired by the Holy Spirit, then perfumed with the merits of Christ's propitiation the incense comes up before God holy and entirely acceptable. Then gracious answers are returned. Oh, that all may see that everything in obedience must be placed upon the glowing fire of the righteousness of Christ. Why? Because there is an evil element in it in our obedience. And that fire has to purge it. That's the evil that Paul is talking about. Verse 23, "But I see another law in my members warring against the law of my mind and bringing me into captivity to the law of sin which is in my members. Now please note with me that there is a vast difference between being brought captive and being a slave. Is Paul a slave to this old man. Absolutely, most emphatically, he is not. He used to be, but now he is just a captive. There is a difference. He was an abject slave before, now he is simply a prisoner. There is a difference. Note what he longs for. He moves on in Romans 8:20, "For the creation was subject to futility, not willingly but because of him who subjected it in hope; because the creation itself also will be delivered from the bondage of corruption into the glorious liberty of the children of God. We know that the whole creation groans and labours with birth pangs together until now. And not only they but we also who have the first fruits of the spirit. Even we ourselves groan within eagerly waiting for the adoption, the redemption of our body. But in the meantime, we are in bondage to corruption. We are prisoners, not slaves. How does he groan within himself? Verse 24, "Oh wretched man that I am. Who shall deliver me from the body of this death. That's why he goes on to long for the redemption of his body. His will has been redeemed. He has come to the place where that will is so totally redeemed that he is not even in a thought yielding to the desires of the flesh. But he is not fully redeemed. His redemption still draweth nigh. What dimension of the redemption does he await and eagerly hope for? The redemption of his body. And in the meantime, he is a prisoner though. Do you see it? I don't ask you to believe it, but I just want to know whether we are communicating. Verse 25, "I thank God through Jesus Christ our Lord. So then, what's his conclusion? "So then with the mind I myself serve the law of God but the flesh the law of sin." Whose experience is that alone? The flesh sets its desire against the spirit and the spirit against the flesh. This side of glorification--will our bodies ever serve the law of God--that lower corrupt nature? No. We have within us a dimension that continually serves the law of sin. But what does God hold us responsible for? The mind. That's where our character is. And we can have Christian character perfection. Why? Because we can come to the place where our will is so committed to the lordship of Jesus Christ that it refuses consistently to yield to the lust of the flesh. It consistently puts to death the deeds of the body and consistently yields to the desires of the spirit. It consistently chooses to conceive them and bear the fruit of the spirit unto the glory of God. But what is the condition of that fruit? It is so defiled passing through the corrupt channels that unless purified by blood it can never be of value with God. We have in the physical realm a very tangible illustration of this. When a woman is in labour. What happens to that precious little baby. It's all distorted. Because of what? The opposition of the flesh. It's head is all malformed. And it comes out with a bad odour I want you to know, a very foul odour. I've been through it three times. But, brothers and sister, is that an avoidable deficiency? It is not. It is an unavoidable deficiency. Let the object lessons that God has given us teach us something. In labour shall you bring forth children--the fruit of the spirit unto the glory of God. It takes labour, why? Because of the opposition of the flesh--that lower corrupt nature. And that opposition distorts, hinders, and defiles what we are seeking to bring forth. Therefore, that little baby can only be acceptable as it's washed and rubbed with salt. That's the Old Testament. That's teaching a profound truth. Do you see what it's teaching? This is so important. Do you see now what the conclusion is though in verse 8. Let me at least go this far with Paul. "There is therefore now no condemnation to those who are in Christ Jesus who do not walk according to the flesh but according to the spirit." With his mind he serves the law of God, and with the flesh he serves the law of sin. And that is condemnable. There is a dimension in him that causes his obedience to be evil. But what can he conclude because his mind serves God, because he's doing the very best he can given his sin-damaged resources--what can he conclude? "There is therefore now no condemnation for those who are in Christ Jesus." Do you see it? Why is there no condemnation? Because it is not that which is condemnable is not in the realm of that which he can do something about. And God doesn't hold us under condemnation for something that we can't do anything about. He doesn't condemn a dear mother for producing a distorted baby that smells bad. No. He accepts that and he loves her for all of her labour to bring it into the world. And he has provision to make that baby totally acceptable to him. And that's the blood and righteousness of the intercessor. Do you see it? But please note why there is no condemnation. Because it is unavoidable deficiencies. That's why. It's unavoidable. Verse 2, "For the law of the spirit of life in Christ Jesus has made me free from the law of sin and death." We are no longer in slavery. We are free from that law of the husband. By the way, this is one in the same law. And whether it's the law of the spirit and life or the law of sin and death. Whether the law of God to us is the law of spirit of life or the law of sin and death depends entirely upon whom we are married. If our will is married to the old man, what is God's law? The law of sin and death. If our will is married to Jesus Christ, what is the law of God?

The law of spirit and life. It makes all the difference, then, who's got our will, doesn't it. Now please note verse 3, "For what the law could not do in that it was weak through the flesh, God did by sending his own son in the likeness of sinful flesh." Why does he have to say likeness? Because he's just told us what sinful flesh causes, and he's got to say likeness; because if he came in sinful flesh, he's got the same problem we do. He's in the likeness of sinful flesh, brothers and sisters. If he wanted us to think that he was in sinful flesh, he would have said sinful flesh. But he put an essential word in there, "likeness." It's like us enough to be our sympathetic elder brother and valid example. But praise God it's different enough to be our sinless substitute. And where we get in trouble if we try to make it so like us that we destroy his substitutionary capacity. He was like us, I assure you. He was like us enough to be a valid example for us. He was like us enough to know what it's like to be tempted in all things as like as we are, and we will study this together. But let's don't make him so like us that he becomes that same corrupt channel we are so that his religious services, his prayer, his praise is so defiled that it has to be purified by blood. If we make him that like us, we are without hope. Do you see it? "In the likeness of sinful flesh, God did, sending his Son in the likeness of sinful flesh and for sin." You know what that Greek phrase is? That is the expression used for the sin offering. And what is the sin offering? That is the continual offering that was a provision for the unavoidable deficiency of the children of Israel. The sin offering. With this he condemned sin in the flesh. Now he condemned sin in the flesh both as our example and as our substitute. He condemned sin in the flesh because he was in the likeness of sinful flesh. And he showed us that by his grace we can overcome sin in the flesh. And if we don't, we are under condemnation for it. That's how he condemned sin in the flesh as our example. But he also condemned sin in the flesh as our substitute in that he became the sin offering for it. And he took the condemnation for it in himself. And now the sin issue for which we are held responsible is precisely defined. What are we held responsible for? Walking by the spirit and not by the flesh. Look how precisely defined our responsibility is. In Romans 8:13,

"For if you live according to the flesh, you will die. But if by the spirit you put to death the deeds of the body, you will live." What realm of the sin problem has been because of the atonement delineated for us to deal with in his strength? Only the consent of the will. That is all that we are responsible for. If our will through the energy and the power of the Holy Spirit puts to death the deeds of the body by reckoning that old man dead and consents to the desires of the spirit, we are assured of acceptance and eternal life in Christ Jesus because he makes up for all the rest in the deficiencies. Praise God. If God is for us, who can be against us? Let's pray."[405]

A very special Thank-you to, Pastor Stephen Wallace from all of us! Also, I wish to give a very special Thank-you to, his wonderful staff that has freely and graciously supported this endeavor as well for no other motive than to get the truth to those who are seeking the Pearl of Great price!

---

[405]. Stephen Wallace, "*Our Sinless Yet Sympathetic Savior*," revivalseminars.org. See also: americanchristianministries.org.

5

The Real Gospel Stands Up

The jury is in and the verdict is out, *Not Guilty*! Chapters 1-4 have proven without question that the Defendant, the organized church's position at large on the everlasting gospel is in perfect harmony with the Scriptures and Inspiration. With this verdict legally in place for all to witness for oneself the organized church has been given the following legal options and directions by Heaven:

> "Whosoever sins ye remit," said Christ, "they are remitted; . . . and whosoever sins ye retain, they are retained." Christ here gives no liberty for any man to pass judgment upon others. In the Sermon on the Mount He forbade this. It is the prerogative of God. But on the church in its organized capacity He places a responsibility for the individual members. Toward those who fall into sin, the church has a duty, to warn, to instruct, and if possible to restore. "Reprove, rebuke, exhort," the Lord says, "with all long-suffering and doctrine." 2 Timothy 4:2. Deal faithfully with wrongdoing. Warn every soul that is in danger. Leave none to deceive themselves. Call sin by its right name. Declare what God has said in regard to lying, Sabbathbreaking, stealing, idolatry, and every other evil. "They which do such things shall not inherit the kingdom of God." Galatians 5:21. If they persist in sin, the judgment you have declared from God's word is pronounced upon them in heaven. In choosing to sin, they disown Christ; the church must show that she does not sanction their deeds, or she herself dishonors her Lord. She must say about sin what God says about it. She must deal with it as God directs, and her action is ratified in heaven. He who despises the authority of the church despises the authority of Christ Himself.
>
> But there is a brighter side to the picture. "Whosoever sins ye remit, they are remitted." Let this thought be kept uppermost. In labor for the erring, let every eye be directed to Christ. Let the shepherds have a tender care for the flock of the Lord's pasture. Let them speak to the erring of the forgiving mercy of the Saviour. Let them encourage the sinner to repent, and believe in Him who can pardon. Let them declare, on the authority of God's word, "If we confess our sins, He is faithful and just to forgive us our sins, and to cleanse us from all unrighteousness." 1 John 1:9. All who repent have the assurance, "He will have compassion upon us; He will subdue our iniquities; and Thou wilt cast all their sins into the depths of the sea." Micah 7:19."[406]

---

[406] Ellen White, *The Desire Ages*, 805-806.

Nevertheless, the just verdict has been placed squarely into the hands of the independents and Heaven is waiting for a humble but honest response. It is hoped that the leading men of the independents and their followers will come forward and ask for forgiveness from the church and its members by falsely accusing them of apostasy pertaining to the gospel and unite with the Brethren in proclaiming the real gospel of the Scriptures that is so soon to be heralded among the nations. The hour is late and a house divided sends the wrong message to the world that is to be the depository of His truth. That truth is now set before all and I fully believe with all my heart that this may be the last plea by Heaven to unite His Church in the unity of the faith of John 17 before the judgements of God begin to fall as He begins to "thoroughly purge his floor" by separating the wheat from the chaff (Matt. 3:12) in the church. Humble yourselves therefore Brethren for this is no time to be fighting against God and His Church. And if these Brethren of the independents should step forward in humility and confess their errors we must receive them with a genuine embrace, forgive and forget and all must ask, what can I do to strengthen the hands of the Brethren and the truth? Here is an opportunity of a lifetime for all too visibly see the mighty hand of God Almighty work in behalf of His people if we all humble ourselves like Ezra and the multitude and are willing to be taught like little children, the ball is in our hands!

Since there has been such a huge departure from the Scriptures and Inspiration regarding the simplicity of the gospel we must commence from the ground up, step by step and assume nothing and illustrate everything. In this chapter we begin by submitting numerous chapters from Pastor Frank Phillips book, *His Robe Or Mine*. I could not have said it better myself as Brother Phillips has a wonderful way of illustrating these simple steps that all may grasp for themselves. In this way no one will ever be confused again upon what God does for and in us and what God expects from us in return. Chapter titles and pg. numbering [ ] is in the original. Please welcome Pastor Frank Phillips:

Perfectly Legal

[21] "Be ye therefore perfect even as your Father which is in heaven is perfect." Matthew 5:48. This statement from Christ's Sermon on the Mount clearly tells us that God's plan for man has never changed. He created man perfect. When Adam fell from that state of perfection, the human family inherited his guilt. Nevertheless, man's fallen condition has not lessened one bit the perfection requirement that Jesus clearly states in Matthew 5:48. However, God has a plan through which man can meet His requirements. That plan is simple enough to be understood by man, yet it is so comprehensive that only God can ever probe its depths. John 3:16. Satan, by misrepresenting God's character to man, has caused that plan to be misunderstood. As a result, man has devised many methods to reach perfection. We feel sorry for the Hindu who might roll on a bed of spikes. Yet, we try to reach that same goal by doing good things that we are led to believe a good Christian should do if he expects to reach heaven. It doesn't matter how close to

the genuine a counterfeit is. A counterfeit is still a counterfeit. The closer it looks to the genuine, the more deceptive it becomes which is why:

> "The strongest bulwark of vice in our world is not the . . . life of the abandoned sinner or the degraded outcast; it is that life which otherwise appears virtuous, honorable, and noble, but in which one sin is fostered, one vice indulged."[407]

[22] That sin may be small. But it is not the size of the sin that is so important as is the refusal to recognize sin's malignant nature and surrender our rebellion to Jesus. It is resistance to His work in our lives that grieves His heart, for there is nothing He can do until we are willing to be yielded as the clay in the potter's hands. God's plan is succinctly stated in Steps to Christ.

> "It was possible for Adam, before the fall, to form a righteous character by obedience to God's law. But he failed to do this, and because of his sin our natures are fallen and we cannot make ourselves righteous. Since we are sinful, unholy, we cannot perfectly obey the holy law. We have no righteousness of our own with which to meet the claims of the law of God. But Christ has made a way of escape for us. He lived on earth amid trials and temptations such as we have to meet. He lived a sinless life. He died for us, and now He offers to take our sins and give us His righteousness. If you give yourself to Him, and accept Him as your Saviour, then, sinful as your life may have been, for His sake you are accounted righteous. Christ's character stands in place of your character, and you are accepted of God just as if you had not sinned."[408]

Here we have God's marvelous plan in one passage. This plan, however, is more comprehensive than we see at first glance. Paul tells us:

> "He [God] has made known to us His hidden purpose—such was His will and pleasure determined beforehand in Christ—to be put into effect when the time was ripe: namely, that the universe, all in heaven and on earth, might be brought into a unity in Christ." Ephesians 1:10, NEB.

Think of it! The entire universe all drawn together in perfect harmony by the magnetic force of the love of God through Jesus Christ our Lord. [23] But this is not all. We obtain an inheritance:

> ". . . being predestinated (pre-planned for) according to the purpose of Him [God] who worketh all things after the counsel of His [God's] own will." Ephesians 1:11.

---

[407] Ellen White, *Thoughts From the Mount of Blessing*, p. 94.
[408] Ellen White, *Steps to Christ*, p. 62.

Can you imagine what is involved when we become inheritors? This means that we are actual members of His family—His flesh and bones. We are more than adopted; we are grafted into the true vine. We shall speak more of this in a later chapter. Now since in God's plan Jesus is the cohesive power around which the entire universe revolves, and every being is bound to Him with cords of love, we can see that Christ's character of love (His robe of righteousness) given to me—a sinner, would be the only way that angels, inhabitants of other worlds and men and women of all countries of earth could agree without question that we are safe for eternity. Only as we become like Him in character can we reveal stability that cannot be shaken. I am certain that by now we have discovered that the only way to perfection is through justification—just as if I had never sinned. I hope that it is equally clear that justification is the crediting of Christ's perfect character to an imperfect and helpless sinner.

> "What is justification by faith? It is the work of God in laying the glory of man in the dust, and doing for man that which is not in his power to do for himself. When men see their own nothingness, they are prepared to be clothed with the righteousness of Christ."[409]

Let us now look at the *process* of justification. The Bible says it well in one sentence. "Therefore being justified by faith, we have peace with God through our Lord Jesus Christ." Romans 5:1. In other words, Christ's death enables Him to justify everyone who wishes to be justified:

> "On the cross of Calvary He paid the redemption price of the race. And thus He gained the right to rescue the captives from the grasp of [24] the great deceiver."[410]

We can readily see that faith is only the *means* and *not the basis* of justification. We do not stand on the ground of faith, but faith enables me to stand, trusting God's word. Faith is more real than any or all of our five senses. (See The SDA Bible Commentary, vol 6, p. 1073.) Now there is another side to look at when we consider this matter of faith. Paul states:

> "Knowing that a man is not justified by the works of the law, but by the faith of Jesus Christ, even we have believed in Jesus Christ, that we might be justified by the faith of Christ, and not by the works of the law: for by the works of the law shall no flesh be justified." Galatians 2:16.

Let us examine a statement from the Review & Herald, April 24, 1888:

> "We should study the life of our Redeemer, for He is the only perfect example for men. We should contemplate the infinite sacrifice of Calvary, and

---

[409] Ellen White, *The Review and Herald*, September 16, 1902, Christ Our Righteousness, p. 104.
[410] *Questions on Doctrine*, p. 672.

behold the exceeding sinfulness of sin and the righteousness of the law. You will come from a concentrated study of the theme of redemption strengthened and ennobled. Your comprehension of the character of God will be deepened; and with the whole plan of salvation clearly defined in your mind, you will be better able to fulfill your divine commission. From a sense of thorough conviction, you can then testify to men of the immutable character of the law manifested by the death of Christ on the cross, the malignant nature of sin, and the righteousness of God in justifying the believer in Jesus on condition of his future obedience to the statutes of God's government in heaven and earth."[411]

Please read again the last sentence of the foregoing paragraph and notice upon which condition God justifies men. We cannot understand this kind of faith. This is God's wonderful faith in His own plan of salvation as it applies [25] to me—a sinner. All we can say is, "Lord, I believe, help Thou my unbelief." I am so glad that God has given to every man *the* measure of faith. And how much faith is that? Just enough faith to reach out like the poor father with the demon-possessed son. Our faith simply opens the door for Christ to help us according to our need and His glory. Jesus is not only the author, but the finisher of our faith. Hebrews 12:2. The process of justification is therefore a legal one. When we have a legal work to be done we must find someone qualified to do it. Jesus is the only One qualified to do our legal work.

> "On the cross of Calvary He paid the redemption price of the race. And thus He gained the right to rescue the captives from the grasp of the great deceiver."[412]

As the soldiers were driving the nails through the Saviour's hands:

> "Jesus was earning the right to become the advocate [our attorney] of men in the Father's presence."[413]

Justification, being a legal work, can only deal with our legal standing (our record) and not with us personally. When a criminal is pardoned by the legal process of law, his standing before the law is changed but his character is unaffected. For this same reason, justification is credited righteousness. This is in no way an inferior or incomplete righteousness. There is nothing that time, experience, talent or effort can add to this marvelous gift. Jesus lived in this world for thirty-three and one-half years and developed a perfect character. This is His unspeakable gift to us. Let your imagination stretch to its utmost limits and still it is impossible to conceive of anything that you could add to that unspeakable gift of His perfection credited to us. Here is where the human nature is tempted to believe that perfection cannot be ours in reality unless we do some of the work of developing it. There is a work, of course, a most trying and painstaking

---

[411] Ellen White, *Review & Herald,* April 24, 1888, Christ Our Righteousness, p. 35.
[412] *Questions on Doctrine*, p. 672.
[413] Ellen White, *The Desire of Ages*, p. 744.

work for us to do which we will soon see clearly. However, we must keep in mind that only God can do His work and only man can do his work. It is [26] as impossible for God to do man's work, and be consistent with His own laws, as it is for man to do God's work which he has no power to do anyway. Sanctification—the imparted righteousness of God—is the process which clearly defines and clarifies our work from His. We will discuss sanctification in another chapter. It is through justification that we are credited as obeying God's commandments. (See Christ Our Righteousness, p. 99, Review & Herald, August 22, 1893.)

> "Therefore being justified by faith, we have peace with God through our Lord Jesus Christ." Romans 5:1.

Jesus not only justifies me but also makes peace between me, the sinner, and God, my Maker whom I have been rebelling against:

> "The believer is not called upon to make his peace with God; he never has nor ever can do this. He is to accept Christ as his peace, for with Christ is God and peace."[414]

" . . . The carnal mind is enmity against God: for it is not subject to the law of God, neither indeed can be. So then they that are in the flesh cannot please God." Romans 8:7-8. Carnality is a term that should shock every church member into action. Contrary to common belief, carnality does not refer to the man of the world who does not know God, but rather to the man of the church who knows God but does not follow on to know Him better. Paul refers to three levels of life of human beings: the natural man, the carnal man, and the spiritual man. 1 Corinthians 2:14, 15 & 3:1. We are all living on one of these levels. The natural is the nature we inherited from birth. The spiritual is the nature given by God when we are born again and when we continue to grow in Christ. The carnal nature is between the two. It is that new nature given to man when he is born of the Spirit and not of the flesh, but who did not grow ". . . unto the measure of the stature of the fullness of Christ." Ephesians 4:13. This is the condition of man as described by John in Revelation 3:14-22 ". . . neither cold nor hot . . . lukewarm, and neither cold nor hot . . . I will spew thee out of my mouth . . ." [27]

> "The figure of spewing out of His mouth means that He cannot offer up your prayers or your expressions of love to God. He cannot endorse your teaching of His word or your spiritual work in anywise. He cannot present your religious exercises with the request that grace be given you."[415]

We are well aware of the fact that unless our prayers are anointed with the Spirit of the Lord Jesus, God does not hear us:

---

[414] Ellen White, *Selected Messages*, book 1, p. 395.
[415] Ellen White, *Testimonies*, vol. 6, p. 408.

". . . No man cometh unto the Father, but by me," said Jesus in John 14:6.

This leaves us in a position where we must make a decision. This is why Jesus said, " . . . I would thou wert cold or hot." Revelation 3:15. Revelation 3:18 carefully follows with, "I counsel thee to buy of me gold tried in the fire . . ." We must keep in mind that man makes this purchase without money and without price. Isaiah 55:1. Someone has said "victory is born out of crisis." Our crisis is to see the utter foolishness of the lukewarm condition and sense our real need of the gold God advises us to obtain. Here we need special wisdom, for many have come to this point but followed Satan's plan. They think they are walking out of their problems when he is only leading them into deeper problems. To "turn over a new leaf," to "determine to do better," to "be more faithful" are good ideas but they are powerless to change the life:

> "As the leaven, when mingled with the meal, works from within outward, so it is by the renewing of the heart that the grace of God works to transform the life. No mere external change is sufficient to bring us into harmony with God. There are many who try to reform by correcting this or that bad habit, and they hope in this way to become Christians, but they are beginning in the wrong [28] place. Our first work is with the heart."[416]

The decision we must make is to allow the mind of Christ to become ours. "Let this mind be in you, which was also in Christ Jesus." Philippians 2:5.

"God has made provision that we may become like Him, and He will accomplish this for all who do not interpose a perverse will and thus frustrate His grace." "With untold love our God has loved us, and our love awakens toward Him as we comprehend something of the length and breadth and depth and height of this love that passeth knowledge. By the revelation of the attractive loveliness of Christ, by the knowledge of His love expressed to us while we were yet sinners, the stubborn heart is melted and subdued, and the sinner is transformed and becomes a child of heaven. God does not employ compulsory measures; love is the agent which He uses to expel sin from the heart. By it He changes pride into humility, and enmity and unbelief into love and faith."[417]

With faith as the vehicle and love as the power, each originating with and coming from Christ, we can easily see that the process must be His also. Praise God! It is His by right of His own purchase through His willing death upon the cross.

> "On the cross of Calvary He paid the redemption price of the race. And thus He gained the right to rescue the captives from the grasp of the great deceiver."[418]

---

[416] Ellen White, *Christ's Object Lessons*, p. 97. (See also *Selected Messages*, book 1, p. 353.)
[417] Ellen White, *Thoughts from the Mount of Blessing*, pp. 76, 77.
[418] *Questions on Doctrines*, p. 672

This makes it clear that Christ took care of every conceivable legal consideration that God's holy law demanded before He attempted to rescue man from the pit of sin into which he had fallen. For Christ is " . . . the Lamb slain from the foundation of the world." Revelation 13:8. [29] Now, of course, we recognize that God's plan effectively silences Satan's charges that since man had sinned, he belonged to him. Oh, the blessedness of the most precious gift God gives to man when He gives back the will that Adam surrendered at the time when he fell! This gift of a returned will enables us to choose to love, serve, and obey another master even if we know that we do not have power to accomplish that which we have chosen to do. This we will understand fully when we come to study *The Man of Romans* 7 in chapter 3 That choice freed God to carry out His plan to legally justify and credit to me, a sinner, His perfect character that He developed here on this earth while buffeted by the most severe temptations of Satan. That is why our record reads "just as if I'd never sinned," and Satan can do nothing about it. That is the reason why when "the Son makes you free you are free indeed." Let me repeat: The vehicle is faith, the power is love, the process is the plan of redemption, and praise His holy name! it's legal anywhere in the entire world. It is not only legal, but it also constitutes the only source of real joy and happiness for the entire world."[419]

How Good is Perfect?

[30] "What do ye imagine against the Lord? He will make an utter end; affliction shall not rise up the second time." Nahum 1:9. These words of Scripture constitute one of the most amazing promises found in all of the Bible. God's Word also declares, "If the Son therefore shall make you free, ye shall be free indeed." John 8:36. This amazing promise, that man will never fail again, *will* be carried out in this freedom which He gives to us. Here we have pictured to us a time that is coming in the near future when, not even in thought, will sin raise its ugly head again. Our first response to this thought is apt to be that with all evil removed there will be no inclination to sin, so obedience will be natural. However, this was the condition in heaven when sin started. And let me further remind you that in times of ease and prosperity man strays farthest from the Lord. Isn't this one of the major problems of the church today? "Rich and increased with goods," but destitute of love. How is God able to make such a sweeping promise? In Malachi 4:1 God says that the cleansing fire that purifies the earth will, in the process, also remove sin—both root and branch. In John 15:5 Jesus says, "I am the vine, ye are the branches . . . ." Here Jesus was speaking to His disciples after one had separated himself from the twelve. Would it not be just as true to say that Satan is also the root from which the branches of the world are growing? These are to be consumed in the cleansing fire. [31] But we must look much deeper to see what is involved in God's promise of Nahum 1:9, which declares an enemy shall not arise the second time. The first enemy arose by looking to himself! There has always been the possibility within the freedom of God's creation for the root of sin to spring up. How can God promise that not one of His redeemed, or someone from an unfallen world, or even an angel

---

[419] Frank Philipps, *His Cross Or Mine*, Chapter 2 – Perfectly Legal, 21-29.

from heaven will ever, even in thought, rebel against Him? Marvel of marvels, this will be the impact of the plan of salvation throughout God's creation! God, who knows the future, assures us that this will be so. God's work is already finished for those who dwell in the heavens. Inhabited worlds and angels have been able to rejoice that they have been liberated from the presence of evil angels and from Satan. Revelation 12:12. However, this quarantined earth and its inhabitants are fully aware of the presence of Satan and his workers. Even so, to some of us sin has not yet become exceedingly sinful. Its deadly nature has not come through to us as malignant (deadly). Somehow we think that we can drop its bewitching influence upon us just before we are permitted to enter heaven.

> "Angelic perfection failed in heaven. Human perfection failed in Eden . . . Our only hope is perfect trust in the blood of Him who can save to the uttermost all that come unto God by Him."[420]

To the *uttermost* means saving *from* self not *in* self. The malignant nature of sin is revealed as we trust in self rather than in God's Word! Could this be the reason why there is in our world today an unprecedented call from every class of society for self-expression? Nations are demanding independence. Cities, towns and villages are all declaring their own authority. Families are being broken almost as fast as they are formed. Children are "doing their own thing" as a direct result of the self-expression atmosphere that permeates the world. [32] Satan is doing his work well. Thus, self-assertiveness and self-worth are declared to be the answer to personal, as well as public, problems. Think what this spirit started in heaven so long ago:

> "We cannot retain self and yet enter the kingdom of God. If we ever attain unto holiness, it will be through the renunciation of self and the reception of the mind of Christ."[421]

Selfish thoughts not only unfit us for heaven, but:

> "When self is woven into our labors, then the truth we bear to others does not sanctify, refine, and ennoble our own hearts; it will not testify that we are fit vessels for the Master's use."[422]

How are we to be free from self? Hebrews 12:6 tells us, ". . . He chasteneth . . . every son whom he receiveth." This is to remove every root of bitterness (self) that could spring up to trouble us. "See that ye refuse not him that speaketh . . ." Hebrews 12:25. How easy to hide self behind a screen of not understanding when He speaks. God does not promise that we shall understand everything before we follow His calling. Hebrews 11 reveals a large number of faithful who did not understand God's purposes, yet they all obeyed. Abel, Enoch, Noah and

---

[420] Ellen White, *The SDA Bible Commentary*, vol. 5, p. 1132, *The Signs of the Times*, Dec. 30, 1889.
[421] Ellen White, *Thoughts from the Mount of Blessing*, p. 143.
[422] Ellen White, *Selected Messages*, book 1, p. 405.

Abraham are just a few. Some might call this blind faith. But I would remind you that God's children ". . . walk by faith, not by sight." 2 Corinthians 5:7. How good is perfect? Perfection is not a state of goodness to be attained, but rather a state of trusting God implicitly without doubting or questioning. It was this characteristic that marked Job's life and enabled God to say that Job was " . . . a perfect and an upright man. . ." Job 1:8. This commendation from the Lord came in spite of the fact that Job testifies in chapter 42:6, ". . . I abhor myself, and repent in dust and ashes." Noah was declared to be ". . . just. . . and perfect . . ." Genesis 6:9. Yet, like Lot, Moses, Abraham, David and Solomon, the Bible record of their lives reveals personal imperfection. [33] How good, then, is perfect? That depends:

> "As the leaven, when mingled with the meal, works from within outward, so it is by the renewing of the heart that the grace of God works to transform the life. No mere external change is sufficient to bring us into harmony with God. There are many who try to reform by correcting this or that bad habit, and they hope in this way to become Christians, but they are beginning in the wrong place. Our first work is with the heart."[423]

"The man who attempts to keep the commandments of God from a sense of obligation merely— because he is required to do so—will never enter the joy of obedience. He does not obey. When the requirements of God are accounted a burden because they cut across human inclination, we may know that the life is not a Christian life. True obedience is the outworking of a principle within. It springs from a love of righteousness, the love of the law of God. The essence of all righteousness is loyalty to our Redeemer. This will lead us to do right because it is right—because right doing is pleasing to God."[424]

God has a plan whereby we may be found perfect—not by human effort "lest any man should boast." This perfection is a marvelous gift from Jesus Christ that is given to all who believe.

> "The law requires righteousness,—a righteous life, a perfect character; and this man has not to give. He cannot meet the claims of God's holy law. But Christ, coming to earth as man, lived a holy life, and developed a perfect character. These He offers as a free gift to all who will receive them."[425]

How good is perfect? Perfection is a divine accomplishment revealed in the life of Jesus our Lord during His [34] earthly life on this planet. His life reveals perfect trust, total dependence upon His Father for daily living and accomplishing the will of God. Now, He finished His work—completed everything in our behalf—knowing that we could never in our strength do what God's law requires. What is our part? Exercise the will! Choose to trust Him! Even if we know that we cannot do what we choose to do, by choosing we open the door for Christ to do in

---

[423] Ellen White, *Christ's Object Lessons*, p. 97.
[424] Ellen White, *Christ's Object Lessons*, pp. 97, 98.
[425] Ellen White, *The Desire of Ages*, p. 762.

us what we are unable to do for ourselves. So, in truth, the child of God chooses to trust in all things. Then his work is to let Christ do the trusting through him and refuse to allow circumstances or situations to create doubts in the method Christ is using to do His work. If we refuse to doubt *His methods of working* in us and simply believe He knows what He is doing, then we will have learned Christ's secret of victory—even in the face of apparent defeat. Let me close this chapter by quoting my favorite and most helpful paragraph from the pen of one who lived what she wrote:

> "The Father's presence encircled Christ, and nothing befell Him but that which infinite love permitted for the blessing of the world. Here was His source of comfort, and it is for us. He who is imbued with the Spirit of Christ abides in Christ. The blow that is aimed at him falls upon the Saviour, who surrounds him with His presence. Whatever comes to him comes from Christ. He has no need to resist evil, for Christ is his defense. Nothing can touch him except by our Lord's permission, and 'all things' that are permitted 'work together for good to them that love God.' Romans 8:28."[426]

How good is perfect? All the goodness we will ever have is simply a perfect trust in Jesus.

> "Through the merits [35] of Christ, through His righteousness, which by faith is imputed unto us, we are to attain to the perfection of Christian character."[427] [428]

Graveyard Religion

[36] "Know ye not, that so many of us as were baptized into Jesus Christ were baptized into his death?" Romans 6:3. Most Christians who have been baptized by immersion are fully aware of being baptized in the name of the Father, Son, and Holy Spirit. But all too few are aware of the fact that baptism is into Christ's death. Paul says, "Therefore we are buried with him by baptism into death: that like as Christ was raised up from the dead by the glory of the Father, even so we also should walk in newness of life." Romans 6:4. Baptism symbolizes a death experience that already should have taken place in the believer's life. The death here spoken of is the death of the nature we were born with. That incorrigible old nature is fit only for death. The natural result of death is burial from which there would be no resurrection. In fact, Paul states that ". . . our old man is crucified with him, that the body of sin might be destroyed, that henceforth we should not serve sin." Romans 6:6.

---

[426] Ellen White, *Thoughts from the Mount of Blessing*, p. 71.
[427] Ellen White, *Testimonies*, vol. 5, p. 744.
[428] Frank Phillips, *His Robe Or Mine*, Chapter 3: How Good Is Perfect, 30-35.

> "Undoubtedly the great difficulty with the majority of believers is that they are trying to live Christ's life without first having died Christ's death. They seem to have the notion that Christ died so that we need not die, and so through faith in Christ they hope to live without dying. Paul said, 'They that are in the flesh cannot please God' Romans 8:8, [37] and 'they that are Christ's have crucified the flesh' Galatians 5:24."[429]

A clear understanding of the importance of this fact is absolutely necessary if we are to have a successful walk with the Lord.

> "The new birth is a rare experience in this age of the world. This is the reason why there are so many perplexities in the churches. Many, so many, who assume the name of Christ are unsanctified and unholy. They have been baptized, but they were buried alive. Self did not die, and therefore they did not rise to newness of life in Christ."[430]

The foregoing statement was written in 1897. Undoubtedly it would be equally true today. Paul states further:

> "Therefore if any man be in Christ, he is a new creature: (creation) old things are passed away; behold, all things are become new." 2 Corinthians 5:17.

Why is it necessary for the old nature to die? Jesus answers, "For whosoever will save his life shall lose it: and whosoever will lose his life for my sake shall find it." Matthew 16:25. Apparently there is nothing that can be done to cure the old sinful nature of man. It just simply must die. If there is to be a new life, the old must pass away. Meade MacGuire, in his book, His Cross and Mine, gives us an insight that is very helpful.

> "There is a great difference between sins and sin. Many find serious difficulty in their Christian life because they do not understand this distinction. Beneath all our acts of transgression is the principle of sin from which they spring. Though all our evil deeds were pardoned, we would still go on sinning. Something more must be done for us than simply to pardon our sins."[431]

[38] MacGuire continues:

> "Here it is necessary to consider the distinction between sin and sins. Sins, acts of disobedience, transgressions of the divine law, God is always ready to forgive, through the merits of Christ, in response to the prayer of penitence and

---

[429] Ellen White, *The Life of Victory*, by Meade MacGuire, p. 35.
[430] Ellen White, *The SDA Bible Commentary*, vol. 6, p. 1075, *Manuscript* 148, 1897.
[431] His Cross and Mine, by Meade MacGuire, p. 80.

faith. But sin God cannot forgive. Sin is the nature which leads us to disobey God's law. The nature with which we come into the world does not change, as we read in the Saviour's words: 'That which is born of the flesh is flesh; and that which is born of the Spirit is spirit.' The only way to be rid of a bad nature is by death. The only way to receive a good nature is to be born again."[432]

Death is the only way to deal with the old nature. Here is how this death takes place in the believer. The lower passions have their seat in the body and work through it. The words *flesh* or *fleshly* or *carnal lusts* refer to the lower nature. We are commanded to crucify the flesh, with the affections and lusts. How? By inflicting pain on the body? No. What I want to do is to put to death the temptation to sin. Kill the corrupt thought. I want every thought controlled by Jesus Christ.[433]   In Romans 6, Paul declares that the death of the old nature is real. In verse 11 we are told to reckon this to be a fact! Here is where many Christians fail. It is so easy to believe this experience to be a theological expression, but not something that is real or practical. Satan is responsible for this reasoning. When God states a fact, Satan will oppose, modify or attempt to change the fact to suit his cause. Satan knows that if the Christian truly believes his old nature is really dead, his power is broken. In order to reinforce his claim that the death experience is not real, Satan tries to get the Christian to live more and [39] more in his feelings rather than by his faith. And so he gets the believer to fall into sin. Then he turns around and blames him for falling into sin. And he uses this experience of falling as proof that the old nature is not dead. He simply uses perfectly rational reasoning and says, "If the old nature were dead, you would not have been tempted." At this point, it is necessary for the Christian to stop trying to reason his way through the maze of feelings he has coursing through his being. He must, in spite of feelings, believe God's Word. If he has given himself to Christ he knows that ". . . they that are Christ's have crucified the flesh with the affections and lusts." Galatians 5:24. We must always return to God's Word and stop trying to reason with Satan's suggestions if we are to remain Christians. God says that your old nature is dead even if you have fallen into sin through being tempted. Satan says that it is not dead. Now the question for us to answer is not *what* do we believe, but *who* do we believe? How can I handle these feelings? Read chapter one again and observe the fact that Satan is the master of our feelings. The following statements underscore this fact:

> "We should daily dedicate ourselves to God and believe He accepts the sacrifice, without examining whether we have that degree of feeling that corresponds with our faith. Feeling and faith are as distinct as the east is from the west. Faith is not dependent upon feeling. We must earnestly cry to God in faith, feeling or no feeling, and then live our prayers. Our assurance and

---

[432] *His Cross and Mine*, by Meade MacGuire, p. 91.
[433] Ellen White, *The Acts of the Apostles*, pp. 127, 128.

evidence is God's word, and after we have asked we must believe without doubting."[434]

In order to help us see how subtle this question of faith versus feelings is, let us think clearly as we read this next quotation: [40]

> ". . . God must be served from principle instead of from feeling . . . Confound not faith and feeling together. They are distinct. Faith is ours to exercise. This faith we must keep in exercise. Believe, believe. Let your faith take hold of the blessing, and it is yours. Your feelings have nothing to do with this faith. When faith brings the blessing to your heart, and you rejoice in the blessing, it is no more faith, but feeling."[435]

The last sentence in the foregoing paragraph is not the easiest to grasp. Please read it again. Now let's take a closer look. Obviously, it is a very short step from faith to feeling. Or can we say that living by faith requires constant vigilance lest we slip into living by feeling. A clear Biblical example might help us at this point. In Luke 10:17 the Bible says, "And the seventy returned again with joy, saying, Lord, even the devils are subject unto us through Thy name." Catch the excitement that must have been shown by these returning missionaries. Never had they had an experience like that before. Their joy must have been very evident, for it is especially mentioned. Now listen to Christ's response in verse 18: "And he said unto them, I beheld Satan as lightning fall from heaven." What a response! I can almost see the expressions on the faces of those workers, can't you? There must have been some talking among those men. "He must not have understood what we said. Why is He so sad? I can't figure Him out." Some may have even tried to clarify their report. Jesus, however, was responding from a wealth of experience that they knew nothing about. Christ's mind went back to the fall of Lucifer and He simply was saying, "I saw that same spirit in Satan long ago and now I am seeing it here." To Satan had been given the blessing of great power. He thrilled to the power but forgot the greater blessing of his relationship to the source of that power. The key words here that reveal the solemn truth are "subject unto us." [41] Listen now to verses 19 and 20: "Behold, I give unto you power to tread on serpents and scorpions, and over all the power of the enemy: and nothing shall by any means hurt you. Notwithstanding in this rejoice not, that the spirits are subject unto you; but rather rejoice, because your names are written in heaven." The greatest blessing possible for God to bestow—a blessing that cost the life of the Son of God—was set aside and relegated to an insignificant place when compared to the casting out of devils. Calvary was the price paid that we might have our names written in heaven. The power to cast out devils Christ could give at no cost to Himself. How often we think more of a basket of groceries miraculously set on our front steps when needed, than the gift of God in allowing us to become members of His family, ". . . of

---

[434] Ellen White, *Selected Messages*, book 2, p. 243.
[435] Ellen White, *Testimonies*, vol. 1, p. 167.

his flesh, and of his bones." Ephesians 5:30. Now that we have pointed out the problems of living by our feelings, let us return to the question of how we handle these feelings. Do we grit our teeth and bear them? Do we ignore them and hope that they will go away? Is it better to express our feelings and thereby let the tension or stress out? These and many other solutions would receive support from some very responsible people. All our feelings are much easier to deal with by first checking their source. We must keep in mind the fact that God works first with the heart (mind) and His work is from inside outward. Satan, on the other hand, works through the feelings and his work is from the outside inward. (See Appendix D) God motivates all of our actions through the mind. Satan motivates through the senses. He bypasses the reasoning process. Please remember:

> "There are but two powers that control the minds of men—the power of God and the power of Satan."[436]

With these facts in mind it is easier to ascertain the source of the feelings and know what to do with them. But how do we handle the feelings even when we know [42] they are from the devil? We must remember the counsel in The Adventist Home, p.128. "Put to death the temptation to sin." This is impossible for us to do in our own strength. Right here is where we must use the power of the will. We must *choose* to believe God in spite of our feelings. Having done this, then we must frankly admit to ourselves that we cannot control our feelings. Then flee to the Lord in prayer, admitting our inability, and thank Him for His great power and willingness to deliver us. He will deliver! The feelings will pass away and peace will reign in our heart. It may be necessary to do this often for a time until we convince Satan that we will not willingly be controlled by feelings. Walk by faith—feelings or no feelings. Keepthinking, I am dead, and my life is hid with Christ in God. Colossians 3:3. What can the devil do with a dead person? When the will is used to choose even that which we cannot do, God is glorified, for He loves to do for us that which it is not possible for us to do for ourselves. Graveyard religion may not have much appeal for us, I'm sure it didn't for Jesus. Yet, it is the only way out of this sin problem. He said to the Greeks who came to see Him just before His death ". . . Except a corn of wheat fall into the ground and die, it abideth alone; but if it die, it bringeth forth much fruit." John 12:24. May I suggest that your graveyard may be in your own home, workshop, office or anywhere that self may arise during each day's activities. Remaining a Christian takes much more than a daily dying to self. With Paul we must be "always bearing about in the body the dying of the Lord Jesus, that the life also of Jesus might be made manifest in our body. So then death worketh in us, but life in you." 2 Corinthians 4:10 & 12. There is only one way to attract others to Jesus and not to ourselves. If self is hidden (crucified) Jesus is revealed.

---

[436] Ellen White, *Temperance*, p. 276.

"Christ is waiting with longing desire for the manifestation of Himself in His church. When the character of Christ shall [43] be perfectly reproduced in His people, then He will come to claim them as His own."[437] [438]

Christians are Born not Made

[44] "The born-again experience spoken of more than a dozen times in the New Testament is often grossly misunderstood. To many, it is simply believing in Jesus. To others, accepting Jesus as Saviour is to be born-again. To still others, baptism by immersion equals being born-again.

May I suggest that the new birth is such a dynamic, vitalizing experience, as pictured in God's Word, that many people find it difficult to accept literally what the Scriptures teach.

"The man who is really God's son does not practice sin, for God's nature is in him, for good, and such a heredity is incapable of sin." 1 John 3:9, Phillips.

"Everyone who believes that Jesus is the Christ is born of God, and everyone who loves the father loves his child as well." 1 John 5:1, N.I.V.

"For whatsoever is born of God overcometh the world: and this is the victory that overcometh the world, even our faith." 1 John 5:4.

We can see that being born-again is where the power of the Christian life resides. Now we must discover what makes this power a real experience to us personally. John declares, "And this is the record, that God hath given to us eternal life, and this life is in his Son. He that hath the Son hath life, and he that hath not the Son of God hath not life." 1 John 5:11, 12. [45]

Could it be that in our eagerness to learn what is truth we have neglected to see who is the Truth? In our search for truth there may be something that is blinding us to truth. We shall try to discover what it is that blinds, so effectively, honest searchers and thus learn how to clear the way for this marvelous experience of the new birth.

"Behold, I stand at the door, and knock: if any man hear my voice, and open the door, I will come in to him, and will sup with him, and he with me." Revelation 3:20. Apparently these words are addressed to God's Laodicean church of today, for they are a part of the special message of Jesus to His last church. It is, therefore, imperative that we know the answer to the oft repeated question, "How am I born again?" Or is this merely a verbal experience? Is it literal? If literal, how much of my life does this give Jesus access to? My religious life? My business life? My recreational life? Just how much is necessary before He will enter my life?

> "Every thought is to be brought into captivity to Jesus Christ. All animal propensities are to be subjected to the higher powers of the soul. The love of God must reign supreme; Christ must occupy an undivided throne. Our bodies are to be regarded as His purchased possession. The members of the body are to become the instruments of righteousness."[439]

---

[437] Ellen White, *Christ's Object Lessons*, p. 69.
[438] Frank Phillips, *His Robe Or Mine*, Chapter 4 Graveyard Religion, 36-43.
[439] Ellen White, *The Adventist Home*, p. 128.

Obviously, this experience involves much more than being willing to part with our bad habits, our evil natures, our love of the world, and our earthly possessions. Every thought must be under His control. All natural inclinations and members of the body itself must reflect His righteousness.

In order to accomplish this, Jesus says, "I counsel thee to buy of me gold tried in the fire, that thou mayest be rich; and white raiment, that thou mayest be clothed, and that the shame of thy nakedness do not appear; and anoint thine eyes with eye-salve, that thou mayest see." Revelation 3:18. [46]

> "What is it that constitutes the wretchedness, the nakedness, of those who feel rich and increased with goods? It is the want of the righteousness of Christ."[440]

Even a strong belief in the correct doctrinal teachings of the church cannot save anyone. Jesus must have full control of every facet of our lives. This is not an arbitrary demand of our Saviour; it is simply one of God's divine natural laws. It is the law that says, ". . . the carnal mind is enmity against God . . ." Romans 8:7.

For this reason, Nicodemus came to Jesus by night. His heart was heavy, for he desired the covering of Christ's righteousness, the assurance of salvation, but he did not know how to get it. Jesus saw his need and went straight to the point. ". . . Except a man be born again, he cannot see the kingdom of God." John 3:3. Nicodemus' wealth, influence, personal achievements were of no value in meeting Jesus' requirements of a new birth.

Here was Nicodemus' crisis. Unable to see the answer, he declared, " . . . How can these things be?" John 3:9. Jesus had already told him, "That which is born of the flesh is flesh; and that which is born of the Spirit is spirit." Verse 6. Nicodemus did not wish to see this. Self was very much alive in him.

Christ's statement to Nicodemus still stands. Flesh cannot crucify flesh, no matter how many promises, pledges, commitments we might make, or how much sincere effort we might expend. There is always a little bit of flesh-self still alive to take over again. Someone has said that self would rather be thought evil of than not to be thought of at all.

Christ is standing at the door of His church with His voice pleading, ". . . If any man hear my voice, and open the door, I will come in . . . " Revelation 3:20. Why does Jesus picture Himself thus? Because we, like Nicodemus, are still blind to self. We have yet to see that Christians are born and not made. [47]

Many earnest Christian people have the idea that with God's help their old nature—the flesh—can be cleansed, purified, freed from the evil within and then they will be able to live victorious lives for God. This is Satan's counterfeit! His plan is to lead human beings to believe that human nature can be changed. He knows that it is only fit to die, but he tries to cover the truth with lies and keep us blinded.

> "The Christian's life is not a modification or improvement of the old, but a transformation of nature. There is a death to self and sin, and a new life altogether. This change can be brought about only by the effectual working of the Holy Spirit."[441]

---

[440] Ellen White, *Christ Our Righteousness*, p. 90.
[441] Ellen White, *The Desire of Ages*, p. 172.

> "Christ came to earth, taking humanity and standing as man's representative, to show in the controversy with Satan that man, as God created him, connected with the Father and the Son, could obey every divine requirement."[442]

This quotation deserves some very serious thought. In it we find the reason why it was absolutely necessary for Jesus to be born with a sinless nature such as the first Adam had. It is only that which is born of the Spirit that God can work with to mold and fashion according to His will. Sinful nature is unstable and will not respond to the Master Worker. The desire may be in the mind, but the flesh is incorrigible. The result is failure.

When Jesus said, ". . . Except a corn of wheat fall in the ground and die, it abideth alone . . ." John 12:24, He was obviously speaking of baptism which, in truth, symbolizes death.

> "The new birth is a rare experience in this age of the world. This is the reason why there are so many perplexities in the churches. Many, so many, who assume the name of Christ are unsanctified and unholy. They have been baptized, but they were buried alive. Self did not die, and therefore they did not rise to newness of life in Christ."[443]

[48] "But as many as received him, to them gave he power to become the sons of God, even to them that believe on his name: Which were born, not of blood, nor the will of the flesh, nor of the will of man, but of God." John 1:12,13. It is quite clear that Inspiration teaches the necessity of the spiritual birth before one becomes a son of God or a member of His family. However, death must precede life.

The solution to this problem is beyond man's abilities. Man, even in his sinful nature, can exercise his God-given will and choose to die and be born again.

This process is described in chapter one of this book. We had nothing to do with our natural birth but, praise God, we do have a God-given part in the born-again experience. We can choose to be born again. However, even in this new birth there must be a connection with the Father and the Son. This is what justification accomplishes.

The Father justifies the believer on the basis of his acceptance of Jesus and His atonement on the cross in the believer's behalf.

Jesus lived His life in direct connection with His Father. He said, ". . . The Son can do nothing of himself . . ." John 5:19. His life of obedience to every divine requirement was not independent from His Father but 100 percent dependent upon His Father. It is thus that His life is a perfect example for us to follow. Jesus tells us, " . . . without me ye can do nothing." John 15:5. Independent of Jesus, even in the new birth experience, we cannot obey the divine requirements. But Jesus living in us, as the Father lived in Him, makes it possible to obey. He does this in us. And that is good news, isn't it? The question we must ask is, "What is the divine requirement I must meet?" We find the answer in the following quotation:

> "God requires the entire surrender of the heart before justification can take place; and in order for man to retain justification, there must be continual

---

[442] Ellen White, *The SDA Bible Commentary*, vol. 7A, p. 650, *The Signs of the Times*, June 9, 1898.
[443] Ellen White, *The SDA Bible Commentary*, vol. 6, p. 1075, *Manuscript* 148, 1897.

obedience, through active, living faith that works by love and purifies the soul."[444]

[49] You will notice that while the condition for justification is surrender, the condition for retaining justification is continual obedience. Does justification enable us to obey? No. Justification deals only with our legal record—our standing before God. How can we meet the second condition? Here is how:

> "As God works in the heart, and man surrenders his will to God, and cooperates with God, he works out in the life what God works in by the Holy Spirit, and there is harmony between the purpose of the heart and the practice of the life. Every sin must be renounced as the hateful thing that crucified the Lord of life and glory, and the believer must have a progressive experience by continually doing the works of Christ. It is by continual surrender of the will, by continual obedience, that the blessing of justification is retained."[445]

Please notice that man's work is to surrender his will. Christ's life was one of continual surrender. We will speak more of this in a later chapter. Continual obedience is the result of the process of sanctification, which we will consider in the next chapters. It may seem to some that human nature has been pictured as totally insignificant. That is, indeed, the point.

> "When the soul surrenders itself to Christ, a new power takes possession of the new heart. A change is wrought which man can never accomplish for himself. It is a supernatural work, bringing a supernatural element into human nature. The soul that is yielded to Christ becomes His own fortress, which He holds in a revolted world, and He intends that no authority shall be known in it but His own. A soul thus kept in possession by the heavenly agencies is impregnable to the assaults of Satan. . . . The only [50] defense against evil is the indwelling of Christ in the heart through faith in His righteousness. Unless we become vitally connected with God, we can never resist the unhallowed effects of self-love, self-indulgence, and temptation to sin. We may leave off many bad habits, for the time we may part company with Satan; but without a vital connection with God, through the surrender of ourselves to Him moment by moment, we shall be overcome."[446]

> "What is justification by faith? It is the work of God in laying the glory of man in the dust, and doing for man that which it is not in his power to do for himself. When men see their own nothingness, they are prepared to be clothed with the righteousness of Christ."[447]

---

[444] Ellen White, *Selected Messages*, book 1, p. 366.
[445] Ellen White, *Selected Messages*, book 1, p. 397.
[446] Ellen White, *The Desire of Ages*, p. 324.
[447] Ellen White, *Christ Our Righteousness*, p. 104.

"Why is it so hard to lead a self-denying, humble life? Because professed Christians are not dead to the world. It is easy living after we are dead."[448]

Remember that God's ways are not our ways. His way may look like failure, but His way is the only way to true success. For when we are truly born again— We live by dying. Strength comes through weakness. The battle is won by *surrendering*. Then we can know that Christians are born and not made."[449]

From Justification to What?

[52] "If one is justified and his record in heaven reads "just as if I'd never sinned," it would seem strange to desire anything added to that kind of a record. To express this kind of thinking is to reveal the fact that one is still thinking legally. There is still a desire to do something to make ourselves feel that it is real. The highest goal for the justified person is to, by faith, maintain that undeserved position that God, by His love, has given to us as a free gift. However, the moment we are justified, that moment we are also sanctified. Both of these conditions are attained solely by faith.

Justification deals with your record in heaven. It changes this record from that of a condemned criminal to that of a free man with a perfect record, including your past life.

Sanctification is heaven's ordained plan whereby the freed criminal (now a member of God's family) can continuously say thank you to God for this unspeakable gift of justification to an undeserving wretch. How does he do this? By every day allowing God to work in him according to His good will and pleasure. Philippians 2:13.

Our part is to allow God to work in our lives, rehabituating us to continuously say yes every time Jesus says, "This is the way, walk ye in it." Heaven's requirement for those who enter heaven is a complete trust in Jesus without doubting, delaying or even questioning why or how. Our response to His leading must be as natural as the flower's turning to the sun. [53]

Obviously, there must be no doubting along the way for our justification (imputed righteousness) or our sanctification (imparted righteousness). It is through justification that obedience is credited to us, now and for the future.

> "Through His imputed righteousness, they are accepted of God as those who are manifesting to the world that they acknowledge allegiance to God, keeping all His commandments."[450]

> "We should study the life of our Redeemer, for He is the only perfect example for men. We should contemplate the infinite sacrifice of Calvary, and behold the exceeding sinfulness of sin and the righteousness of the law. You will come from a concentrated study of the theme of redemption strengthened

---

[448] Ellen White, *Messages to Young People*, p. 127.
[449] Frank Phillips, *His Robe Or Mine*, Chapter 5 - Christians Are Born Not Made, 45-50.
[450] Ellen White, *Christ Our Righteousness*, p. 99.

and ennobled. Your comprehension of the character of God will be deepened; and with the whole plan of salvation clearly defined in your mind, you will be better able to fulfill your divine commission. From a sense of thorough conviction, you can then testify to men of the immutable character of the law manifested by the death of Christ on the cross, the malignant nature of sin, and the righteousness of God in justifying the believer in Jesus on condition of his future obedience to the statutes of God's government in heaven and earth."[451]

"Personal religion among us as a people is at a low ebb. There is much form, much machinery, much tongue religion; but something deeper and more solid must be brought into our religious experience . . . What we need is to know God and the power of His love, as revealed in Christ, by an experimental knowledge . . . Through the merits of Christ, through His righteousness, which by faith is imputed unto us, we are to attain to the perfection of Christian character."[452]

[54] Perfection also comes through justification. It is through sanctification that this position is retained. This will be our position not only until Jesus comes but throughout eternity. It will be our happy lot to express our appreciation to the entire universe for Christ's unspeakable gift in our behalf.

Salvation is dependent upon justification as a free gift from God. Our attitude toward that gift is expressed by our relationship to sanctification and our willingness to allow Jesus to remold our characters so that they will reflect His own. This is His work no matter what methods He uses to accomplish His goal. Our work is to submit to Him.

Is sanctification the evidence of justification? Jesus, in John 15:5 says, ". . . He that abideth in me and I in him, the same bringeth forth much fruit . . ." The fruit of the Spirit is to be seen in all who are truly justified. Galatians 5:22, 23. The believer has only to abide in this relationship (position) in Christ and He will produce the fruit. Christ is the Vine; the believer is the branch. Our *position* as members of the family of God is the cause of our rejoicing. We must refuse to indulge ourselves in *conditional* thinking. When we are grafted into the Vine, we become a part of Him. Justification will always be needed. Christ's character is the only covering that could completely meet all of the demands of God's perfect law, therefore, it must always be retained.

"The enemy of man and God is not willing that this truth [justification by faith] should be clearly presented; for he knows that if the people receive it fully, *his power will be broken*. If he can control minds so that doubt and

---

[451] Ellen White, *Christ Our Righteousness*, p. 35.
[452] Ellen White, *Christ Our Righteousness*, pp. 81, 82.

unbelief and darkness shall compose the experience of those who claim to be the children of God, he can overcome them with temptation."[453]

"Behold, I give unto you power to tread on serpents and scorpions, and over all the power of the enemy . . ." Luke 10:19. [55] Obviously, Christians in general have not experientially been aware that they can live free from Satan's power. This does not imply freedom from his temptations. The temptations will, along with sin, have lost their *power*. This is good news for all of us.

Sin has a powerful influence in the human family. It is attractive to the sinful nature. It offers pleasure for a season. Being forbidden, it is exciting. It builds the spirit of independence. It is an abuse of the power of choice or use of the will. All these are taken care of in the truly born-again Christian as he walks with his Lord in righteousness.

There is another much more subtle aspect of the power of sin which we must consider: ". . . the strength of sin is the law." 1 Corinthians 15:56. *Dunamis* (ability) in the Greek is here translated strength. It is more often rendered power. We get our word "dynamite" from the same root. The ability of dynamite is in its explosive power. If the "strength of sin" is the law, we should know how this is true. God did not reveal His law as a transcript of His character and also the "strength of sin." God's law of love did cause Him to create man with the ability to sin. He gave him the power of choice. Could this be where the power of sin rests?

"Temptation is resisted when man is powerfully influenced to do a wrong action and, knowing that he can do it, resists, by faith, with a firm hold upon divine power."[454]

It is interesting to know that the power Jesus gave His disciples recorded in Luke 10:19 was *exousia* (authority), not ability. But the power of the enemy in the same verse is *dunamis* (ability). We can say, then, that God gives men the authority over all Satan's ability, but He retains the ability and authority over Satan in His own control. Through Christ all the power of Satan is broken for he is a defeated foe.

Colossians 1:13 says, "Who hath delivered us from the power (authority) of darkness, and hath translated us into the kingdom of his dear Son." Deliverance from Satan's authority and being members of the kingdom of God are one and the same thing:

"When you give up your own will, your own wisdom, and learn of Christ, you will find admittance into the kingdom of God."[455]

Since God's law is a transcript of His character, and Satan is trying constantly to misrepresent His character, we should find here a clue as to the law being the "strength of sin."

---

[453] Ellen White, *Christ Our Righteousness*, p. 54.
[454] Ellen White, *The SDA Bible Commentary*, vol. 5, p. 1082, *The Youth's Instructor*, July 20, 1899.
[455] Ellen White, *Selected Messages*, book 1, p. 110.

Through a misunderstanding and misuse of God's law, Israel of old was held in Satan's control for centuries of time. It was God's plan that His law, as written and revealed at Sinai, would be as a schoolmaster to bring His people to Christ. Galatians 3:24. Satan had other plans. That very law of liberty he would use to enslave. How? By focusing all of his efforts on one function of the law—its ability to convict. Paul writes, "Therefore as by the offence of one judgement came upon all men to condemnation. . ." Romans 5:18. Here is Satan's focal point and his power over men. He seeks to blind our eyes to the rest of the same verse: ". . .even so by the righteousness of one the free gift came upon all men unto justification of life."

Satan has always magnified the condemnation and then presented strict obedience to the law as the only acceptable solution to the problem. Thus, man has gone down in defeat under miserable discouragement trying to keep that which he cannot keep in his own ability—*dunamis*, or authority, *exousia*. Condemnation and guilt are associated together and form the powerhouse of Satan's work in deceiving Christians.

Conviction and guilt were intended to point man to his own nothingness, and in his extremity he would turn to God who sent His Son to solve the whole sin problem. The loving parent, when dealing with a wayward child, often reveals both authority and ability even though he be misunderstood. Sin made necessary the revealing of a law that had existed from eternity but was misunderstood and wrongly applied. By condemnation, the major function of the law as schoolmaster was hidden from human eyes. [57]

Condemnation is a harsh, compelling force among heathen and Christian religions. Many of the reformers suffered under its power. Christianity, in general, has battled with this problem only to find human answers which fail to generate the love for God and produce a right attitude toward His law. David had his eyes opened and saw the law as the schoolmaster, or pathway, to Christ. His response was, "O how I love thy law! It is my meditation all the day." Psalm 119:97.

From the beginning of Satan's apostasy he has hated God's law, continually working to have it changed or modified. Any attempt to use justification, the imputing of Christ's character to man's account, as a means of changing or doing away with God's law is to agree with Satan and to cooperate with him in his rebellion against God.

Antinomianism, the doing away with God's law, is a human answer to man's sin problem that agrees with Satan's original accusation against God.

Modern man may think the law is incapable of meeting his needs. However, he still needs the Saviour to whom the law brings him. The truth is that man needs to be changed completely, not the law. This change is brought about in two related, but distinctly different, processes. First, a legal process was accomplished for man by Christ on Calvary's cross when He took our rightful place and paid the debt we could not pay, and yet live. Thus, man's record is changed the moment he accepts Christ as his Saviour and surrenders his life to Christ's control.

> "When men see their own nothingness, they are prepared to be clothed with the righteousness of Christ."[456]

Calvary stands as undeniable proof of the immutability of God's law. If it had been possible to change or do away with the law, Calvary would have been unnecessary. Thank God for His gift on Calvary where Jesus gained the right to rescue the captives from the grasp of the great deceiver.[457]

[58] "There is therefore now no condemnation to them which are in Christ Jesus, who walk not after the flesh, but after the Spirit." Romans 8:1. Justification takes care of condemnation for the surrendered Christian. The Saviour said, "For God sent not his Son into the world to condemn the world; but that the world through him might be saved." John 3:17. The law still convicts, but only Satan is in the business of condemnation. The born-again (justified) Christian learns that, even though Satan works through his feelings to condemn, Christ is not in the condemning business. "For if our heart condemn us, God is greater than our heart, and knoweth all things. Beloved, if our heart condemn us not, then have we confidence toward God." 1 John 3:20, 21.

Can we see that it is only as we understand God in His true relation to man—that of love and not condemnation—that we can have confidence in Him? This is also true of a parent-child relationship. Only in a true relationship is there true confidence. "For the law of the Spirit of life in Christ Jesus hath made me free from the law of sin and death." Romans 8:2. The law of the Spirit is to teach us about life in Christ Jesus which sets us free from the law of sin and death. This is what Paul was set free from in Romans 7.

That law of sin, which says ". . . the wages of sin is death . . ." Romans 6:23 has a terrible condemning force in our lives when pressed home by Satan. It is his plan to force us to repentance through these miserable feelings. Much of the repentance of Christians is a desire to be free from these strong feelings. If we are honest we can see that selfishness is the root of this repentance. God's Word declares, " . . . the goodness of God leadeth thee to repentance." Romans 2:4. It is not by condemnation but by looking at Jesus on Calvary's cross that we are brought to true repentance. Knowing that He condemns sin but loves the sinner sets us free. "If the Son therefore shall make you free, ye shall be free indeed." John 8:36. [59]

As we see that we are victims of a deadly disease called sin that has left many scars called habits in our flesh—which must be eradicated—we can understand how patiently, yet persistently, Christ must work to rid us of these habits. Only then can we see why sanctification—the second process—is God's way of changing these habits of ours and is the work of a lifetime. It isn't that a lifetime would make us sinless, but it must establish in us a pattern of total surrender and willingness which enables God to " . . . will and to do of his good pleasure" in us. Philippians 2:13.

---

[456] Ellen White, *Christ Our Righteousness*, p. 104.
[457] Ellen White, *The Desire of Ages*, p. 744.

Justification deals with our nature. As we die to self, surrender our will, and invite Him to take over our lives, a new nature is given to the newborn Christian. This nature is capable of being made subject to the law of God, whereas the old nature hated God's law. Romans 8:7. Sanctification takes over the task of rehabituating the character and removing the habits that were developed through the old nature. These habits and hereditary tendencies are the remainder of the old self-life. They are the strongest hold that Satan has in the life of the newborn Christian. Thank God even that hold can be broken through this marvelous plan of redemption."[458]

Ladders are for Climbing

[60] "Peter's second letter is addressed to a group of people who, like himself, had obtained ". . . like precious faith with us through the righteousness of God and our Saviour Jesus Christ." 2 Peter 1:1.

It would be difficult to express in more beautiful language the fact that these people were like Peter, justified—freed from their old sins—and were walking in newness of life. Then Peter, under inspiration, clearly sets before these born-again Christians God's plan for His righteousness to be imparted to them and to us.

Peter talks plainly and authoritatively on the subject of sanctification. He makes the sweeping claim that " . . . all things that pertain unto life and godliness. . . " are given unto us. He even states fully the process by which these gifts come to the believer—by believing the great and precious promises that point us to the fact that the born-again believer can be a partaker of the divine nature.

Further, he states that he escapes the corruption of the world through this same process. 2 Peter 1:3,4. The corruption of lust spoken of here is selfishness, which is initially destroyed in the death of the old nature, by faith. This results in Jesus being able to justify the believer as he reckons himself to be dead indeed unto sin. Romans 6:12.

The believer then, according to Paul, is not only justified by the blood of Christ (His death), but he is saved by the life of Jesus. Romans 5:10. What life is that? Praise His [61] holy name! It is His perfect life (character) that He worked out on earth for thirty-three and one-half years.

It is Jesus' character that is first credited to the believer in justification, resulting in a life record of the past that reads, "just as if I'd never sinned." This character is then made real in the believer's life as he learns to walk in this newness of life, trusting his Lord to supply the "all things" that pertain to this new life.

Of course, the goal in learning to walk in this new life is to completely rely upon the divine nature to crush out the habits of the old nature that are a carry-over from the old, but recently crucified, nature.

---

[458] Frank Phillips, *His Robe Or Mine*, Chapter 6 From Justification To What, 52-59.

> "As God works in the heart, and man surrenders his will to God, and cooperates with God, he works out in the life what God works in by the Holy Spirit, and there is harmony between the purpose of the heart and the practice of the life. Every sin must be renounced as the hateful thing that crucified the Lord of life and glory, and the believer must have a progressive experience by continually doing the works of Christ. It is by continual surrender of the will, by obedience, that the blessing of justification is retained."[459]

It is quite natural, at this point, to focus upon the thought of having to be obedient. This is where the Christian often fails. Our focus should be on surrender. If we are consistent in our surrender, then God will work in us " . . . to will and to do of his good pleasure." Philippians 2:13.

Character is what we are. Reputation is what people think we are. The first is revealed by our habit patterns, the second by thoughtful control.

> "The character is revealed, not by occasional good deeds and occasional misdeeds, but by the tendency of the habitual words and acts."[460]

[62] Habitual living is that which we do before we consciously think about what to do. Much of our living day by day is motivated by the subconscious mind. Our surrender to Christ's leading in our lives must become habitual. That is, it must become the natural thing to do.

> "We may keep so near to God that in every unexpected trial our thoughts will turn to Him as naturally as the flower turns to the sun."[461]

Paul urges us by saying, "Let this mind be in you, which was also in Christ Jesus." Philippians 2:5. Then follows a surrender so complete that it was ". . . unto death, even the death of the cross." Verse 8.

By the word "let," we understand that the controlling power is in our hands.

> "Christ is waiting with longing desire for the manifestation of Himself in His church. When the character of Christ shall be perfectly reproduced in His people, then He will come to claim them as His own."[462]

This goal can only be reached through the new birth experience in the context of righteousness by faith. The credited righteousness of justification and the given righteousness of sanctification are the " . . . all things that pertain unto life and godliness . . ." 2 Peter 1:3. These marvelous gifts of God become ours as we let Him do for us that which we cannot do for ourselves.

---

[459] Ellen White, *Selected Messages*, book 1, p.397.
[460] Ellen White, *Steps to Christ*, pp. 57, 58.
[461] Ellen White, *Steps to Christ*, pp. 99, 100. (Italics supplied.)
[462] Ellen White, *Christ's Object Lessons*, p. 69.

Daniel's prayer should be ours: "O Lord, righteousness belongeth unto thee, but unto us confusion of faces. . ." Daniel 9:7. It is hard for man to face the fact that in him dwells nothing good. It is

> "When men see their own nothingness, they are prepared to be clothed with the righteousness of Christ."[463]

When the term "two-faced" is used, we know what the speaker means. I believe that Daniel was simply saying, "Lord, no matter which face I try to wear, it all ends in confusion for it is not real."

Oh, that God would be allowed to make Himself real in us so that we could say with Paul, "For God, who commanded the light to shine out of darkness, hath shined in [63] our hearts, to give the light of the knowledge of the glory of God in the *face of Jesus Christ*. But we have this treasure in earthen vessels, that the excellency of the power may be of God, and not of us." 2 Corinthians 4:6,7. (Italics supplied.)

Peter's ladder of sanctification is given to us in 2 Peter 1:5-7. "Add to your faith virtue; and to virtue knowledge; and to knowledge temperance; and to temperance patience; and to patience godliness; and to godliness brotherly kindness; and to brotherly kindness charity (love)." Here Peter sets before us the steps by which Bible sanctification can be attained.

> "Faith, virtue, knowledge, temperance, patience, godliness, brotherly kindness, and charity are the rounds of the ladder. We are saved by climbing round after round, mounting step after step, to the height of Christ's ideal for us. Thus He is made unto us wisdom, and righteousness, and sanctification, and redemption."[464]

Before we start ascending this ladder we must learn more of the characteristics that comprise its unique structure. Each round in this ladder is a step in character development. However, we do not perfect each stage before we move up the ladder.

We might say that this ladder is like a rope ladder hung from above. This is what makes it a ladder of faith, its support is from above. The climber beginning on the bottom rung picks up the steps one at a time as he goes, adding to his character and

> " . . . as he thus works on the plan of addition, God works for him on the plan of multiplication."[465]

---

[463] Ellen White, *Christ Our Righteousness*, p. 104, *The Review and Herald*, September 16, 1902.
[464] Ellen White, *The Acts of the Apostles*, p. 530.
[465] Ellen White, *The Acts of the Apostles*, p. 532.

Each step must be taken in *order* for they are tied together and are interdependent. The second depends upon the first for its foundation upon which to build. Each character step continues to be multiplied by the Lord as long as we continue to grow spiritually.

[64] There is one thing further we need to know about this ladder:

> "Before the believer is held out the wonderful possibility of being like Christ, obedient to all the principles of the law. But of himself man is utterly unable to reach this condition. The holiness that God's word declares he must have before he can be saved, is the result of the working of divine grace, as he bows in submission to the discipline and restraining influences of the Spirit of truth . . . . The part of the Christian is to persevere in overcoming every fault. Constantly he is to pray to the Saviour to heal the disorders of his sin-sick soul. *He has not the wisdom or the strength to overcome; these belong to the Lord,* and He bestows them on those who in humiliation and contrition seek Him for help."[466]

Did you notice that our work is to submit to life's experiences, without complaint, accepting everything as coming from Christ even though it may have originated with Satan? Because Christ's robe of righteousness surrounds us, we must recognize that nothing can touch us except by His permission. Romans 8:28.

Christ permits to touch us only that which will help our character to become like His. (See Thoughts from the Mount of Blessing p. 71). By accepting this truth we learn to trust Him in every experience of life. Thus, we live by faith and not by sight. It was thus that Jesus lived here as our example.

Here is another picture:

> "This work of transformation from unholiness to holiness is a continuous one. Day by day God labors for man's sanctification, and man is to cooperate with Him, putting forth persevering efforts in the cultivation of right habits."[467]

Once again God's work and man's work are defined. God's work is the daily work of sanctification. Our work is to cooperate by "cultivating right habits."

[65] If we are to cultivate right habits, the natural question is, how? We might try by exercising the will, by determined effort, by repetition of the desired habit, or we might try prayer.

---

[466] Ellen White, *The Acts of the Apostles*, p. 532. (Italics supplied.)
[467] Ellen White, *The Acts of the Apostles*, p. 532.

May I suggest that the word cultivate was, no doubt, chosen because of its depth of meaning. If we would change the wording from habits to carrots we would have less trouble understanding the how. Now if we are cultivating carrots we all know how to do that. We simply remove weeds and break up the hard soil so the carrots can grow. But what do we do with the carrots? We leave them in the Lord's care. Only He can cause them to grow. We can only remove hindrances to that growth.

> "He longs to reveal His grace. If His people will remove the obstructions, He will pour forth the waters of salvation in abundant streams through the human channels."[468]

> "There is nothing that Satan fears so much as that the people of God shall clear the way by removing every hindrance, so that the Lord can pour out His Spirit upon a languishing church and an impenitent congregation."[469]

We already have learned that we can't change ourselves. "Can the Ethiopian change his skin, or the leopard his spots? Then may ye also do good, that are accustomed to do evil." Jeremiah 13:23. Our work in removing hindrances and obstacles in our character formation is to recognize them when we see them. Then we are to be persevering in our prayers to God to heal our sin-sick souls. He will remove these hindrances when we are ready to stop protecting these hindering factors. We need to recognize a weed from the true plant.

The fruits of the Spirit are tender plants that need careful cultivation until they are well rooted. Then they become dominant to the point where we can say with Paul, " . . . none of these things move me . . ." Acts 20:24.

[66] All this preparatory work, as well as the climbing of Peter's ladder, is a work of faith. "There are those who attempt to ascend the ladder of Christian progress; but as they advance, they begin to put their trust in the power of man, and soon lose sight of Jesus, the author and finisher of their faith. The result is failure." (See The Acts of the Apostles, p. 532.) [Please read the entire chapter 52 in, *The Acts of the Apostles*].

Let us clearly understand that sanctification, like justification, is a work of faith at every step.

> "The followers of Christ are to become like him— by the grace of God to form characters in harmony with the principles of His holy law. This is Bible sanctification. This work can be accomplished only through faith in Christ, by the power of the indwelling Spirit of God."[470]

---

[468] Ellen White, *The Desire of Ages*, p. 251. (Italics supplied.)
[469] Ellen White, *Selected Messages*, book 1, p. 124.
[470] Ellen White, *The Great Controversy*, p. 469.

> "In ourselves we are incapable of doing any good thing; but that which we cannot do will be wrought by the power of God in every submissive and believing soul. It is through faith that spiritual life is begotten, and we are enabled to do the works of righteousness."[471]

> "None but Christ can fashion anew the character that has been ruined by sin. He came to expel the demons that had controlled the will."[472]

> "It is through the impartation of the grace of Christ that sin is discerned in its hateful nature, and finally driven from the soul temple."[473]

These statements make it very clear that only as Christ's character is imparted to us in sanctification are we able to see sin for what it really is—a malignant disease. Only then can we learn to hate it. This fact will become clear as we begin to ascend the ladder. You will notice sin is in the singular, which points to the disease and not sins, which are the symptoms of the disease.

[67] We can very easily work up quite a strong feeling of hatred for the sins that reveal that there is a sinful nature from which they spring. Yet our efforts are most often directed toward the symptoms and not the disease. And this is what Satan would have us do. For until the disease is taken care of, he knows that the symptoms will be there to keep us battling and defeated.

It is a fact that we overlook the reality that every human being in his human (fleshly) nature is infected with the same deadly disease of sin. From God's viewpoint the disease in any stage is still deadly. Some symptoms, however, are quite acceptable in the best of society, while others would be rejected as making one incorrigible.

God must be allowed to reveal to us this deadly nature and bring us to the point where we look at sin as He does. Then we will long to be free from its vicious tentacles. Why is this so hard for human beings to see? Because we are sin hardened, calloused to the point where we hardly recognize sin when we come in contact with it. The tragedy of this is the fact that as we live in this condition we forget that:

> "He [Christ] was free from the taint of sin, the refined sensibilities of His holy nature rendered contact with evil unspeakably painful to Him."[474]

What a work must be accomplished in us that we might reflect His image perfectly. Before we begin climbing this ladder of sanctification, let us take an overview of the chart (Appendix C, pages 154, 155). [See Phillips book, *His Cross Or Mine*] Here we attempt to show how Satan has

---

[471] Ellen White, *The Desire of Ages*, p. 98.
[472] Ellen White, *The Desire of Ages*, p. 38.
[473] Ellen White, *Selected Messages*, book 1, p. 366.
[474] Ellen White, *The SDA Bible Commentary*, vol. 7A, p. 451, *The Review and Herald*, Nov. 8, 1887.

a counterfeit plan for sanctification as he does for every Bible truth. God's plan begins with faith and ends with love (divine love).

Satan's plan begins with self, very much alive, and ends with emotionalism. Satan's plan develops hindrances, obstacles, that prevent the Christian from developing the character of Christ. These characteristics become stronger and stronger, thus preventing the end result of divine love from being attained. In its place is a very entrancing, bewitching, and deceptive [68] substitute which we call emotionalism. It is in this area of emotional living where Satan holds spellbound millions of deceived Christian people.

I do not mean to convey the thought that there is no emotion in the way of the Lord. There truly is. But it is the love of Christ that constraineth us. 2 Corinthians 5:14. That is, the love of Christ holds us together. This is the effect of divine love.

Emotionalism tends toward strong feelings, especially toward those who understand each other. The love of Christ, on the other hand, reaches out and engulfs even those who oppose and even fight against us. It accepts any kind of treatment and still reacts only with love. Obviously, this is not natural to the human being. It must be a gift from God. That is what sanctification accomplishes.

We must remember also that the Christian, while allowing God to develop His character in man, grows *in grace* (God's character), *not into grace* (God's character).[475] The growth process is hard to recognize as it operates, but the result is evident both to the believer and to those with whom he comes in contact.

Keep in mind as we ascend the ladder that each step is one of faith as is shown in the statements between the two ladders on our chart.

Yes, ladders are for climbing, and we are about ready to begin. So let us pray that God will reveal any hindrances or obstacles that would prevent His working in us to produce the fruit of righteousness. It might be a good idea to take a quick look at the character fruit we can expect to be revealed as He does this marvelous work in us. ". . . The fruit of the Spirit is love, joy, peace, longsuffering, gentleness, goodness, faith, meekness, temperance . . . ." Galatians 5:22, 23."[476]

[To climb the rungs of the ladder with Brother Phillips see his book, *His Cross Or Mine*, Chapters 8-15, pgs; 70-101. We conclude with one more chapter from Brother Phillips.]

Follow Me

---

[475] Ellen White, *Christ's Object Lessons*, p. 271.
[476] Frank Phillips, *His Robe Or Mine*, Chapter 7 – Ladders Are For Climbing, 60-68.

[110] "Then said Jesus unto his disciples, If any man will come after me, let him deny himself, and take up his cross, and follow me." Matthew 16:24.

> "Jesus now explained to His disciples that His own life of self-abnegation was an example of what theirs should be. Calling about Him, with the disciples, the people who had been lingering near, He said, 'If any man will come after Me, let him deny himself, and take up his cross daily, and follow Me.' The cross was associated with the power of Rome. It was the instrument of the most cruel and humiliating form of death. The lowest criminals were required to bear the cross to the place of execution; and often as it was about to be laid upon their shoulders, they resisted with desperate violence, until they were overpowered, and the instrument of torture was bound upon them. But Jesus bade His followers take up the cross and bear it after Him. To the disciples His words, though dimly comprehended, pointed to their submission to the most bitter humiliation,— submission even unto death for the sake of Christ. No more complete self-surrender could the Saviour's words have pictured."[477]

You will notice that Luke adds another dimension with the word "daily." Webster defines abnegation as "surrender" or "relinquish." When we realize this surrender [111] is even unto death, it takes on a very significant meaning, especially when coupled with the word "daily." It sounds strangely familiar, for it was Paul who said, "I die daily." 1 Corinthians 15:31, and again, "Always bearing about in the body the dying of the Lord Jesus, that the life also of Jesus might be made manifest in our body. For we which live are always delivered unto death for Jesus' sake, that the life also of Jesus might be made manifest in our mortal flesh. So then death worketh in us, but life in you." 2 Corinthians 4:10-12.

Obviously, there is only one way to reflect the image of Jesus and that is not by trying but by dying. Since this is made so clear in the Scriptures, Satan has fought this principle with all his power. He has focused our attention on Christ's words and emphasized the word "deny." However, he has made us think that denying self is the same as self-denial. By the simple act of reversing the order of the two words, the meaning is completely changed in the human mind.

To practice self-denial can be a real beneficial experience in the character building process. This must never be equated with denying self, which is the process of crucifying self and keeping self-crucified. When Christ is enthroned in the heart, self is dethroned; and when self is enthroned, Christ is dethroned. Every decision we make must be made by using the same formula that Christ used, "Not my will but Thine." The Saviour followed this practice so completely that He said, " . . . The words that I speak unto you I speak not of myself: but the Father that dwelleth in me, he doeth the works." John 14:10.

---

[477] Ellen White, *The Desire of Ages* p. 416-17.

It is this secret that Paul learned and passed on to Timothy as the foundation of our life with Christ here and now. He said, "It is a faithful saying: For if we be dead with Him, we shall also live with Him." 2 Timothy 2:11.

Jesus not only said that we must deny self, but also take up our cross. It is an amazing fact that Christ uses the cross as the agent to bind the believer to Himself. [112]

> "The yoke and the cross are symbols representing the same thing,—*the giving up of the will to God.* Wearing the yoke unites finite man in a companionship with the dearly beloved Son of God. Lifting the cross cuts away self from the soul, and places man where he learns how to bear Christ's burdens. *We cannot follow Christ* without wearing His yoke, without lifting the cross and bearing it after Him."[478]

> *"We cannot retain self and yet enter the kingdom of God.* If we ever attain unto holiness, it will be through the renunciation of self and the reception of the mind of Christ."[479]

> "The reason many in this age of the world make no greater advancement in the divine life is because they interpret the will of God to be just what they will to do. While following their own desires, they flatter themselves that they are conforming to God's will. These have no conflicts with self. There are others who for a time are successful in the struggle against their selfish desire for pleasure and ease. They are sincere and earnest, but grow weary of protracted effort, of daily death, of ceaseless turmoil. Indolence seems inviting, death to self-repulsive; and they close their drowsy eyes, and fall under the power of temptation instead of resisting it."[480]

Christ's emphatic statement, "follow Me," is utterly impossible unless we experience that which goes before in the same verse. He was not urging His disciples and followers to *do* what He did but to *live* as He lived.

The Father did, through Christ, that which He sent Him into the world to do. This was made possible by Christ choosing, every moment of His life, to be as the clay in His Father's hands. In His sphere this surrender brought [113] the only hope of peace to a universe that had been thrown into confusion by the rebellion of Lucifer who became Satan. In our sphere this surrender brings the only hope of our personal salvation. It is our privilege to live a life here which He can use as a magnetic force to persuade men and women of *God's plan of salvation*. This plan is,

---

[478] Ellen White, *The SDA Bible Commentary*, vol. 5, pp. 1090-91, *The Review and Herald*, October 23, 1900. (Italics supplied.)
[479] Ellen White, *Thoughts from the Mount of Blessing*, p. 143. (Italics supplied.)
[480] Ellen White, *The Acts of the Apostles*, p. 565.

indeed, the only process conceivable that can prepare human beings to live eternally in the perfect environment of the home of the saved.

> "Implicit belief in Christ's word is true humility, true self-surrender."[481]

> "Self-surrender is the substance of the teachings of Christ."[482]

It is only as we see the importance of trusting Christ perfectly, even though all things seem impossible, that we can grasp the urgency of Christ's words to Nicodemus, "Ye must be born again."

We had no choice in our first birth, but the new birth depends entirely upon our exercising the free will that can only be kept free by our choosing to die to self and letting Christ reign within. Matthew closes his gospel by quoting the words of Jesus, ". . . All power [authority, *exousia*] is given unto me in heaven and in earth." Matthew 28:18. This was the Father's response to His Son for a life of total surrender while here on earth as He lived in the human flesh that He had assumed.

Christ was offered short cut routes. In the wilderness, at the very beginning of His public ministry, Satan tried to bargain with Him. After showing Him all the kingdoms of this world and the glory of them, Satan said, " . . . All these things will I give Thee, if Thou wilt fall down and worship me." Matthew 4:9. What a short cut! But by choosing to believe and trust God, even though it was by the way of the cross, and a willingness to die, He received from His Father *all power in heaven and in earth*. We must keep in mind that Christ made this choice in human flesh with *no power that is not available to each of us.* [114]

> "Jesus revealed no qualities, and exercised no powers, that men may not have through faith in Him. His perfect humanity is that which all His followers may possess, if they will be in subjection to God as He was."[483]

Probably the most subtle short cut Satan offered to Jesus was at the beginning of the wilderness experience.

> "He [Satan] tried to make Christ believe that God did not require Him to pass through self-denial and the sufferings He anticipated; that he had been sent from heaven to bear to Him the message that God only designed to prove His willingness to endure. Satan told Christ that He was only to set His feet in the bloodstained path, but not to travel it. He also stated that he was the angel that stayed the hand of Abraham as the knife was raised to slay Isaac, and he had now come to save His life; that it was not necessary for Him to endure the

---

[481] Ellen White, *The Desire of Ages*, p. 535.
[482] Ellen White, *The Desire of Ages*, p. 523.
[483] Ellen White, *The Desire of Ages*, p. 664. (Italics supplied.)

painful hunger and death from starvation; he would help Him bear a part of the work in the plan of salvation."[484]

Satan has come to every child of Adam, since the beginning, with the same message, "Christ died for you so that you do not have to die." It sounds so good because it is a partial truth. Christ *did die* to deliver us from the *wages of sin,* which is *eternal death*. However, He also lived a life of total self-abnegation (relinquishment) as an example of what ours must be. Satan will try to bring every kind of short cut to the struggling Christian, but the only route to the kingdom of God is in following Jesus."[485]

[It has been a wonderful privilege to have Pastor Frank Phillips on board along with his wonderful staff that has freely and graciously supported this endeavor for no other motive than to get the truth to those who are struggling with their walk with the Lord. I am confident I can speak for the reader as well, Thank-you ever so kindly!

With the mechanics of the real gospel fresh in the readers mind as presented by Brother Phillips we directly turn to the writings of Ellen White, for in just three small paragraphs we are able to compare how the two authors perfectly mirror one another with one and the same gospel. Emphasis in italics:

> "The law reveals to man his sins, but it provides no remedy.
> While it promises life to the obedient, it declares that death is the portion of the transgressor. The gospel of Christ alone can free him from the condemnation or the defilement of sin. He must exercise *repentance toward God,* whose law has been transgressed; and *faith in Christ,* his atoning sacrifice. *Thus he obtains "remission of sins that are past"* and *becomes a partaker of the divine nature.* [The new birth] He is a child of God, having received the spirit of adoption, whereby he cries: "Abba, Father!"
> *Is he now free to transgress God's law? Says Paul: "Do we then make void the law through faith? God forbid: yea, we establish the law."* [The converted man of Rom. 7] "How shall we, that are dead to sin, live any longer therein?" And John declares: "This is the love of God, that we keep His commandments: and His commandments are not grievous." Romans 3:31; 6:2; 1 John 5:3. *In the new birth the heart is brought into harmony with God,* as it is brought into accord with *His law. When this mighty change has taken place in the sinner, he has passed from death unto life,* from sin unto holiness, from transgression and rebellion to obedience and loyalty. *The old life of alienation from God has ended; the new life of reconciliation, of faith and love, has begun.* Then "the righteousness of the law" will "be fulfilled in us, *who walk not after the flesh, but after the Spirit."* Romans 8:4. And the language of the soul will be: "O how love I Thy law! it is my meditation all the day." Psalm 119:97.

---

[484] Ellen White, *Selected Messages*, book 1, p. 273.
[485] Frank Phillips, *His Robe Or Mine*, Chapter 17, Follow Me, 110-114.

"The law of the Lord is perfect, converting the soul." Psalm 19:7. Without the law, men have no just conception of the purity and holiness of God or of their own guilt and uncleanness. They have no true conviction of sin and feel no need of repentance. Not seeing their lost condition as violators of God's law, they do not realize their need of the atoning blood of Christ. The hope of salvation is accepted *without a radical change of heart* or reformation of life. Thus *superficial conversions abound*, and multitudes are joined to the church who have *never* been united to Christ."[486]

Perfect harmony indeed! This concludes my use of Pastor Frank Phillips and Pastor Stephen Wallace's excellent material on the everlasting gospel. There is much more material including CD's, books and tracts that I highly recommend the reader to obtain from the contact info provided in my Introduction that further explains and reinstates other aspects of the simplicity of the gospel not submitted here due to space limitations.

---

[486] Ellen White, *The Great Controversy*, 467-8.

6

The Final Generation/144,000

Certain concepts of the final generation were technically introduced into Adventism by A. T. Jones and E. J. Waggoner. It found new and advanced meaning with M. L. Andreasen[487] and after *Questions on Doctrine* came out in 1957 the leadership of the independents has propelled their views to new heights with what is called today as **Last Generation Theology (LGT)**. One of the main proponents of the independents of LGT is Robert J. Wieland and Donald. K. Short of the *1888 Message Study Committee*. Bill Ikswezdyr has publically and correctly commentated in a blog in Spectrum Magazine of April 2014 some of the wayward teachings of LGT that we will address and further expose here. Wieland wants us to believe that, *The Glad Tidings* of Waggoner's commentary on Paul's Epistle to the Galatians is Waggoner's 1888 lectures that Wieland had reprinted in 1972 by the Pacific Press Publishing Association. In truth, Waggoner's commentary on Paul's Epistle to the Galatians was published in the *Signs of the Times* in 1898-1899 and then in the Review and it finally appeared in book form in 1900. A thoroughly researched and documented biography of E J Waggoner will show the pantheism in *Glad Tidings* and many of Waggoner's other articles. The 1972 edition of *Glad Tidings* was edited by Robert Weiland to exclude most of the obvious pantheism sentiments. It you read Robert Weiland's book, *In Search of the Cross*, you will see that he takes a very similar mystical view of the cross as Waggoner does in his post-1888 theology. Also in common with Waggoner, Robert Weiland teaches that our Lord had a sinful human nature and that the final generation can be and will be as sinless as the Lord was. This perfectionism view is called "Last Generation Theology".

Also Wieland's teaching confused the pleading and calling of the Holy Spirit (prevenient grace) to all men, with the infilling and baptism of the Holy Spirit of the believer. Only the believer is "in Christ" personally and unto personal justification. The unbelieving world is offered eternal life "in Christ" *if* they believe in the atoning sacrifice the Lord made for "all" and for the "many" Rom. 5:15. The whole world was not personally saved at the death of our Lord on the cross. Rather, because the Lord substitutionally died for the sins of the whole world, the individual person is only accepted by God when he as a repentant sinner personally puts his trust in the death of Christ for his sins and calls upon His name in faith. I think that Jack Sequeira has a similar view as Wieland that since Christ supposedly mystically took our "sinful flesh" then all humanity was mystically all crucified at the cross because all humanity was contained the *flesh* of Christ. The Pauline legal categories are ignored in this mystical view of how sin was supposedly contained in Christ's flesh and thus sin was expiated for the whole world. The Pauline view is that the sins of the world were legally imputed to Christ on the cross. The Sequeira / Wieland view is that sin was actually in Christ's flesh and thus when He died the entire world and all the sin of the world died with Christ. The Pauline phrase, "In Christ"

---

[487] M. L. Andreasen (*The Sanctuary Service*, Washington, D.C.: Review and Herald Pub. Assn., 1937; revised 1947).

means *legally* substitutionally placed upon Christ. It does not mean physically "inside of Christ's body".

Paul is very explicit here:

> "Therefore as through one man's offense judgement came to all men resulting in condemnation, even so through one Man's righteous act the free gift came to all men, resulting in justification of life. For as by one man's disobedience many were made sinners, so also by one Man's obedience **many will be** made righteous." Romans 5:18-19.

Paul is saying that "justification unto life has come to all men" but notice that Paul places their *personal* justification in the future tense when he states in verse 19, "many will be made righteous." In the Gospel we proclaim the good news that "all" have been saved and justified at the cross "in Christ", but also proclaim that to be *personally* justified, all sinners must personally be "in Christ" to receive the benefits of the vicarious death and imputed righteousness of our Lord by personally believing the Gospel, repenting of our sins, and being baptized for the remission of our sins. Thus when the evangelist proclaims the Gospel, he proclaims that "all" have been saved "in Christ" by Christ's death on the Cross, and then urge "all" to believe the good news. Those who do not believe are not saved because they call God a liar; they do not believe and hence blaspheme against the Holy Spirit.

Here is how Elders Robert J. Wieland and Donald K. Short of the *1888 Message Study Committee* (LGT) have been revolutionary in the sense that they have miraculously evolved into another gospel:

> " . . . the message of 1888 was neither a restatement of the doctrines of Luther and Wesley, nor a mere re-emphasis of the teaching of the Adventist pioneers; but that it was rather a more mature conception of the 'everlasting gospel' than had ever been perceived by any previous generation of human beings, a preaching of 'righteousness by faith' more mature and developed, and more practical than had been preached even by the Apostle Paul."[488]

That is an astounding statement. Few of us would be as bold as Wieland and Short in saying that the 1888 message was in advance of Paul, but often the idea has prevailed that the Advent message must contain something more than was preached by the great apostle. Of course, if the last-day message is to be beyond what Paul offered, we would not really expect that that message could be proved by the greatest New Testament writer and if not by the greatest New Testament writer, then certainly not by the lesser ones.

Again:

---

[488] Robert J. Wieland and Donald K. Short, *A Warning and Its Reception* (Adventist Laymen's Foundation of Iowa, Inc. 1970). 50.

> "Abraham was not accounted righteous when he was not righteous. His faith was accounted to him for righteousness. . . . Abraham's faith, being genuine, was righteousness. . . ."[489]

> ". . . justification by faith is a 'declaring' what is now a **fact**—the contrite soul is delivered from the power of known sin."[490]

This is contrary to Paul's doctrine of God justifying the ungodly and the uncircumcised:

> "But to him that worketh not, but believeth on him that justifieth the ungodly, his faith is counted for righteousness." Rom. 4:5.

> "How was it then reckoned? when he was in circumcision, or in uncircumcision? Not in circumcision, but in uncircumcision." Rom. 4:10.
> "And he received the sign of circumcision, a seal of the righteousness of the faith which *he had yet* being uncircumcised: that he might be the father of all them that believe, though they be not circumcised; that righteousness might be imputed unto them also:" Rom. 4:11.

God does not declare the believer righteous because the repentant sinner himself is righteous. No! No! God declares him righteous because He finds that the believer's Substitute is righteous. And as anybody who has read Luther knows, he was forever refuting the idea that the righteousness which is of faith is some quality within a man. There is a world of difference between saying that "righteousness is of faith" and "righteousness is faith." Faith is not righteousness:

> "The faith that is required is not a mere assent to doctrines; it is the faith that works by love and purifies the soul. Humility, meekness, and obedience are not faith; but they are the effects, or fruit, of faith. These graces you have yet to attain by learning in the school of Christ."[491]

There is no merit in faith, but there is merit in the righteousness of Christ.

Wieland and Short's statement reads just like it comes right out of the Council of Trent, or remarkably parallel to the thought of Cardinal John Henry Newman in his celebrated *Lectures on the Doctrine of Justification.*[492]

Having highlighted just a few aspects of the independents gospel for the benefit of the reader according to the teachings of the *1888 Message Study Committee*, Robert Wieland believes that

---

[489] Ibid. 222.
[490] Ibid. 227.
[491] Ellen White, *Testimonies*, 5:437-8.
[492] Cardinal John Henry Newman, *Lectures on the Doctrine of Justification*, (*Present Truth Magazine*, Vol. 47); www.PresentTruthMag.com

the final generation of Adventists would reach a condition of sinlessness perfection prior to the Second Advent because Adventists supposedly had a more mature understanding of the gospel than the apostles did.

Let us never forget as Seventh-day Adventist what our first and only reference point is for all doctrine and reform:

> "God will have a people upon the earth to maintain the Bible, and the Bible only, as the standard of all doctrines and the basis of all reforms. The opinions of learned men, the deductions of science, the creeds or decisions of ecclesiastical councils, as numerous and discordant as are the churches which they represent, the voice of the majority--not one nor all of these should be regarded as evidence for or against any point of religious faith. Before accepting any doctrine or precept, we should demand a plain "Thus saith the Lord" in its support.
>
> Satan is constantly endeavoring to attract attention to man in the place of God. He leads the people to look to bishops, to pastors, to professors of theology, as their guides, instead of searching the Scriptures to learn their duty for themselves. Then, by controlling the minds of these leaders, he can influence the multitudes according to his will."[493]

And to cement this admonition Inspiration leaves us with the following counsel:

> "When persons will speak lightly of the word of God, and set their *impressions, feelings, and exercises above the divine standard, we may know that they have no light in them.*"[494]

We have been warned. These admonitions will prove fundamental to this reading. This then brings us in our study to one of the central issues regarding the independents teachings of The Final Generation, or what is commonly termed, *Last Generation Theology* (LGT). Only three pivotal issues need be addressed as follows but these will more than suffice to lay to rest the folly of human reasoning elevated above divine revelation:

(1) LGT teaches it is the responsibility of the final generation, the 144,000 that will answer Satan's charge and vindicate Gods character by refuting Satan's charge: "that God had made a law which man could not keep":

---

[493] Ellen White, *The Great Controversy*, 595.
[494] Ellen White, *Thoughts from the Mount of Blessing*, 146. [Emphasis mine]

When Satan was able to bring the leading men of the independents to reject the counsel in SDABC 5:1128-9 that we *highlighted* in chapter 2, he was now able to bring them to another calculated point with ease:

> "Jesus victory was remarkable, not because as God He acted like God, but because as man He did not act like every other man. Jesus in man's nature lived a life that Satan said *could not be lived*. The amazing aspect about Jesus life was that he lived a sinless life on *any level other than our fallen level*, [sinful nature] *the question "What does that prove?" would never have been answered.*"[495]

Few of us are as intrepid as Priebe and the independents in bringing Christ down to the same brute level such as ourselves declaring Jesus to be just like us in every way with a "sinful nature" compounding that supposition with a public declaration that Jesus also had a bent to evil in face of such explicit counsel:

> "Never, in any way, leave the slightest impression upon human minds that a taint of, or inclination to, corruption rested upon Christ, or that He in any way yielded to corruption. . . Let every human being be warned from the ground of making Christ altogether human, such an one as ourselves; for it cannot be."[496]

Maybe this is where we got the phrase, "The pot calling the kettle black." Unbelievable! Priebe says, "Jesus in man's nature [Post fall] lived a life that *Satan said could not be lived.*" Therefore, we turn to the writings of Ellen White to see if Satan or herself made just such a claim. Here is what she had to say:

> "After the fall of man, Satan declared that human beings were proved...." ["Were proved". Past tense.] "To be incapable of keeping the law of God, and he sought to carry the universe with him in this belief. Satan's words appeared to be true and Christ came to unmask the deceiver."[497]

Three significant points are made clear here thus far. 1. Christ, not the final generation comes along to unmask the deceiver. 2. The era is not that of the final generation but of the cross. 3. "Were proved" designated time and place in the placement of human history and will be illustrated again momentarily below:

Are Priebe, Weiland, Standish brothers and the independents once again diametrically opposed to Ellen White?

---

[495] Dennis Priebe, *Face-to-Face With the Real Gospel* (Boise Idaho, Pacific Press Publishing Association, 1985), 61. [Emphasis mine]
[496] Ellen White, *Letter* 8, 1895; *SDABC*, 5:1128-9. [Emphasis mine]
[497] Ellen White, *Selected Messages*, 1:252. [Emphasis mine]

"Christ is called the *Second Adam*. In purity and holiness, connected with God and beloved by God, *he began where the first Adam began.* Willingly he passed over the ground where Adam fell and redeemed Adam's failure."[498]

Christ came to disprove the lie that man, *as God created him*, could perfectly obey. In order to do that, in order to pass over the same ground where Adam stumbled and fell, where would he logically have to begin? Where Adam began, before he fell! In order to unmask the deceiver, how did He have to come? As a man, yes, but as a man separated from God, or as a man in perfect union with God? Ellen White answers this vital question for us:

"*Christ* came to the earth, taking *humanity* and standing as man's representative, *to show in the great controversy with Satan that man, as God created him*, connected with the Father and the Son, *could obey every divine requirement*."[499]

Again:

"Satan had claimed that it was impossible for man to obey God's commandments; *and in our own strength it is true that we cannot obey them.* But *Christ came in the form of humanity*, and by *His perfect obedience He proved* that humanity and divinity *combined* [with a fully surrendered will] can obey every one of God's precepts."[500]

"Christ came to give moral power to man; to elevate, ennoble, and strengthen him. He came to prove the falsity of Satan's charge that God had made a law which man could not keep. *While possessing man's nature, Christ kept the Ten Commandments. Thus He proved to the inhabitants of the unfallen worlds and to human beings that it is possible for man perfectly to obey the law. He vindicated God's justice in demanding obedience to His law.* Those who accept Christ as their Saviour, becoming partakers of the *divine nature*,

---

[498] Ellen White, *Youth's Instructor*, June 2, 1898. [Emphasis mine]
[499] Ellen White, *SDABC*, 7:926. [Emphasis mine]
[500] Ellen White, *Christ Object Lessons*, 314. [Emphasis mine]

[sinless nature] are *enabled* to follow His example of obedience to every divine precept."[501]

Ellen White has shown us just the *opposite of what Priebe and the independents teach*. She declares Jesus had lived a life in man's nature (sinless nature) "as God created him." This would be in Adams (pre fall) "sinless nature" that *Satan said* could not be lived. That is diametrically opposed to what Priebe teaches. The burden of proof was upon the second Adam, Christ, not man, not the 144,000! Priebe places the burden of proof on (post fall) humanity and this changes the dynamics of the gospel dramatically as the ramifications here are huge! Here is where the independents have out-foxed themselves. Inspiration has just defined the gospel of grace in a nutshell. Our righteousness is in Christ and it is indeed a free gift!

> "Our hope is to be constantly strengthened by the knowledge that *Christ is our righteousness*."[502]

Priebe and the independents gospel have now been fully unmasked as the most subtle form of legalism the world has ever witnessed! Its righteousness is measured in ones performance by trying to do what the Father did in Christ instead of living the life of Christ! All this talk by Priebe about "relying upon God for power" and "daily surrender" is all just a ploy to keep the reader off balance. The sole driving force behind Priebe's gospel and unscriptural teaching of overcoming in a "sinful nature" is *all measured* in doing not dying!

Christ came to prove what? To show in the great controversy, not that *man or the final generation as he was separated from God and alienated from God by "nature" could perfectly obey every requirement*, but that what? Man as God *"created him"*, connected with the Father and the Son, could obey every divine requirement! Now that we have completely dismantled that private supposition by Priebe, LGT and the independents that it was "Christ," the second Adam in a "sinless nature," not "man" or the "final generation," the 144,000 in a "sinful nature" that had met and refuted the charge of Satan according to Inspiration. Ellen White goes further on record to say:

> "By His life and His death, Christ *proved* that God's justice did not destroy His mercy, but that sin could be forgiven, and that the *law is righteous, and can be perfectly obeyed. Satan's charges were refuted [past tense]*. God had given man unmistakable evidence of His love."[503]

---

[501] Ellen White, *Signs of the Times*, May 14, 1902. [Emphasis mine]
[502] Ellen White, *Testimonies*, 5:742. [Emphasis mine]
[503] Ellen G. White, *The Desire of Ages* 762. [Emphasis mine]

Even in the executive judgement before the lost multitude the cross *alone* stands to vindicate the Father and His dear Son:

> "Satan sees that his voluntary rebellion has unfitted him for Heaven. He has trained his powers to war against God; the purity, peace, and harmony of Heaven would be to him supreme torture. His accusations against the mercy and justice of God are now silenced. The reproach which he has endeavored to cast upon Jehovah rests wholly upon himself. And now Satan bows down, and confesses the justice of his sentence.
>
> Every question of truth and error in the long-standing controversy is made plain. *God's justice stands fully vindicated. Before the whole world is clearly presented the great sacrifice made by the Father and the Son in man's behalf.*"[504]

Again:

> "So deep was the Lord's interest in the beings He had created, so great His love for the world, that He "gave his only begotten Son, that whosoever believeth in him should not perish, but have everlasting life" (John 3:16). Christ came to bring moral power to man, to elevate, ennoble, and strengthen him, enabling him to be a partaker of the *divine nature*, having escaped the corruption that is in the world through lust. He [Christ] *proved* [not the final generation] to the inhabitants of the unfallen worlds and to human beings that the law can be kept. While possessing the nature of man, He obeyed the law of God, *vindicating God's justice in demanding that it be obeyed. In the judgment [executive] His life will be an unanswerable argument in favor of God's law.*"[505]

---

[504] Ellen White, *Spirit of Prophecy*, 4:486. [Emphasis mine]
[505] Ellen White, *In Heavenly Places*, 38. [Emphasis mine]

Again:

"But the plan of redemption had a yet broader and deeper purpose than the salvation of man. *It was not for this alone that Christ came to the earth*; it was not merely that the inhabitants of this little world might regard the law of God as it should be regarded; but it was to *vindicate the character of God before the universe*. To this result of His great sacrifice--its influence upon the intelligences of other worlds, as well as upon man--the Saviour looked forward when just before His crucifixion He said: "Now is the judgment of this world: now shall the prince of this world be cast out. And I, if I be lifted up from the earth, will draw all unto Me." John 12:31, 32. The act of Christ in dying for the salvation of man would not only make heaven accessible to men, *but before all the universe it would justify God and His Son in their dealing with the rebellion of Satan. It would establish the perpetuity of the law of God and would reveal the nature and the results of sin.*

From the first the great controversy had been upon the law of God. Satan had sought to prove that God was unjust, that His law was faulty, and that the good of the universe required it to be changed. In attacking the law he aimed to overthrow the authority of its Author. In the controversy it was to be shown whether the divine statutes were defective and subject to change, or perfect and immutable.

When Satan was thrust out of heaven, he determined to make the earth his kingdom. When he tempted and overcame Adam and Eve, he thought that he had gained possession of this world; "because," said he, "they have chosen me as their ruler." He claimed that it was impossible that forgiveness should be granted to the sinner, and therefore the fallen race were his rightful subjects, and the world was his. But God gave His own dear Son--one equal with Himself--to bear the penalty of transgression, and thus He provided a way by which they might be restored to His favor, and brought back to their Eden home. Christ undertook to redeem man and to rescue the world from the grasp of Satan. The great controversy begun in heaven was to be decided in the very world, on the very same field, that Satan claimed as his.

It was the marvel of all the universe that Christ should humble Himself to save fallen man. That He who had passed from star to star, from world to world, superintending all, by His providence supplying the needs of every order of being in His vast creation--that He should consent to leave His glory and take upon Himself human nature, was a mystery which the sinless intelligences of other worlds desired to understand. When Christ came to our world in the form of humanity, all were intensely interested in following Him as He traversed, step by step, the bloodstained path from the manger to

Calvary. Heaven marked the insult and mockery that He received, and knew that it was at Satan's instigation. They marked the work of counter-agencies going forward; Satan constantly pressing darkness, sorrow, and suffering upon the race, and Christ counteracting it. They watched the battle between light and darkness as it waxed stronger. And as Christ in His expiring agony upon the cross cried out, "*It is finished*" (John 19:30), *a shout of triumph rang through every world and through heaven itself. The great contest that had been so long in progress in this world was now decided, and Christ was conqueror. His death had answered the question whether the Father and the Son had sufficient love for man to exercise self-denial and a spirit of sacrifice.* Satan had revealed his true character as a liar and a murderer. It was seen that the very same spirit with which he had ruled the children of men who were under his power, he would have manifested if permitted to control the intelligences of heaven. *With one voice the loyal universe united in extolling the divine administration.*"[506]

While there was more to be revealed after the cross[507] concerning the Great Controversy it is summed up with the following quote of which the 144,000 play no part:

"The Father has given the world into the hands of Christ, that through his mediatorial work he may *completely vindicate* the binding claims and the holiness of *every principle of his law*."[508]

If something is said to be *completely* finished by God Almighty can *we* add anything to it to make it *complete*? To even suggest it is sheer folly! Yes, the government of God was upon his shoulder, Isa. 9:6. And it was Jesus and Jesus alone that also came to this world to vindicate the government of God!

"And Jesus said, For judgment I am come into this world" John 9:39.

Once again, just the opposite is the truth of the matter as Inspiration declares it is God Almighty that will "vindicate" His people at the end of time:

"He has often permitted matters to come to a *crisis*, that His interference might become marked. Then He has made manifest that there is a God in Israel who will maintain His law and *vindicate His people*."[509]

---

[506] Ellen White, *Patriarchs and Prophets* 68-70. [Emphasis mine]
[507] Ellen White, *The Desire of Ages,* 761.
[508] Ellen White, *Signs of the Times*, August 7, 1879. [Emphasis mine]
[509] Ellen White, *Christ Object Lessons*, 178. [Emphasis mine]

Inspiration is abundantly clear; it was Christ alone, not the final generation/144,000 that *completely* vindicates the binding claims and the holiness of *every principle of his law.* The supposition proposed by the proponents of LGT has just been *completely* dismantled by the very source they say sustains their supposition. That charge has been and was indeed answered and *completely* refuted by Christ at the cross and sustained through His mediatorial work by none other and no other than Christ Himself. Ellen White never says *anywhere* in her writings that the final generation or the 144,000 are responsible for refuting Satan's charge: "that it was impossible for man to obey God's commandments" *after* the fall of Adam! That is solely of human origin and the private work of LGT. I personally challenge the proponents of LGT to produce just such a statement!!!

This brings us to another theological position of the independents as promised in chapter 2 that we said would be addressed in this chapter because it likewise has theological applications for the final generation/144,000 as well. This segment comes to us from Dennis Priebe and the Standish brothers. The following statement was stated in chapter 2. No. 14, by Dennis Priebe however, this supposition is upheld by all the independents:

Therefore, this brings us to our 2nd pivotal issue:

(2) [They assert] "If He did not have man's nature, [sinful nature] He could not be our example."[510]

We have already witnessed in chapter 2 that the Scriptures and Inspiration teach that Jesus did *not* have a "sinful nature" because He "never sinned" and there was "no sin in Him." Therefore, we see no need to reiterate those definitive statements again. Our issue at hand is the clause, *"He could not be our example."* Our *"example"* as proclaimed by the independents is to mean that Christ overcame all manner of sin in a "sinful nature" and so must we in our "sinful nature." Priebe concludes with the following:

> "In our conclusions, we make many mistakes because of our erroneous views of the human nature of our Lord. When we give His human nature a power that is not possible for man to have in his conflicts with Satan, we destroy the completeness of His humanity." – Ellen G. White Comments, S.D.A. Bible Commentary, vol. 7, p. 929. We simply do not have the power of

---
[510] Dennis Priebe, *Face-to-Face With the Real Gospel* (Boise Idaho, Pacific Press Publishing Association, 1985), 60.

Adam's nature available to us. The warning is clear that by giving to Jesus' human nature a power that we cannot have, we destroy the completeness of His humanity. "The Lord now demands that every son and daughter of Adam… serve Him in human nature which we now have…. Jesus….could only keep the commandments of God in the same way that humanity can keep them." –Ibid. How can we keep them? Certainly not in Adam's nature. We can only keep them in that nature which we now have-fallen nature. And Jesus kept the commandments of God in the same way we are to keep them. Jesus overcame as we are to overcome."[511]

Again:

"If He was truly coming to enter into our weakness and our temptations, then it must be true that He took all that makes us the way we are, so He can show us the way to overcome those weaknesses and temptations. "If He did not have man's nature, *He could not be our example*. If He was not a partaker of our nature, He could not have been tempted as man has been. If it were not possible for Him to yield to temptation, He could not be our helper." Select Messages, bk. 1, p. 408. In other words, He must live at our level. He must live the way we live."[512]

Since Priebe correlates "sinful nature" with "our example" it becomes necessary to illustrate the following to refresh the reader:

"For what the law could not do, in that it was weak through the flesh,"—it could not justify man, *because in his sinful nature he could not keep the law*."[513]

Ellen White says we *cannot* keep the law in "sinful nature," Priebe says we *can*! However, Inspiration was just echoing Paul:

"Because the carnal mind [sinful nature] *is* enmity against God: <u>for it is not subject to the law of God, neither indeed can be</u>." Rom. 8:7.

---

[511] Ibid. 61-62.
[512] Ibid. 60.
[513] Ellen White, *Patriarchs and Prophets*, 373. [Emphasis mine]

The "carnal mind," "sinful nature" or "old man" is all one and the same and this class has not experienced the "new birth"! Instead of accepting the fact that we must be "born again" (John 3:3,7) and fully surrender our will to Christ and *then* we are given a "new nature" (2 Cor. 5:17) as Christ abides in us by faith of which we *then* become subject to the law of God as seen in our character by a change in our habits and pursuits. This procedure is based upon "it is written" and is the *only* means that Heaven will work *with* and *within* humanity after receiving the invitation:

> "*Entire self-renunciation is required.* Unless this takes place, we carry with us the evil that destroys our happiness. But *when self is crucified, Christ lives in us*, and the power of the Spirit attends our efforts."[514]

> "Man must be emptied of self before he can be, in the fullest sense, a believer in Jesus. *When self* is renounced, *then* the Lord can make man a *new creature.*"[515]

> "Let no one despair of gaining the victory. Victory is sure *when self is surrendered to God.*"[516]

"When *self* is crucified" what takes place? "Christ lives *in us.*" Is that a "sinful nature" that now resides within us? Of course not! Would it be safe to say then that this is a "new nature" from above that lives within us? Absolutely! On the other hand, the independents brush right over this vital lifesaving instruction and concentrate on the impossible without one mandate from above. Inspiration admonishes all the absolute necessity of being "born again" and that we rest not until we *experience* this transformation for ourselves by making this the all-important business of our lives:

> "A change so marked as to be represented by death. From living, active life, to death! What a striking figure! None need be deceived here. If this transformation has not been experienced by you, rest not. Seek the Lord with all your hearts. Make this the all-important business of your lives."[517]

How does one experience this transformation of character?

> "Transformation of character is wrought through the operation of the Holy Spirit, which works upon the human agent, implanting in him, according to his desire and consent to have it done, *a new nature*. The image of God is restored to the soul, and day by day he is strengthened and renewed by grace, and is enabled more and more perfectly to reflect the character of Christ in righteousness and true holiness."[518]

---

[514] Ellen White, *Our High Calling*, 21.
[515] Ellen White, *The Desire of Ages*, 280.
[516] Ellen White, *MS* 2, 1903.
[517] Ellen White, *Testimonies*, 2:178.
[518] Ellen White, *Review & Herald*, September 17, 1895.

The independents have a Christ with a *sinful nature* like themselves with a *bent toward evil* as *their example*, a nature *condemned* of God, and all who possess such a nature are in need of a *Saviour*, (Rom. 5:19) Christ being exempt of course, (Acts 10:34) yet trying to *keep the law* (Gal. 2:16) in a nature that Paul and Inspiration has plainly declared it to be an *impossibility* to overcome sin in! (Rom. 8:7) With the emphasis on, "All that the Lord hath spoken *we will do.*" Talk about discouragement! Talk about Self-righteousness! Wow! In contrast Christ says, "For my yoke *is* easy, and my burden is light." (Matt. 11:30). Try to harmonize those two views! However, I have never seen or been given any Scripture or Ellen White statements for confirmation for these private suppositions because there is none! If the reader will reason from cause to effect on every issue submitted one will clearly be able to discern very quickly that which is of human origin in contrast to that which is of divine revelation. Continuing now from where we left off if you please.

It behooves us to reiterate one very important aspect that was covered by Bro. Pfandl before we begin unmasking the truth of what the Scriptures declares to be "our example". Since the Bible and Inspiration make this critical definitive distinction then so must the reader if he is to see and understand the seriousness of this masterpiece of a deception! This is done because the Standish brothers, Priebe and the independents reject this section of the Bible and S.O.P. and their followers know little or next to nothing about this part of the Bible and S.O.P. teaching on this subject. Therefore I bring Pfandl to the front again and then I will present additional documentation to explain and illustrate to the reader this vital understanding that is not taught among the independents and why:

"Again, the book *Deceptions of the New Theology* claims:

> "*To separate Christ's physical nature from His mental and moral nature would take us both to the Greek pagan concept of the distinction between an evil body and a good soul. No right thinking Seventh-day Adventist dare accept that dualistic view of man. It is a satanic deception.* If Christ had a fallen physical nature, and He did, then His entire nature was fallen." (p.53).

However, this is not what we find in the writing of E.G. White. In *Signs of the Times*, Dec. 9, 1897 she wrote, "The human nature of Christ is likened to ours, and suffering was more keenly felt by Him; *for His spiritual nature was free from every taint of sin.*" She clearly distinguished between his physical and spiritual nature.

To distinguish between these two aspects in man's nature only becomes wrong when we say that each can exist separately from each other, as is the case in the belief that the soul is immortal.

After all, the Bible clearly states that man consists of "spirit, soul and body" (2. Thess. 5:23); and E.G. White wrote that "the nature of man is threefold" (Child Guidance, p.39), and that every follower of Christ should "dedicate all his powers of mind and soul and body to Him who has paid the ransom money for our souls" (Selected Messages, vol.2, p.124).

"On the one hand, Jesus' physical human nature was the nature of humanity after the fall (Rom. 8:3; Heb. 2:16, 17). Ellen White said, "He took upon his sinless nature the fallen nature of man" (*Medical Ministry*, p.181). That is, Jesus had a deteriorated human nature, a nature that did not have all the strength, vitality and capacity that Adam had at his creation.

On the other hand, Jesus' spiritual nature was the sinless nature of Adam before the fall, i.e., He had no evil propensities (with which we are born), no inclinations to sin (with which we are born) and no tendencies to sin (which we all have).

One will search in vain for expressions like "sinful nature of Christ", "fallen human nature of Christ", or "fallen nature of Christ" in the writings of Ellen White. What she does say repeatedly is that Christ took our "fallen" or "sinful" nature upon Himself (e.g., *Medical Ministry*, p.181; Manuscript 80, 1903).

At times she quotes Romans 8:3, e.g., "Christ, the second Adam, came in `the likeness of sinful flesh'" (Manuscript 99, 1903). This is in harmony with the view that Christ had the sinful physical nature of Adam after the fall, but the sinless spiritual nature of Adam before the fall."[519]

That concludes what we wanted reiterated from the pen of Brother Pfandl but let's take this a few steps further:

The Standish brothers again as we expand this exposure of Satan's counterfeit gospel:

> "Associated with the view that we sin because we are sinful, the notion has developed that Christ had a composite human nature, one which displayed the characteristics of that possessed by Adam both before and after the Fall. An analysis of this fence-sitting position usually reveals that the proposer believes that Christ inherited the physical fallen nature of Adam but possessed an unfallen moral nature. This proposition, found neither in Scripture nor the Spirit of Prophecy, is most dangerous. Again we would emphasize that unthinkingly its supporters are accepting the dualistic theories of Greek paganism. Seventh-day Adventists have never separated the soul from the body. Our health reform message is based upon our rejection of dualism. It is

---

[519] Gerhard Pfandl, *What Is New In The New Theology*, PDF 5-6.

totally impossible for one's physical nature to be fallen and his moral nature unfallen. Either man possesses a fallen nature or an unfallen nature. There can be no composite nature. Again it needs to be emphasized that character is distinct from nature. *Christ possessed a fallen human nature, but His character was ever perfect. In this He provided an example to us.*"

For even hereunto were ye called: because Christ also suffered for us, leaving us an example, that ye should follow his steps: Who did no sin, neither was guile found in his mouth (1 Peter 2:21, 22).

That Jesus possessed a fallen nature is seen by His collapse when bearing the cross. This was the response of a nature weakened by 4,000 years of sin."[520]

Even though we just saw the Bible clearly states that man consists of "spirit, soul and body" II. Thess. 5:23; and Ellen White wrote that "the nature of man is threefold,"[521] the Standish brothers have the audacity to accuse the organized church of following after "Greek paganism" rather than the Bible and Spirit of Prophecy. Unbelievable! If you would have asked the Standish brothers, what does it mean to be "born again" you would have gotten the following answer after they quote John 3:5. To be born of the water they would cite Matt. 3:11, "water unto repentance". To be born of the Spirit they would cite Acts 5:32, "so is also the Holy Ghost, whom God hath given to them that obey him". But they will go no further and never do the independents as a whole reference or acknowledge the Scripture in II Thess. 5:23 or Ellen White[522] in this regard. Hence, the laity remains in the dark just where they want them. They know if they did they would have to acknowledge II Cor. 5:17 as well and this in turn would force them to acknowledge that when we are "born again" John 3:3, 7 we receive a "new nature" from above that was so elegantly defined by Pastor Frank Phillips that we witnessed in chapter 5:

"Transformation of character is wrought through the operation of the Holy Spirit, which works upon the human agent, implanting in him, according to *his desire* and *consent* to have it done, *a new nature*. The image of God is *restored* to the soul, and day by day he is strengthened and renewed by grace, and is enabled more and more perfectly to reflect the character of Christ in righteousness and true holiness."[523]

Again:

---
[520] Colin D. Standish & Russell R. Standish, *Deceptions of the New Theology* (Hartland Publications, 1989). 137-8.
[521] Ellen White, *Child Guidance*, 39.
[522] Ibid. 39.
[523] Ellen White, *Review & Herald*, September 17, 1895. [Emphasis mine]

> "The *new birth* is a rare experience in this age of the world. This is the reason why there are so many perplexities in the churches. Many, so many, who assume the name of Christ are unsanctified and unholy. They have been baptized, but they were buried alive. *Self did not die*, and therefore they did not rise to newness of life in Christ."[524]

If the laity of the independents should ever see and understand this aspect of the Scriptures no honest free thinking individual would continue to buy their moldy bread. Neither could it be taught that this "new nature" could be passed off as a "sinful nature". But this un-ethical mentality does not stop here! Standish brothers go on to say *"Christ possessed a fallen human nature* [sinful nature] . . . *In this He provided an example to us."* Then the Standish brothers misuse I Peter 2:20-21, for their confirmation of the Bibles "example" for humanity that we will expose momentarily.

We submit several quotes from Inspiration that defines *precisely* what it means for Jesus to be *our example* and once again it is *not* what Priebe, Standish brothers and the independents say it is:

> *"If we have made Christ our pattern*, [example] if we have walked and worked as he has given us *an example in his own life*, we shall be able to meet the solemn surprises that will come upon us in our experience, and say from our heart, *"Not my will, but thine, be done."*[525]

> "Jesus now explained to His disciples that His own life of *self-abnegation* [denial] *was an example of what theirs should be."*[526]

> "It was a solemn reality that Christ came to fight the battles as man, in man's behalf. His temptation and victory tell us that *humanity must copy the Pattern; man must become a partaker of the divine nature."*[527]

> "Jesus said of Himself before He came to earth, *"I delight to do Thy will, O My God: yea, Thy law is within My heart."* Psalm 40:8. And just before He ascended again to heaven He declared, *""I have kept My Father's commandments, and abide in His love."* John 15:10. The Scripture says, "Hereby we do know that we know Him, if we keep His commandments. . . . *He that saith he abideth in Him ought himself also so to walk even as He walked."* 1 John 2:3-6. *"Because Christ also suffered*

---

[524] Ellen White, *SDABC* 6:1075. [Emphasis mine]
[525] Ellen White, *Review & Herald*, September 17, 1895. [Emphasis mine]
[526] Ellen White, *The Desire of Ages*, 416. [Emphasis mine]
[527] Ellen White, *Selected Messages*, 1: 408. [Emphasis mine]

> *for us, leaving us an example, that ye should follow His steps."* <u>1 Peter 2:21</u>."[528]

> "But the Son of God was *surrendered to the Father's will*, and *dependent upon His power*. So *utterly was Christ emptied of self that He made no plans for Himself*. He accepted God's plans for Him, and day by day the Father unfolded His plans. *So should we depend upon God, that our lives may be the simple outworking of His will*. . . . Christ, the true temple for God's indwelling, molded every detail of His earthly life in harmony with God's ideal. . . . So our characters are to be builded "for an habitation of God through the Spirit." Ephesians 2:22. And *we are to "make all things according to the pattern,"* even Him who "*suffered for us, leaving us an example, that ye should follow His steps."* Hebrews 8:5; 1 Peter 2:21.[529]

Please do not miss Ellen White's last quote and Scripture reference in her use, context and interpretation of 1 Peter 2:21 and now again the Standish brothers use, context and interpretation of 1 Peter 2:21 that we had just read:

> " . . . *Christ possessed a fallen human nature, but His character was ever perfect. In this He provided an example to us."*
> For even hereunto were ye called: because Christ also suffered for us, , *leaving us an example that ye should follow his steps: Who did no sin, neither was guile found in his mouth (1 Peter 2:21, 22).*
> That Jesus possessed a fallen nature is seen by His collapse when bearing the cross. This was the response of a nature weakened by 4,000 years of sin."[530]

Our *true example* is that man must become a partaker of the divine nature (sinless nature) just as Christ had to be a partaker of His Fathers nature. *This* in turn leads to *true conversion*:

> "Father, if it be possible, let this cup pass from me." Three times was the prayer offered, but was followed by, "Nevertheless, not my will, but thine, O God, be done." This must be our attitude: "*Not my will, but thine*, O God, be done." *This is true conversion*."[531]

Once again two different authors coming from two completely different sources, one from above, one from beneath, both claim, all in the name of Jesus. Incredible! Willful ignorance exalts opinions above a "Thus saith the Lord," and willful ignorance leads to willful disobedience. Most importantly for those who follow Inspiration is that we find her in perfect harmony with the Scriptures as to what our real example consist of:

---

[528] Ellen White, *Steps to Christ*, 61-62. [Emphasis mine]
[529] Ellen White, *Desire of Ages*, 208-209. [Emphasis mine]
[530] Colin D. Standish & Russell R. Standish, *Deceptions of the New Theology* (Hartland Publications, 1989). 137-8. [Emphasis mine]
[531] Ellen White, *Signs of the Times*, November 21, 1892. [Emphasis mine]

> "Then answered Jesus and said unto them, Verily, verily, I say unto you, The Son can do nothing of himself, but what he seeth the Father do: for what things soever he doeth, these also doeth the Son likewise." John 5:19.

> "I can of mine own self do nothing: as I hear, I judge: and my judgment is just; because I seek not mine own will, but the will of the Father which hath sent me." John 5:30.

1 Peter 2:19-21 is demonstrating this very principal and example. Our example is not in doing what Jesus [the Father] has done but in living the life Jesus has lived; in complete submission unto His Father. Complete surrender of our *will* to Christ to form and mould according to His own good pleasure. This is the *example* given us by the Scriptures and confirmed by Inspiration:

> "For this *is* thankworthy, if a man for conscience toward God endure grief, suffering wrongfully. 1 Peter. 2:19.
> For what glory *is it*, if, when ye be buffeted for your faults, ye shall take it patiently? but if, when ye do well, and suffer *for it*, ye take it patiently, this *is* acceptable with God. 1 Peter. 2:20.
> For even hereunto were ye called: because Christ also suffered for us, leaving us an example, that ye should follow his steps:" 1 Peter. 2:21.

Once again the reader comes face to face with the real gospel, alongside with the counterfeit gospel for all to see for themselves. The counterfeit gospel stresses the need to perform the impossible with a sinful nature that Heaven has condemned that can never achieve victory. This in turn renders the probationer in a state of hopelessness which is precisely the game plan of the Devil for you to get so discouraged that you let go of your "faith" in Christ. Then to fully secure his objective he presents another counterfeit as to what our "example" is and with that he is then able to side step the real issue that all must be "born again" and receive a "new nature" that Heaven can and will work with. This "new nature" produces willing, loving obedience *after* we "surrender our will" fully to Christ. Proof? Believers now enjoy studying their Bibles with like-minded seekers of truth and enjoy fellowship with their new found friend, Jesus Christ! Before conversion this was unthinkable! However, Satan knows full well that "his nature," the "sinful nature" of fallen man is *not* subject to the law of God, Rom 8:7. This becomes ever so clear after we understand the threefold nature of man as presented by Scripture and Ellen White as it was so persuasively illustrated by Brother Pfandl above. Why is this deception of our "will" so important to the Devil?

> "If you cling to *self*, refusing to yield your *will* to God, you are choosing death." [532]

Will this require a struggle?

---

[532] Ellen White, *Thoughts from The Mount Of Blessing*, 62. [Emphasis mine]

> "The warfare against *self* is the greatest battle that was ever fought. The yielding of self, *surrendering all to the will of God*, requires a struggle; but the soul *must* submit to God *before it can be renewed in holiness.*"[533]

> "Everyone who enters the pearly gates of the city of God will enter there as a conqueror, *and his greatest conquest will have been the conquest of self.*"[534]

The Devil also understands that with us:

> "*Everything* depends on the right action of the *will.*"[535]

This is why the Devil must introduce a counterfeit of such huge proportions that will keep us from seeing what our "real example" is and why this is so important. If the right action of the *will* is not understood aright, then there will be no victory, no latter rain. Therefore he will and has used *every* device to deceive and distract from the real gospel of Jesus Christ:

> "*Nothing but the baptism of the Holy Spirit* can bring up the church to its right position, and prepare the people of God for the *fast approaching conflict.*"[536]

Therefore, let's deepen our understanding here:

> "Many are inquiring, "How am I to make the surrender of myself to God?" You desire to give yourself to Him, but you are weak in moral power, in slavery to doubt, and controlled by the habits of your life of sin. Your promises and resolutions are like ropes of sand. You cannot control your thoughts, your impulses, your affections. The knowledge of your broken promises and forfeited pledges weakens your confidence in your own sincerity, and causes you to feel that God cannot accept you; but you need not despair. What you need to understand is the true force of the will. This is the governing power in the nature of man, the power of decision, or of choice. *Everything depends on the right action of the will*. The power of choice God has given to men; it is theirs to exercise. You cannot change your heart, you cannot of yourself give to God its affections; but you can choose to serve Him. You can give Him your will; He will then work in you to will and to do according to His good pleasure. Thus your whole nature will be brought under the control of the Spirit of Christ; your affections will be centered upon Him, your thoughts will be in harmony with Him.
> Desires for goodness and holiness are right as far as they go; but if you stop here, they will avail nothing. Many will be lost while hoping and desiring to be

---

[533] Ellen White, *Steps To Christ* 43.
[534] Ellen White, *Testimonies* 9:182.
[535] Ellen White, *Steps to Christ*, 47. [Emphasis mine]
[536] Ellen White, *Letter* 15, 1889. [Emphasis mine]

Christians. They do not come to the point of yielding the will to God. They do not now choose to be Christians.

Through the right exercise of the will, an entire change may be made in your life. By yielding up your will to Christ, you ally yourself with the power that is above all principalities and powers. You will have strength from above to hold you steadfast, and *thus through constant surrender* to God you will be enabled to live the new life, *even the life of faith*."[537]

Let's consider the practical implications of a fully surrendered will! If we have fully submitted our will to Christ without *any resistance* like Christ had done with His Father, is there anything that deity could not do, undertake or overcome in such an earthen vessel? I think not! The difference between Christ and us, the difference between victory and defeat is that Christ made no plans for himself; we do, and constantly frustrate the outworking of His will:

"So utterly was Christ emptied of self that He made no plans for Himself. He accepted God's plans for Him, and *day by day the Father unfolded His plans.* So should we depend upon God, that our lives may be the *simple outworking of His will.*"[538]

When *this* gospel is understood and experienced and the gift is accepted just as it reads, by faith, the burden becomes light and love, joy and peace captivate the mind as perfect love casteth out all fear:

"The sinner is justified through the merits of Jesus, and this is God's acknowledgment of the *perfection* of the ransom paid for man. That Christ was obedient even unto the death of the cross is a pledge of the repenting sinner's acceptance with the Father. Then shall we permit ourselves to have a vacillating experience of doubting and believing, believing and doubting? Jesus is the pledge of our acceptance with God. We stand in favor before God, *not because of any merit in ourselves, but because of our faith in "the Lord our righteousness."* Jesus stands in the holy of holies, now to appear in the presence of God for us. There he ceases not to present his people moment by moment, complete in himself. But because we are thus represented before the Father, we are not to imagine that we are to presume upon his mercy, and become careless, indifferent, and self-indulgent. Christ is not the minister of sin. We are complete in him, accepted in the Beloved, only as we abide in him by faith.

Perfection through our own good works we can never attain. The soul who sees Jesus by faith, repudiates his own righteousness. He sees himself as *incomplete*, his repentance *insufficient*, his strongest faith but *feebleness*, his most costly sacrifice as *meager*, and he sinks in *humility at the foot of the cross.* But a voice speaks to him from the *oracles of God's word*. In amazement he hears the message, "Ye are complete in him". Now *all* is at

---

[537] Ellen White, *Steps to Christ*, 47-48. [Emphasis mine]
[538] Ellen White, *The Desire of Ages*, 208. [Emphasis mine]

rest in his soul. No longer must he *strive to find some worthiness in himself, some meritorious deed by which to gain the favor of God.*

Beholding the Lamb of God, which taketh away the sin of the world, he finds the peace of Christ; for *pardon is written against his name, and he accepts the word of God, "Ye are complete in him."* How hard is it for humanity, long accustomed to cherish doubt, to grasp this *great truth*! But what *peace it brings to the soul*, what vital life! In looking to ourselves for righteousness, by which to find acceptance with God, *we look to the wrong place,* "for all have sinned, and come short of the glory of God." We are to look to Jesus; "for we all, with open face beholding as in a glass the glory of the Lord, are changed into the same image from glory to glory." You are to find your *completeness* by *beholding the Lamb of God, which taketh away the sin of the world.*"[539]

"The law requires righteousness,--a righteous life, *a perfect character*; and this man has not to give. He cannot meet the claims of God's holy law. But Christ, coming to the earth as man, lived a holy life, and developed *a perfect character*. These He offers as a *free gift to all who will receive them.*"[540]

With a *gift* like *that* how can one fail not fall in love with the man Christ Jesus and render willing loving obedience to all His commands!

Inspiration clearly exposes the end game of Satan's counterfeit gospel and his henchmen that promote it and lays out the destiny of all who come under its influence. When the soul fully surrenders his or her will to Christ, then Christ becomes our Righteousness, then Christ becomes our Perfection.

Be not deceived, we prove absolutely nothing and we vindicate absolutely nothing this side of the sun because apart from Christ we overcome nothing, we can do nothing apart from Christ! Apart from the Father, the Son overcame nothing. It should have been a clue to the independents when Jesus said:

"I can of mine own self do nothing. . ." John 5:30.

It should have been a clue to the independents when Jesus said:

". . . Without me ye can do nothing." John 15:5.

An ingenious counter measure pulled directly from Satan's arsenal to rob Seventh-day Adventist of receiving the latter rain. And wholly unfit them of what then would lie just ahead by trying to accomplish the impossible. A mandate not found among the Scriptures or among the writings of Ellen G. White! Thus when it is too late to remedy their course of action they will

---

[539] Ellen White, *Signs of the Times*, July 4, 1892. [Emphasis mine]
[540] Ellen White, *The Desire of Ages*, 762. [Emphasis mine]

find themselves among the "superficial, conservative class, whose influence has steadily retarded the progress of the work" and will become our most bitter enemies from within the Seventh-day Adventist Church. After all:

> "We have far more to fear from within than from without."[541]

This does not line up well with the private doctrine of *sinlessness perfection* as advocated by LGT in a sinful nature! Ellen White never says *anywhere* in her writings that the final generation or the 144,000 are *responsible* for *vindicating* God's *law* or *character* that we have proven previously. And as we have illustrated previously as well, there is no argument that if a man has fully surrendered his will to Christ he receives a "new nature" because it is now Christ *in him* that can keep him from falling. But it is also contrary to the teachings of the Scriptures and Inspiration that Priebe's gospel concludes with the emphasis on the *deeds performed in a "sinful nature"* merits salvation! Ellen White is very forthright about overcoming sin[542] but it will *never* be accomplished by the "old man" in his "sinful nature" as advocated by LGT because:

> "The old nature, born of blood and of the will of the flesh, *cannot inherit the kingdom of God.*"[543]

Can it get any clearer! It is just as wrong to claim their "example" is Jesus overcoming all manner of sin in a "sinful nature" with the emphasis again on *performance* rather than *submission* while *their* Jesus was struggling with the same bent to evil as they themselves. Instead of accepting the *free gift* of a "perfect character"[544] from Christ that man cannot give, Priebe chooses (or thinks) to do it himself and even the *impossible* in a "*sinful nature*"! And then to add insult to injury, Priebe further claims to even match the *performance* of that of *Jesus Christ Himself* in overcoming sin *in his* "*sinful nature*":

> "*We will have reached perfection of character in a fallen nature that is still able to sin.* No longer will we have occasional forays into the land of self-indulgence. *We will always say No as Jesus said No to all temptations.* To silence the last lingering question that perhaps Jesus was sinless because He was God, *the final generation will prove beyond a shadow of a doubt that men and woman with fallen natures can live without sinning. This final demonstration will contribute to the vindication of God's character*, His government, His justice, and His mercy-and the great controversy will be very near its conclusion."[545]

---

[541] Ellen White, *Review & Herald*, March 22, 1887.
[542] Ellen White, *Spirit of Prophecy* 4:440; *The Great Controversy*, 623.
[543] Ellen White, *Thoughts from the Mount of Blessing*, 141.
[544] Ellen White, *The Desire of Ages*, 762. "The law requires righteousness,--a righteous life, *a perfect character*; and this man has not to give. He cannot meet the claims of God's holy law. But Christ, coming to the earth as man, lived a holy life, and developed *a perfect character*. These He offers as a *free gift to all who will receive them.*" [Emphasis mine]
[545] Dennis Priebe, *Face-to-Face With the Real Gospel* (Boise Idaho, Pacific Press Publishing Association, 1985), 89-90. [Emphasis mine]

To the surface reader this may come across as being politically correct but these unfounded humanistic theories cannot be found in the word of God and are solely the private work of LGT and the independents. This is precisely why Inspiration warned us about when taking the humanity of Christ too far and disregarding her counsel all in the same source when she said:

> *"I perceive that there is danger in approaching subjects which dwell on the humanity of the Son of the infinite God."*[546]

Again, I personally challenge the proponents of LGT to produce just such a definitive statement! This is sheer fanaticism and legalism at its best or worst! Unbelievable! As we will soon illustrate this is *not* the issue the final generation/144,000 will be confronted with as both the Bible and Ellen White speak ever so clearly with one voice on this vital issue.

The following quote, taken out of its context is often cited but again, be not deceived dear reader:

> "Should they prove unworthy, and lose their lives because of their own defects of character, then God's holy name would be reproached."[547]

There is no mandate behind this wording, action or by implication. This is nothing more than a natural response from any born again Christian of any generation that loves their Lord that would be placed under similar circumstances. Let's not read into something of which is not there please.

Since the 144,000 do not answer Satan's initial charge that Christ alone answered and completely refuted and vindicated the Father at the cross, than what do they answer if anything? This brings us to the million dollar question. Since the gospel is one and the same for all generations of all six millenniums, including the 144,000 because God never changes, Mal. 3:6; Heb. 13:8 (along with the writings of Paul) then why the names of the 144,000 are engraved in letters of gold as depicted in the Heavenly temple:

> "I saw there tables of stone in which the names of the 144,000 were engraved in letters of gold."[548]

Since there is no Bible or S.O.P. to validate the teachings of LGT regarding the role the 144,000 are said to perform in achieving *sinlessness perfection* in a "sinful nature." Then what do they accomplish in the eyes of Heaven that sets them apart from any other generation as seen just from the privileges granted them? Scripture and Ellen White answers this question in robust clarity in our 3rd and final segment presented below:

(3) "Here is the patience of the saints: here are they that keep the commandments of God, and the <u>faith of Jesus</u>." Rev. 14:12:

---

[546] Ellen White, *SDABC*, 5:1128-9.
[547] Ellen White, *The Great Controversy*, 619.
[548] Ellen White, *Early Writings*, 19.

Luke complements John but leaves no one guessing as to what the real end game issue is that is to confront the final generation/144,000:

> "I tell you that he will avenge them speedily. Nevertheless when the Son of man cometh, <u>shall he find faith on the earth</u>?" Luke 18:8.

While Jones and Waggoner missed it in 1888, Ellen White did not:

> "The third angel's message is the proclamation of the commandments of God and the faith of Jesus Christ. The commandments of God have been proclaimed, but *the faith of Jesus Christ has not been proclaimed by Seventh-day Adventists as of equal importance, the law and the gospel going hand in hand. I cannot find language to express this subject in its fullness.*
>
> "<u>*The faith of Jesus*</u>." It is talked of, <u>but not understood</u>. What constitutes the faith of Jesus, that belongs, to the third angel's message? Jesus becoming our sin-bearer that He might become our sin-pardoning Saviour. He was treated as we deserve to be treated. He came to our world and took our sins that we might take His righteousness. *Faith in the ability of Christ to save us amply and fully and entirely is the faith of Jesus.*"[549]

The following dream that Ellen White relates speaks volumes and perhaps largely forgotten by many but harmonizes perfectly with the emphasis placed squarely upon the Scriptural account:

> "While at Battle Creek, Michigan, in August, 1868, I dreamed of being with a large body of people. A portion of this assembly started out prepared to journey. We had heavily loaded wagons. As we journeyed, the road seemed to ascend. On one side of this road was a deep precipice; on the other was a high, smooth, white wall. . . . As we journeyed on, the road grew narrower and steeper. In some places it seemed so very narrow that we concluded that we could no longer travel with the loaded wagons. We then loosed them from the horses, took a portion of the luggage from the wagons and placed it upon the horses, and journeyed on horseback.

---

[549] Ellen White, *1888 Materials*, 1:217. [Emphasis mine]

As we progressed, the path still continued to grow narrow. We were obliged to press close to the wall, to save ourselves from falling off the narrow road down the steep precipice. As we did this, the luggage on the horses pressed against the wall, and caused us to sway toward the precipice. We feared that we should fall, and be dashed in pieces on the rocks. We then cut the luggage from the horses, and it fell over the precipice. We continued on horseback, greatly fearing, as we came to the narrower places in the road, that we should lose our balance and fall. At such times, a hand seemed to take the bridle, and guide us over the perilous way.

As the path grew more narrow, we decided that we could no longer go with safety on horseback, and we left the horses and went on foot, in single file, one following in the footsteps of another. At this point small cords were let down from the top of the pure white wall; these we eagerly grasped, to aid us in keeping our balance upon the path. As we traveled,

the cord moved along with us. The path finally became so narrow that we concluded that we could travel more safely without our shoes; so we slipped them from our feet, and went on some distance without them. Soon it was decided that we could travel more safely without our stockings; these were removed, and we journeyed on with bare feet.

We then thought of those who had not accustomed themselves to privations and hardships. Where were such now? They were not in the company. At every change, some were left behind, and those only remained who had accustomed themselves to endure hardships. The privations of the way only made these more eager to press on to the end.

Our danger of falling from the pathway increased. We pressed close to the white wall, yet could not place our feet fully upon the path; for it was too narrow.

We then suspended nearly our whole weight upon the cords, exclaiming: "We have hold from above! We have hold from above!" The same words were uttered by all the company in the narrow pathway.

As we heard the sounds of mirth and revelry that seemed to come from the abyss below, we shuddered. We heard the profane oath, the vulgar jest, and low, vile songs. We heard the war song and the dance song. We heard instrumental music, and loud laughter, mingled with cursing and cries of anguish and bitter wailing, and were more anxious than ever to keep upon the narrow, difficult pathway. Much of the time we were compelled to suspend our whole weight upon the cords, which increased in size as we progressed.

I noticed that the beautiful white wall was stained with blood. It caused a feeling of regret to see the wall thus stained. This feeling, however, lasted but for a moment, as I soon thought that it was all as it should be. Those who are following after will know that others have passed the narrow, difficult way before them, and will conclude that if others were able to pursue their onward course, they can do the same. And as the blood shall be pressed from their aching feet, they will not faint with discouragement; but seeing the blood upon the wall, they will know that others have endured the same pain.

At length we came to a large chasm, at which our path ended. There was nothing now to guide the feet, nothing upon which to rest them. Our whole reliance must be upon the cords, which had increased in size, until they were as large as our bodies. Here we were for a time thrown into perplexity and distress. We inquired in fearful whispers, "To what is the cord attached?" My husband was just before me. Large drops of sweat were falling from his brow, the veins in his neck and temples were increased to double their usual size, and suppressed, agonizing groans came from his lips. The sweat was dropping from my face, and I felt such anguish as I had never felt before. A fearful struggle was before us. Should we fail here, all the difficulties of our journey had been experienced for nought.

Before us, on the other side of the chasm, was a beautiful field of green grass, about six inches high. I could not see the sun, but bright soft beams of light, resembling fine gold and silver, were resting upon this field. Nothing I had seen upon earth could compare in beauty and glory with this field. But could we succeed in reaching it? was the anxious inquiry. Should the cord break, we must perish. Again, in whispered anguish, the words were breathed, "What holds the cord?"

For a moment we hesitated to venture. Then we exclaimed: "Our only hope is to trust wholly to the cord. It has been our dependence all the difficult way. It will not fail us now." Still we were hesitating and distressed. The words were then spoken: "God holds the cord. We need not fear." These words were then repeated by those behind us, accompanied with: "He will not fail us now. He has brought us thus far in safety."

My husband then swung himself over the fearful abyss into the beautiful field beyond. I immediately followed. And oh, what a sense of relief and gratitude to God we felt! I heard voices raised in triumphant praise to God. I was happy, perfectly happy.

I awoke, and found that from the anxiety I had experienced in passing over the difficult route, every nerve in my body seemed to be in a tremor. This dream needs no comment. It made such an impression upon my mind that probably every item in it will be vivid before me while my memory shall continue."[550]

Indeed, this dream needs no comment because the solitary theme of "faith" is written all over it as their baggage (earthliness) is being discarded (consumed) but we have only just scratched the surface here:

> "The assaults of Satan are fierce and determined, his delusions are terrible; but the Lord's eye is upon His people, and His ear listens to their cries. *Their affliction is great, the flames of the furnace seem about to consume them*; but the Refiner will bring them forth as gold tried in the fire. God's love for His children during the period of their severest trial is as strong and tender as in the days of their sunniest prosperity; *but it is needful for them to be placed in the furnace of fire; their earthliness must be consumed, that the image of Christ may be perfectly reflected.*"[551]

Notice in the sequence of time and events this is taking place, contrary to popular thinking!

It is by "Faith" but this should be of no surprise because it has always been by faith as illustrated in Hebrews the 11th chapter. Since the gospel is one and the same for all humanity what then is so different in the experience of the final generation/144,000? First, Intensity:

> "The "time of trouble, such as never was," is soon to open upon us; and we shall need an *experience* which we do not now possess and which many are too indolent to obtain. It is often the case that trouble is greater in anticipation than in reality; but this is not true of the crisis before us. *The most vivid presentation cannot reach the magnitude of the ordeal.* In that time of trial, every soul must stand for himself before God. "Though Noah, Daniel, and Job" were in the land, "as I live, saith the Lord God, they shall deliver neither son nor daughter; they shall but deliver their own souls by their righteousness." Ezekiel 14:20."[552]

> "The temptations of Satan are greater now than ever before, for he knows that his time is short."[553]

Inspiration declares all will need a "living experience"[554] in order to reach our ultimate destination on the other side in the coming crisis. If the reader would do a word study using the phrase "living experience" from E.G. White's writings you will find there to be 232 hits. In that, you will find Inspiration's definition of what a "living experience" is and is not, how she obtained it and how we may obtain it and more. Unfortunately, space does not allow for that

---

[550] Ellen White, *Christian Experience and Teachings*, 179- 184.
[551] Ellen White, *The Great Controversy*, 621.
[552] Ellen White, *The Great Controversy*, 622-623. [Emphasis mine]
[553] Ellen White, *Early Writings*, 46. [Emphasis mine]
[554] Ellen White, *The Great Controversy*, 601.

study here. However, I will leave you with one admonition that you may wish to share and encourage the participation of your local church family. All would greatly benefit:

> "Our meetings should be spirited and social, and not too long. Reserve, pride, vanity, and fear of man, should find no place there. Little differences and prejudices should not be taken with us to these meetings. "Ye are the light of the world," says the heavenly Teacher. As in a united family, simplicity, meekness, confidence, and love should exist in the hearts of brethren and sisters who meet to be refreshed and invigorated by bringing their lights together. All have not the same experience in their religious life; but those of diverse exercises come together, and with simplicity and humbleness of mind, talk out their experience. All who are pursuing the onward Christian course, should have, and will have, an experience that is living, that is new and interesting. *A living experience is made up of daily trials, conflicts, and temptations, strong efforts and victories, and great peace and joy gained through Jesus.* A simple relation of such experiences gives light, strength, and knowledge that will aid others in their advancement in the divine life. The worship of God should be both interesting and instructive to those who have any love for divine and heavenly things."[555]

Our study is the final generation/144,000 and we need to differentiate (briefly at this point) between these two terms as for their application in time and place. The final generation is a term that I refer to be used for all that participated in the solemn assembly of Joel 2 and received the latter rain of which I will illustrate shortly. They proclaimed the third angels message with great power but many were martyred for their "faith." The 144,000 also received of the latter rain but remain alive to see Jesus at His second coming when the final seal of protection is to be administrated by Heaven. This takes place when the last great warning message of Rev. 18:1-5 was closing, just before the close of probation of which I will illustrate and document shortly as well.

Therefore, we start by asking what precipitates the coming onslaught that commences the prophecy of Joel chapter 2 and the awaking of the ten virgins?[556] When this visual event takes place "upon the world as an overwhelming surprise"[557] then:

> "Those who follow in the light need have no anxiety lest that in the outpouring of the latter rain they will not be baptized with the Holy Spirit. If we would receive the light of the glorious angel that shall lighten the earth with his glory, let us see to it that our hearts are cleansed, emptied of

---

[555] Ellen White, *Review & Herald*, April 28, 1885.
[556] See my PDF article called, *The Three Woes of Revelation*, for some thoughts regarding these issues from my website at www.thesourcehh.org.
[557] "A *great terror is soon to come upon human beings*. The end is very near. We who know the truth should be preparing for what is soon to *break upon the world as an overwhelming surprise*." Ellen White, *Testimonies*, 8:28.

self, and turned toward heaven, that they may be ready for the latter rain."[558]

Our explicit instruction has at that time all but been outlined for all to follow and there is no need to doubt your standing before God, providing we follow His instructions to the very letter. When the visual crisis has commenced the very first response from faithful pastors and laity alike is to call for a "solemn assembly":

> Joel 2:1 "Blow ye the trumpet in Zion, and sound an alarm in my holy mountain: let all the inhabitants of the land tremble: for the day of the LORD cometh, for *it is* nigh at hand;
> Joel 2:2 A day of darkness and of gloominess, a day of clouds and of thick darkness, as the morning spread upon the mountains: a great people and a strong; there hath not been ever the like, neither shall be any more after it, *even* to the years of many generations. . .
> Joel 2:15 Blow the trumpet in Zion, sanctify a fast, call a solemn assembly:
> Joel 2:16 Gather the people, sanctify the congregation, assemble the elders, gather the children, and those that suck the breasts: let the bridegroom go forth of his chamber, and the bride out of her closet.
> Joel 2:17 Let the priests, the ministers of the LORD, weep between the porch and the altar, and let them say, Spare thy people, O LORD, and give not thine heritage to reproach, that the heathen should rule over them: wherefore should they say among the people, Where *is* their God?
> Joel 2:18 Then will the LORD be jealous for his land, and pity his people.
> Joel 2:19 Yea, the LORD will answer and say unto his people, Behold, I will send you corn, and wine, and oil, and ye shall be satisfied therewith: and I will no more make you a reproach among the heathen:
> Joel 2:20 But I will remove far off from you the northern *army,* and will drive him into a land barren and desolate, with his face toward the east sea, and his hinder part toward the utmost sea, and his stink shall come up, and his ill savour shall come up, because he hath done great things.
> Joel 2:21 Fear not, O land; be glad and rejoice: <u>for the LORD will do great things</u>."

For those who follow the Lord's instructions minutely will witness how the Lord is about to "do *great things*" for His people that we will methodically illustrate.

Ellen White spells it out precisely just what all must accomplish in order to receive the latter rain and receive the final sealing, the seal of protection (EW 71; Eze. 9:1-6)[559] in order to stand (Rev. 6:17) when the 7 last plagues are administered, when probation closes its door and when God's people must stand without a mediator:

> "Those that *overcome* the <u>world</u>, the <u>flesh</u>, and the <u>devil</u>, will be the favored ones who shall receive the seal of the living God. Those whose hands are not

---
[558] Ellen White, *Signs of the Times*, August 1, 1892. [Emphasis mine]
[559] Heidi Heiks, *King of the North* (Teach Services, Brushton, New York, 2009. See my book for an understanding of the three sealing's of the saints in their chronological order.

clean, whose hearts are not pure, will not have the seal of the living God. *Those who are planning sin and acting it will be passed by. Only those who, in their attitude before God, are filling the position of those who are repenting and confessing their sins* in the great anti-typical day of atonement, will be *recognized* and *marked* as worthy of *God's protection.*"[560]

Do not miss the words, "*those who, in their attitude . . . who are repenting and confessing their sins . . .* will be *recognized* and *marked* as worthy of *God's protection*". Immediately after the parable of the unjust judge in Luke 18:1-8 when Christ revealed the central issue that is to confront the 144.000, ". . . When the Son of man cometh, *shall he find faith on the earth*"? Luke then follows up in verses 9-14 with the parable of the, Two Worshipers. In this parable we have two great classes in the church contrasted throughout the history of the world, the legalist and the righteous, the Pharisee and the publican, the 144,000 and the superficial conservative class:

> "The Pharisee and the publican represent two great classes into which those who come to worship God are divided. Their first two representatives are found in the first two children that were born into the world. Cain thought himself righteous, and he came to God with a thank offering only. He made no confession of sin, and acknowledged no need of mercy. But Abel came with the blood that pointed to the Lamb of God. He came as a sinner, confessing himself lost; *his only hope was the unmerited love of God*. The *Lord had respect to his offering*, but to Cain and his offering He had not respect."[561]

Inspiration continues by defining the legalist with his infamous traits of character that God abhors:

> "Unto certain which trusted in themselves that they were righteous, and despised others," Christ spoke the parable of the Pharisee and the publican. The Pharisee goes up to the temple to worship, not because he feels that he is a sinner in need of pardon, but because he thinks himself righteous and hopes to win commendation. His worship he regards as an act of merit that will recommend him to God. At the same time it will give the people a high opinion of his piety. He hopes to secure favor with both God and man. His worship is prompted by self-interest.
> And he is full of self-praise. He looks it, he walks it, he prays it. Drawing apart from others as if to say, ""Which say, Stand by thyself, come not near to me; for I am holier than thou. These are a smoke in my nose, a fire that burneth all the day." (Isaiah 65:5), he stands and prays "with himself." Wholly self-satisfied, he thinks that God and men regard him with the same complacency.
> "God, I thank thee," he says, "that I am not as other men are, extortioners, unjust, adulterers, or even as this publican." He judges his

---

[560] Ellen White, *Testimonies to Ministers*, 445. [Emphasis mine]
[561] Ellen White, *Christ Object Lessons*, 152. [Emphasis mine]

character, not by the holy character of God, but by the character of other men. His mind is turned away from God to humanity. This is the secret of his self-satisfaction.

He proceeds to recount his good deeds: "I fast twice in the week, I give tithes of all that I possess." The religion of the Pharisee does not touch the soul. He is not seeking Godlikeness of character, a heart filled with love and mercy. He is satisfied with a religion that has to do only with outward life. His righteousness is his own--the fruit of his own works--and judged by a human standard.

Whoever trusts in himself that he is righteous, will despise others. As the Pharisee judges himself by other men, so he judges other men by himself. His righteousness is estimated by theirs, and the worse they are the more righteous by contrast he appears. His self-righteousness leads to accusing. "Other men" he condemns as transgressors of God's law. Thus he is making manifest the very spirit of Satan, the accuser of the brethren. With this spirit it is impossible for him to enter into communion with God. He goes down to his house destitute of the divine blessing. . . For each of the classes represented by the Pharisee and the publican there is a lesson in the history of the apostle Peter. In his early discipleship Peter thought himself strong. Like the Pharisee, in his own estimation he was "not as other men are.". . . He thought himself able to withstand temptation; but in a few short hours the test came, and with cursing and swearing he denied his Lord. . . The Lord could not save him from trial, but He could have saved him from defeat. . . The evil that led to Peter's fall and that shut out the Pharisee from communion with God is proving the ruin of thousands today. There is nothing so offensive to God or so dangerous to the human soul as pride and self-sufficiency. Of all sins it is the most hopeless, the most incurable."[562]

Consider now the contrast of the righteous or publican in the eyes of Heaven:

"The publican had gone to the temple with other worshipers, but he soon drew apart from them as unworthy to unite in their devotions. Standing afar off, he "would not lift up so much as his eyes unto heaven, but smote upon his breast," in bitter anguish and self-abhorrence. He felt that he had transgressed against God, that he was sinful and polluted. He could not expect even pity from those around him, for they looked upon him with contempt. He knew that he had no merit to commend him to God, and in utter self-despair he cried, "God be merciful to me, a sinner." He did not compare himself with others.

Overwhelmed with a sense of guilt, he stood as if alone in God's presence. His only desire was for pardon and peace; his only plea was the mercy of God. And he was blessed. "I tell you," Christ said, "this man went down to his house justified rather than the other. . . Thus it must be seen by

---

[562] Ellen White, *Christ Object Lessons*, 150-154.

all who seek God. By faith--faith that renounces all self-trust--the needy suppliant is to lay hold upon infinite power.

No outward observances can take the place of simple faith and entire renunciation of self. But no man can empty himself of self. We can only consent for Christ to accomplish the work. Then the language of the soul will be, Lord, take my heart; for I cannot give it. It is Thy property. Keep it pure, for I cannot keep it for Thee. Save me in spite of myself, my weak, unchristlike self. Mold me, fashion me, raise me into a pure and holy atmosphere, where the rich current of Thy love can flow through my soul.

It is not only at the beginning of the Christian life that this renunciation of self is to be made. At every advance step heavenward it is to be renewed. All our good works are dependent on a power outside of ourselves. Therefore there needs to be a continual reaching out of the heart after God, a continual, earnest, heartbreaking confession of sin and humbling of the soul before Him. *Only by constant renunciation of self and dependence on Christ can we walk safely.* A new heart is given him. He becomes a new creature in Christ Jesus. . . *We shall see that if we are ever saved, it will not be through our own goodness, but through God's infinite grace.*"[563]

Let's come back and take a closer look at the *Testimonies to Ministers* quote we viewed previously. All agree "the *world*, the *flesh*, and the *devil*," have always been the test for all of humanity to overcome and this is correct! There is no different gospel for the 144,000. However, the intensity of these three segments for the final generation/144,000 will be taken to new heights:

The first of the three to be encountered and met with the intensity of the conflict that was presented before us is overcoming "the *flesh*," this takes in a wide spectrum that we have previously covered in chapter 5:

"The word of God tells us how we may become *perfect* Christians and escape the seven last plagues."[564]

Indeed it does as we have previously witnessed:

"For if ye live after the flesh, ye shall die: but if ye through the Spirit do mortify the deeds of the body, ye shall live." Rom. 8:13.

"For he that soweth to his flesh shall of the flesh reap corruption; but he that soweth to the Spirit shall of the Spirit reap life everlasting." Gal. 6:8.

"There is therefore now no condemnation to them which are in Christ Jesus, who walk not after the flesh, but after the Spirit." Rom. 8:1.

---

[563] Ellen White, *Christ Object Lessons*, 151-163.
[564] Ellen White, *Testimonies* 1:126. [Emphasis mine]

While all, including the final generation/144,000 have a part to play in overcoming sin that we will illustrate momentarily the emphasis placed on performance and the means of achievement in a "sinful nature" in obtaining *sinlessness perfection* as advocated by LGT is not part of Heavens curriculum for God never asks us to do what only He can do:

> "Jesus loves His children, *even if they err*. They belong to Jesus, and we are to treat them as the purchase of the blood of Jesus Christ. Any unreasonable course pursued toward them is written in the books as against Jesus Christ. He keeps His eye upon them, and when they do their best, calling upon God for His help, be assured the service will be accepted, *although imperfect*.
>
> *Jesus is perfect. Christ's righteousness is imputed unto them*, and He will say, "Take away the filthy garments from him, and clothe him with change of raiment." *Jesus makes up for our unavoidable deficiencies. Where Christians are faithful to each other, true and loyal to the Captain of the Lord's host, never betraying trusts into the enemy's hands, they will be transformed into Christ's character. Jesus will abide in their hearts by faith*."[565]

Again:

> "When we are clothed with the righteousness of Christ, we shall have no relish for sin; for Christ will be working with us. *We may make mistakes*, but we will hate the *sin* that caused the sufferings of the Son of God."[566]

Again:

> "If in our ignorance we make missteps, Christ does not leave us."[567]

> "Now unto him that is able to keep you from falling, and to present you faultless before the presence of his glory with exceeding joy," Jude 24.

Likewise, the sins of ignorance as specified in the Old Testament in Lev. Chapter 4, God winked at. There is no such thing as salvation in known or practicing sin and that is not what Scripture and Inspiration is referring to. However, the genuine Christian does not seek to excuse or justify any manner of sin as confirmed by Inspiration:

> "In the unregenerate heart there is love of sin and a disposition to cherish and excuse it. In the renewed heart there is hatred of sin and determined resistance against it."[568]

When the ten virgins have been taken unawares this event will also set in motion the final shaking of Adventism when "everything is to be shaken that can be shaken.":

---

[565] Ellen White, *Manuscript Release*, 18:244. [Emphasis mine]
[566] Ellen White, *Review & Herald*, March 18, 1890. [Emphasis mine]
[567] Ellen White, *Christ Object Lessons*, 173.
[568] Ellen White, *The Great Controversy*, 508.

> "There is to be a shaking. . . but this is not the present truth. . . *It will be the result of refusing the truth presented.*"[569]

The Lord had Ellen White pen the following instruction primarily for this very time and event in human history. Contents for this first reading is taken from the chapter called, *The Shaking*, footnotes that are just as important are Ellen White's. Notice especially *my italics* as we will recap on some of these sections after the reader has been given the big picture. The *italics* will demonstrate the central issues Heaven has deemed as fully essential prior to receiving the latter rain and the preservation of those that endure thru Jacob's time of trouble:

> "But before we are delivered from Satan's power without, we must be delivered from his power within."[570]

However, the final remedy that has been provided for us is given only to those who have been preparing themselves for it by daily crucifying the flesh:

> "I was shown that if God's people make no efforts on their part, but wait for the refreshing to come upon them and remove their wrongs and correct their errors; if they depend upon that to cleanse them from filthiness of the flesh and spirit, and fit them to engage in the loud cry of the third angel, they will be found wanting. The refreshing or power of God comes only on those who have *prepared themselves for it* by doing the work which God bids them, namely, cleansing themselves from all filthiness of the flesh and spirit, perfecting holiness in the fear of God."[571]

> "*Before giving us the baptism of the Holy Spirit*, our heavenly Father will *try us*, to see if we can live without *dishonoring Him* [by fulfilling the mandate of Joel 2] . . . . Do not think that you can have great spiritual blessings [the latter rain] without complying with the conditions God Himself has laid down."[572]

> "At this time--a time of overwhelming iniquity-- *a new life*, coming from the Source of all life, is to take possession of those who have the love of God in their hearts, and they are to go forth to proclaim with power the message of a crucified and risen Saviour. They are to put forth earnest, untiring efforts to save souls."[573]

Without the aid of the latter rain, no man will be left standing:

> "When God's wrath is poured out upon the earth, who will then be able to stand? Now is the time for God's people to show themselves true to principle. *When the religion of Christ is most held in contempt, when His law is most*

---

[569] Ellen White, *Selected Messages*, 2:13. [Emphasis mine]
[570] Ellen White, *Christ Object Lessons*, 174.
[571] Ellen White, *Testimonies*, 1:619. [Emphasis mine]
[572] Ellen White, *Letter*, 22, 1902. *Manuscript Releases*, 4:336. [Emphasis mine]
[573] Ellen White, *Testimonies*, 9:44. [Emphasis mine]

despised, then should our zeal be the warmest and our courage and firmness the most unflinching. To stand in defense of truth and righteousness when the majority forsake us, to fight the battles of the Lord when champions are few-- this will be our test. At this time we must gather warmth from the coldness of others, courage from their cowardice, and loyalty from their treason. The nation will be on the side of the great rebel leader."[574]

The mandate of Joel 2 has been graciously spelled out for us by Inspiration in the three following quotes with her own footnotes and emphasis throughout in the original, italics is mine:

> "I was shown the people of God, and saw them mightily shaken. Some, with strong faith and agonizing cries, were pleading with God. Their countenances were pale, and marked with deep anxiety, expressive of their *internal struggle*. Firmness and great earnestness were expressed in their countenances, while large drops of perspiration fell from their foreheads. Now and then their faces would light up with the marks of God's approbation, and again the same solemn, earnest, anxious look would settle upon them.[575]
>
> Evil angels crowded around them, pressing their darkness upon them, to shut out Jesus from their view, that their eyes might be drawn to the darkness that surrounded them, and they distrust God and next murmur against Him. Their only safety was in keeping their eyes directed upward. Angels of God had charge over His people, and as the poisonous atmosphere from the evil angels was pressed around these anxious ones, the heavenly angels were continually wafting their wings over them, to scatter the thick darkness.
>
> Some, I saw, did not participate in this work of *agonizing and pleading*. They seemed indifferent and careless. They were not resisting the darkness around them, and it shut them in like a thick cloud. The angels of God left these, and I saw them hastening to the assistance of those who were struggling with all their energies to resist the evil angels, and trying to help themselves by calling upon God with perseverance. But the angels left those who made no effort to help themselves, and I lost sight of them. As the praying ones continued their earnest cries, a ray of light from Jesus would at times come to them, to encourage their hearts, and light up their countenances.

---

[574] Ellen White, *Testimonies*, 5:136. [Emphasis mine]

[575] Ellen White's footnotes: "Blow the trumpet in Zion, sanctify a fast, call a solemn assembly: gather the people, sanctify the congregation, assemble the elders. . . . Let the priests the ministers of the lord, weep between the porch and the altar and let them say, Spare Thy people, O lord, and give not Thine heritage to reproach, that the heathen should rule over them: wherefore should they say among the people, Where is their God?" Joel 2:15-17.

"Submit yourselves therefore to God. Resist the devil, and he will flee from you. Draw nigh to God, and He will draw nigh to you. Cleanse your hands, ye sinners; and purify your hearts, ye double-minded. Be afflicted, and mourn, and weep: let your laughter be turned to mourning, and your joy to heaviness. Humble yourselves in the sight of the lord, and he shall lift you up." James 4:7-10.

"Gather yourselves together, yea, gather together, O nation not desired; before the decree bring forth, [death degree] before the day pass as the chaff, before the fierce anger of the Lord come upon you, [7 last plagues] before the day of the Lord's anger come upon you.[close of probation] Seek ye the Lord, all ye meek of the earth, which have wrought his judgment; seek righteousness, seek meekness: it may be ye shall be hid in the day of the Lord's anger." Zephaniah 2:1-3.

I asked the meaning of the shaking I had seen, and was shown that it would be caused by the straight testimony called forth by the counsel of the True Witness to the Laodiceans. This will have its effect upon the heart of the receiver, and will lead him to exalt the standard and pour forth the straight truth. Some will not bear this straight testimony. They will rise up against it, and this will cause a shaking among God's people.

The testimony of the True Witness has not been half heeded. The solemn testimony upon which the destiny of the church hangs has been lightly esteemed, if not entirely disregarded. *This testimony must work deep repentance, and all that truly receive it will obey it and be purified.*

Said the angel: "List ye!" Soon I heard a voice that sounded like many musical instruments, all in perfect strains, sweet and harmonious. It surpassed any music I had ever heard. It seemed to be so full of mercy, compassion, and elevating, holy joy. It thrilled through my whole being. Said the angel: "Look ye!" My attention was then turned to the company I had seen, who were mightily shaken. I was shown those whom I had before seen weeping and praying with agony of spirit. The company of guardian angels around them had been doubled, and they were clothed with an armor from their head to their feet. They moved in exact order, firmly, like a company of soldiers. *Their countenances expressed the severe conflict which they had endured, the agonizing struggle they had passed through. Yet their features, marked with severe internal anguish, now shone with the light and glory of heaven. They had obtained the victory, and it called forth from them the deepest gratitude, and holy, sacred joy.*

The numbers of this company had lessened. Some had been shaken out, and left by the way.[576] *The careless and indifferent, who did not join with those who prized victory and salvation enough to perseveringly plead and agonize for it, did not obtain it, and they were left behind in darkness*, but their numbers were immediately made up by others taking hold of the truth and coming into the ranks. Still the evil angels pressed around them, *but they could have no power over them.*[577]

I heard those clothed with the armor speak forth the truth in great power. It had effect. I saw those who had been bound; some wives had been bound by their husbands, and some children had been bound by their parents. The honest who had been held or prevented from hearing the truth, now eagerly laid hold

---

[576] Ellen White's footnotes, "I know thy works, that thou art neither cold nor hot: I would thou wert cold or hot. So then because thou art lukewarm, and neither cold nor hot, I will spew thee out of my mouth. Because thou sayest, I am rich, and increased with goods, and have need of nothing; and knowest not that thou art wretched, and miserable, and poor, and blind, and naked." Revelation 3:15-17.]

[577] Ellen White's footnotes, "For we wrestle not against flesh and blood, but against principalities, against powers, against the rulers of the darkness of this world, against spiritual wickedness in high places. [Or, "wicked spirits in heavenly places," as in the margin.] Wherefore take unto you the whole armor of God, that ye may be able to withstand in the evil day, and having done all, to stand. Stand therefore, having your loins girt about with truth, and having on the breastplate of righteousness; and your feet shod with the preparation of the gospel of peace; above all, taking the shield of faith, wherewith ye shall be able to quench all the fiery darts of the wicked. And take the helmet of salvation, and the sword of the Spirit, which is the word of God: praying always with all prayer and supplication in the spirit, and watching thereunto with all perseverance and supplication for all saints." Ephesians 6:12-18.

of it. All fear of their relatives was gone. The truth alone was exalted to them. It was dearer and more precious than life. They had been hungering and thirsting for truth. I asked what had made this great change. An angel answered: "It is the latter rain, the refreshing from the presence of the Lord, the loud cry of the third angel."

Great power was with these chosen ones. Said the angel: "Look ye!" My attention was turned to the wicked, or unbelievers. They were all astir. The zeal and power with the people of God had aroused and enraged them. Confusion, confusion was on every side. I saw measures taken against this company, who had the power and light of God. Darkness thickened around them, yet there they stood, *approved of God, and trusting in Him. I saw them perplexed. Next I heard them crying unto God earnestly. Through the day and night their cry ceased not.*[578] I heard these words: "Thy will, O God, be done! *If it can glorify Thy name, make a way of escape for Thy people! Deliver us from the heathen round about us!* They have appointed us unto death; but Thine arm can bring salvation." These are all the words that I can bring to mind. All seemed to have a deep sense of their unworthiness, and *manifested entire submission to the will of God*. Yet like *Jacob*, every one, without an exception, was earnestly pleading and wrestling for deliverance.

Soon after they had commenced their earnest cry, the angels, in sympathy, would have gone to their deliverance. But a tall, commanding angel suffered them not. Said he: "*The will of God is not yet fulfilled. They must drink of the cup. They must be baptized with the baptism.*"[579]

This next quote is taken from the very next chapter called, "The Laodicean Church" in what Inspiration just referenced as "the counsel of the True Witness to the Laodiceans.":

"It is designed to arouse the people of God, to discover to them their backslidings, and to lead to *zealous repentance*, that they may be favored with the presence of Jesus, and be fitted for the loud cry of the third angel. As this message affected *the heart*, it led to *deep humility* before God. . . God will prove His people. *Jesus bears patiently with them, and does not spew them out of His mouth in a moment.* Said the angel: "God is weighing His people." If the message had been of as short duration as many of us supposed, there would have been no time for them to develop character. Many moved from feeling, not from *principle and faith*, and this solemn, fearful message stirred them. It wrought upon their feelings, and excited their fears, but did not accomplish the work which God designed that it should. God reads the heart. Lest His people should be deceived in regard to themselves, He gives them time for the excitement to wear off, and then proves them to see if they will obey the counsel of the True Witness.

---

[578] Ellen White's footnote, "And shall not God avenge his own elect, which cry day and night unto Him, though He bear long with them? I tell you that He will avenge them speedily. *Nevertheless when the Son of man cometh, shall he find faith on the earth*?" Luke 18:7, 8. See also revelation 14:14, 15.
[579] Ellen White, *Testimonies*, 1:179-183. [Emphasis mine]

> "God leads His people on, *step by step*. He brings them up to different points calculated to manifest what is in the heart. Some endure at one point, but fall off at the next. At every advanced point the heart is tested and tried a little closer. If the professed people of God find their hearts opposed to this straight work, it should convince them that they have a work to do to overcome, if they would not be spewed out of the mouth of the Lord. Said the angel: "God will bring His work closer and closer to test and prove every one of His people." Some are willing to receive one point; but when God brings them to another testing point, they shrink from it and stand back, because they find that it strikes directly at some *cherished idol*. Here they have opportunity to see what is in their hearts that shuts out Jesus. They prize something higher than the truth, and their hearts are not prepared to receive Jesus. Individuals are tested and proved a length of time to see if they will *sacrifice their idols* and heed the counsel of the True Witness. If any will not be purified through obeying the truth, and overcome their *selfishness*, their *pride*, and *evil passions*, the angels of God have the charge: "They are joined to *their idols*, let them alone," and they pass on to their work, leaving these with their sinful traits unsubdued, to the control of evil angels. Those who come up to *every point*, and *stand every test*, and *overcome,* be the price what it may, have heeded *the counsel of the True Witness*, and *they will receive the latter rain, and thus be fitted for translation.*"[580]

This last quote is taken from *The Great Controversy*, the chapter entitled, "The Time of Trouble":

> "Now, while our great High Priest is making the atonement for us, we should seek to become perfect in Christ. *Not even by a thought could our Saviour be brought to yield to the power of temptation.* Satan finds in human hearts some point where he can gain a foothold; some sinful desire is cherished, by means of which his temptations assert their power. But Christ declared of Himself: "The prince of this world cometh, and hath nothing in Me." John 14:30. Satan could find nothing in the Son of God that would enable him to gain the victory. He had kept His Father's commandments, and there was no sin in Him that Satan could use to his advantage. *This is the condition in which those must be found who shall stand in the time of trouble.*"[581]

If anyone is feeling discouragement you have not been alone but the story does not end there. Yes, we must confess all our sins and sacrifice all our idols and all rebellion must be eradicated from the heart in order that we would be safe to take to Heaven and receive the latter rain but remember, the good news is, this is not accomplished by trying but by dying:

> "*It is for you to yield up your will to the will of Jesus Christ*; and as you do this, *God will immediately take possession and work in you to will and to do of His good pleasure. Your whole nature will then be brought under*

---
[580] Ellen White, *Testimonies*, 1:186-187. [Emphasis mine]
[581] Ellen White, *The Great Controversy*, 623. [Emphasis mine]

the control of the Spirit of Christ, and even your thoughts will be subject to Him. You cannot control your impulses, your emotions, as you may desire; but you can control the will, and you can make an entire change in your life. By yielding up your will to Christ, your life will be hid with Christ in God and allied to the power which is above all principalities and powers. You will have strength from God that will hold you fast to His strength; and a *new life, even the life of living faith, will be possible to you*. But your will must co-operate with God's will, not with the will of associates through whom Satan is constantly working to ensnare and destroy you."[582]

"*We cannot, of ourselves, conquer the evil desires and habits that strive for the mastery. We cannot overcome the mighty foe who holds us in his thrall. God alone can give us the victory*. He desires us to have the mastery over ourselves, our own will and ways. But He cannot work in us *without our consent and co-operation*. The divine Spirit works through the faculties and powers given to man. Our energies are required to co-operate with God.

The victory is not won without much earnest prayer, without the humbling of self at every step. Our will is not to be forced into co-operation with divine agencies, but it must be voluntarily submitted. Were it possible to force upon you with a hundredfold greater intensity the influence of the Spirit of God, it would not make you a Christian, a fit subject for heaven. The stronghold of Satan would not be broken. The will must be placed on the side of God's will. *You are not able, of yourself, to bring your purposes and desires and inclinations into submission to the will of God*; but if you are "willing to be made willing," *God will accomplish the work for you, even "casting down imaginations, and every high thing that exalteth itself against the knowledge of God, and bringing into captivity every thought to the obedience of Christ*." 2 Corinthians 10:5. Then you will "work out your own salvation with fear and trembling. *For it is God which worketh in you both to will and to do of His good pleasure*." Philippians 2:12, 13. . . *The only hope for us if we would overcome is to unite our will to God's will and work in co-operation with Him, hour by hour and day by day*. We cannot retain *self* and yet enter the kingdom of God. If we ever attain unto holiness, it will be through the *renunciation of self* and the *reception* of the *mind of Christ*. Pride and self-sufficiency must be crucified. Are we willing to pay the price required of us? Are we willing to have our will brought into perfect conformity to the will of God? *Until we are willing, the transforming grace of God cannot be manifest upon us*."[583]

Did you see that when we *rightly* tap into the vine (when we fully surrender our will to Christ) it is then, God, casteth down every high thing and bringing into captivity *every thought* to the obedience of Christ." 2 Corinthians 10:5. I don't know about you but that is *extremely encouraging* to me and I love Him all the more for it!

---

[582] Ellen White, *Testimonies for the Church*, 5:514. [Emphasis mine]
[583] Ellen White, *Thoughts from the Mount of blessing*, 142-3. [Emphasis mine]

Contrary to the teachings of LGT we must remember that when the call to the "solemn assembly" is proclaimed that this will usher in all walks of life that it is in Christ at all different levels in their Christian walk. Jesus is the one that reads each individual heart and brings to light what is manifest in the heart that must be made right. Perhaps He may say to some like the Rich Young Ruler of Matt. 19, just one thing thou lacketh. To others, there may be multiple or even dozens of manifestations, but this is *not* a blanket test, one and for all because this is *not* about "sinlessness perfection." We are tested individually because we all have different strengths and weaknesses, sins and idols and or depraved habits or passions that need sacrificed. Or we may yet need to fully die to self, but each and every one of us will know if we are sincere in our endeavor of what will be required. Christ entreats all by announcing:

> ". . . I have no pleasure in the death of the wicked; but that the wicked turn from his way and live: turn ye, turn ye from your evil ways; for why will ye die, O house of Israel?" Eze. 33:11

> "To open their eyes, *and* to turn *them* from darkness to light, and *from* the power of Satan unto God, that they may receive forgiveness of sins, and inheritance among them which are sanctified by faith that is in me." Acts 26:18

The rich young ruler of Matt. 19 consented to turn 170^0 but was it enough? No! We must all turn a full 180^0 because in this race it's all or nothing. If he was to be *perfect* as Jesus had said, it was *not* in the act of selling all that he had but it was first and foremost in the *motive* that would precipitate the act. And what was that? Inspiration rightly connected the dots when she said:

> ". . . His supreme love of self must be *surrendered*."[584]

"That he might receive the love of God." Yes, perfection only comes about from a heart that is completely and fully *surrendered* to Christ, and then we receive His *perfect* robe of righteousness! We never earn anything, it's a gift! Remember perfection is obtained not by doing but by dying:

> "There are many who try to reform by correcting this or that bad habit, and they hope in this way to become Christians, but they are beginning in the wrong place. Our first work is with the *heart*."[585]

Can the leopard change his spots; can we which are accustom to do evil do that which is good? Nay. So what is our part we must undertake when we *turn* back to the Lord:

> "The part we have to act is to *return* unto the Lord by confessing our sins to him and to one another. A broken and contrite heart he will not despise; but our self-righteousness is in his sight as filthy rags. *With many, self is whole*; but when they *fall upon the Rock, and are broken*, then the arms of Jesus will encircle them, and bind them close to his great heart of love. God will not do for us that which

---

[584] Ellen White, *The Desire of Ages*, 519. [Emphasis mine]
[585] Ellen White, *Christ Object Lessons* 97.

we can do for ourselves. But he has said: "Seek ye the Lord while he may be found, call ye upon him while he is near. Let the wicked forsake his way, and the unrighteous man his thoughts; and let him *return* unto the Lord, and he will have mercy upon him; and to our God, for he will abundantly pardon." And when we comply with the conditions, he will fulfill his word."[586]

When we turn a full 180^0 in submission to Christ, Inspiration is clear that all who partake of the "solemn assembly" and allow this agonizing purification process to proceed to fruition will receive of the latter rain and thus be fitted for translation!

> "The season of distress and anguish before us will require a *faith* that can endure weariness, delay, and hunger--a faith that will not faint though severely tried. The period of probation is granted to all to prepare for that time. Jacob prevailed because he was persevering and determined. His victory is an evidence of the power of importunate prayer. *All who will lay hold of God's promises, as he did, and be as earnest and persevering as he was, will succeed as he succeeded.* Those who are unwilling to deny self, to agonize before God, to pray long and earnestly for His blessing, will not obtain it. *Wrestling with God--how few know what it is! How few have ever had their souls drawn out after God with intensity of desire until every power is on the stretch. When waves of despair which no language can express sweep over the supplicant, how few cling with unyielding faith to the promises of God.*"[587]

It is undoubtedly at this juncture we will witness the fulfillment of this prediction before our very eyes:

> "As we near the close of this earth's history, we either rapidly advance in Christian growth, or we rapidly retrograde toward the world."[588]

Throughout the entire writings of Ellen White there are only *two Biblical types* she referenced specifically to describe the experiences and intense circumstances to confront the "faith" of the final generation/144,000. One illustration is "Jacob" as depicted in; *Patriarchs and Prophets* under the chapter titled "The Night of Wrestling" along with *The Great Controversy* under the chapter titled, "The Time of Trouble". The other is "Joshua And The Angel" as depicted in *Testimonies* 5:467-476 as her primary sources with other bits and pieces throughout her writings. Notice the unmistakable language Inspiration uses depicting the final generation/144,000, designating time and place of subject:

> "Zechariah's vision of Joshua and the Angel applies with peculiar force to the experience of God's people in the closing up of the great day of atonement."[589]

---

[586] Ellen White, *Review & Herald*, May 20, 1884. [Emphasis mine]
[587] Ellen White, *The Great Controversy*, 621.
[588] Ellen White, *Review & Herald*, December 13, 1892.
[589] Ellen White, *Testimonies*, 5:472.

Continuing from the same source as we consider the issues said to confront the final generation/144,000:

> "But while we should realize our sinful condition, we are to rely upon Christ as *our righteousness, our sanctification, and our redemption. We cannot answer the charges of Satan against us*. Christ alone can make an effectual plea in our behalf. He is able to silence the accuser with arguments founded *not upon our merits, but on His own*. Yet we should *never be content with a sinful life*."[590]

Ellen White says "*We cannot answer the charges of Satan against us.*" LGT says we can! Whose voice do you follow? It is of the utmost necessity to first understand just what Satan's charges are before we proceed because this quotation is to prove far more enlightening than a first reading may provide:

> "Will God banish me [Satan] and my angels from His presence, *and yet reward those who have been guilty of the same sins? Thou canst not do this, O Lord, in justice. Thy throne will not stand in righteousness and judgment. Justice demands that sentence be pronounced against them*."
>
> But while the followers of Christ have sinned, *they have not given themselves to the control of evil*. They have *put away their sins*, and have sought the Lord in *humility* and *contrition*, and the divine Advocate pleads in their behalf. He who has been most abused by their ingratitude, who knows their sin, and *also* their repentance, declares: '"The Lord rebuke thee, O Satan."[591]

If we are guilty of the same sins as Satan and his angels how could Christ be justified in rebuking Satan?

> "But even as a sinner, man was in a different position from that of Satan. Lucifer in heaven had sinned in the light of God's glory. To him as to no other created being was given a revelation of God's love. Understanding the character of God, knowing His goodness, Satan chose to follow his own selfish, independent will. This choice was final. There was no more that God could do to save him. *But man was deceived; his mind was darkened by Satan's sophistry. The height and depth of the love of God he did not know. For him there was hope in a knowledge of God's love. By beholding His character he might be drawn back to God.*"[592]

How beautiful was that! Returning to where we left off. Satan is forcefully declaring their sins and his are one and of the same magnitude, thus deserving of the same fate and obviously the final generation/144,000 have proven nothing as they rely solely on the merits of Christ for their *righteousness, sanctification, and redemption and perfection*. Then in turn the Lord rebukes

---

[590] Ibid. 472. [Emphasis mine]
[591] Ibid. 474. [Emphasis mine]
[592] Ellen White, *The Desire of Ages*, 761-2. [Emphasis mine]

Satan and points to their *genuine repentance* and *turning from sin* that gave them the *victory*. This is confirmed by Ellen White:

> "Their contrition and self-abasement are infinitely more acceptable in the sight of God than is the *self-sufficient*, haughty spirit of those who see no cause to lament, who scorn the humility of Christ, and who claim *perfection* while transgressing God's holy law. *Meekness and lowliness of heart are the conditions for strength and victory.*"[593]

Yet there is another class who do not receive of the latter rain and Inspiration is exceptionally forthright of why this class of people have failed in obtaining the victory:

> "Christ has promised the gift of the Holy Spirit to His church, and the promise belongs to us as much as to the first disciples. But like every other promise, it is given on *conditions*. There are many who believe and profess to claim the Lord's promise; they talk about Christ and about the Holy Spirit, yet receive no benefit. *They do not surrender the soul to be guided and controlled by the divine agencies.* We cannot use the Holy Spirit. The Spirit is to use us. Through the Spirit God works in His people "*to will and to do of His good pleasure.*" Philippians 2:13. But many will not submit to this. They want to manage themselves. *This is why they do not receive the heavenly gift.* Only to those who wait humbly upon God, who watch for His guidance and grace, is the Spirit given. The power of God awaits their demand and reception."[594]

> "But we must have a knowledge of ourselves, a knowledge that will result in contrition, before we can find pardon and peace."[595]

This brings us to the climax of those who entered into the "solemn assembly" of Joel 2 when the crisis was upon them. We want to know *precisely* what gave them "the victory, that called forth from them the deepest gratitude, and holy, sacred joy." Is it in the performance of "sinlessness perfection" as advocated by LGT? Ellen White answers in robust clarity:

> "Had not Jacob previously repented of his sin in obtaining the birthright by fraud, God could not have heard his prayer and mercifully preserved his life. So in the time of trouble, if the people of God had unconfessed sins to appear before them while tortured with fear and anguish, they would be overwhelmed; *despair would cut off their faith*, and they could not have confidence to plead with God for deliverance. But while they have a deep sense of their unworthiness, they will have no concealed wrongs to reveal. Their sins will have been blotted out by the atoning blood of Christ, and they cannot bring them to remembrance. . . .
> All who endeavor to excuse or conceal their sins, and permit them to remain upon the books of heaven, unconfessed and unforgiven, will be overcome by

---

[593] Ellen White, *Testimonies*, 5:475. [Emphasis mine]
[594] Ellen White, *The Desire of Ages*, 672. [Emphasis mine]
[595] Ellen White, *Christ Object Lessons*, 158.

Satan. The more exalted their profession, and the more honorable the position which they hold, the more grievous is their course in the sight of God, and the more certain the triumph of the great adversary.

Yet Jacob's history is an assurance that God will not cast off those who have been betrayed into sin, but who have returned unto Him with true repentance. It was by *self-surrender and confiding faith* that Jacob gained what he had failed to gain by conflict in his own strength. *God thus taught His servant that divine power and grace alone could give him the blessing he craved. Thus it will be with those who live in the last days.* As dangers surround them, and *despair seizes upon the soul, they must depend solely upon the merits of the atonement. . . . None will ever perish while they do this. . . .*

Jacob prevailed because he was persevering and determined. . . . It is now that we are to learn this lesson of *prevailing prayer*, of *unyielding faith*. The greatest victories to the church of Christ or to the individual Christian are not those that are gained by talent or education, by wealth or the favor of men. They are those victories that are gained in the audience chamber with God, when earnest, agonizing *faith* lays hold upon the mighty arm of power."[596]

It was by *self-surrender and confiding faith*, not sinlessness perfection:

"The Angel urges, "Let Me go, for the day breaketh;" but the patriarch exclaims, "I will not let Thee go, except Thou bless me." What confidence, what firmness and perseverance, are here displayed! *Had this been a boastful, presumptuous claim, Jacob would have been instantly destroyed*; but his was the *assurance* of one who *confesses his weakness* and *unworthiness*, yet trusts the *mercy* of a covenant-keeping God.

"He had power over the Angel, and prevailed." Hosea 12:4. Through *humiliation*, *repentance*, and *self-surrender*, this sinful, erring mortal *prevailed with the Majesty of heaven*. He had fastened his trembling grasp upon the *promises of God, and the heart of Infinite Love could not turn away the sinner's plea*. As an evidence of his triumph and an encouragement to others to imitate his example, his name was changed from one which was a reminder of his sin, *to one that commemorated his victory*. And the fact that *Jacob had prevailed with God was an assurance that he would prevail with men. He no longer feared to encounter his brother's anger, for the Lord was his defence.*"[597] . . . "Their *only hope* is in the *mercy of God*; their *only defence* will be *prayer*."[598]

"We are to kindle our taper at the divine altar; it is to lay our souls before Him *in surrender as did Jacob*. Let *His will prevail*, and then you will have in your hearts a *living connection with God*, and you can tell of Christ to those around you. And you will do this, for you cannot hold your peace."[599]

---

[596] Ellen White, *Conflict and Courage*, 69. [Emphasis mine]
[597] Ellen White, *The Great Controversy*, 617-8. [Emphasis mine]
[598] Ellen White, *Testimonies*, 5:473. [Emphasis mine]
[599] Ellen White, *Sermons and Talks*, 2:51. [Emphasis mine]

As an "encouragement to others to imitate his [Jacob's] example" Inspiration takes us behind the scenes of just how Jacob and others prevailed with the Almighty throughout history and Oh what an encouragement this is for us:

> "*It was Christ* Himself who put into that mother's heart [Luke 18:1-8] the *persistence which would not be repulsed. It was Christ* who gave the pleading widow *courage and determination* before the judge. *It was Christ* who, centuries before, in the mysterious conflict by the Jabbok, had inspired *Jacob* with the same *persevering faith*. And the *confidence which He Himself had implanted, He did not fail to reward.*"[600]

Was that not a whopping truck load of encouragement just dumped at your front door? Wow! Yes, there are giants to overcome as we have all well known in order to possess the land of Canaan but we *can* overcome them! If God Almighty is with us who can be against us! Again, we have nothing to fear providing we follow our Lord's gospel to the very letter. This represents a similar experience that the Lord has prepared for the final generation/144,000 of those that love Him that will soon be gathered together in the solemn assembly of Joel chapter 2 if they walk by "faith" doubting nothing when the Lord "will do great things" Joel 2:21. Through much prayer, humiliation, repentance, and self-surrender, sinful mortals prevailed with the Majesty of Heaven. Having prevailed with God they received the latter rain and was assured that they would prevail with men. They no longer feared to encounter the world's anger, for the Lord was their defence.

> "I was shown those whom I had before seen weeping and praying with agony of spirit. The company of guardian angels around them had been doubled, and they were clothed with an armor from their head to their feet. They moved in exact order, firmly, like a company of soldiers. *Their countenances expressed the severe conflict which they had endured, the agonizing struggle they had passed through.* Yet their features, marked with severe internal anguish, *now shone with the light and glory of heaven.* They had *obtained the victory*, and it called forth from them the *deepest gratitude, and holy, sacred joy.*"[601]

> "Words cannot describe the peace and joy possessed by him who takes God at His word. Trials do not disturb him, slights do not vex him. Self is crucified."[602]

However they have yet to encounter the "fires of affliction" they have yet to "drink of the cup" and "be baptized with the baptism" of Gethsemane. Like Jacob, they have yet to encounter the mob bent on their destruction:

> "Great power was with these chosen ones. Said the angel: "Look ye!" My attention was turned to the wicked, or unbelievers. They were all astir. The

---

[600] Ellen White *Christ Object Lessons*, 175. [Emphasis mine]
[601] Ellen White, *Testimonies*, 1:181-2. [Emphasis mine]
[602] Ellen White, *Messages to Young People*, 98.

zeal and power with the people of God had aroused and enraged them. Confusion, confusion was on every side. I saw measures taken against this company, who had the power and light of God. Darkness thickened around them, yet there they stood, approved of God, and trusting in Him. I saw them perplexed. Next I heard them crying unto God earnestly. Through the day and night their cry ceased not.[603] I heard these words: *"Thy will, O God, be done*! If it can glorify Thy name, make a way of escape for Thy people! Deliver us from the heathen round about us! They have appointed us unto death; but Thine arm can bring salvation." These are all the words that I can bring to mind. All seemed to have a deep sense of their unworthiness, and *manifested entire submission to the will of God.* Yet like *Jacob*, every one, without an exception, was earnestly pleading and wrestling for deliverance.

Soon after they had commenced their earnest cry, the angels, in sympathy, would have gone to their deliverance. But a tall, commanding angel suffered them not. Said he: *"The will of God is not yet fulfilled. They must drink of the cup. They must be baptized with the baptism."*[604]

With the close of probation comes what Inspiration calls "the time of trouble" or "Jacob's time of trouble." Then the focus will be solely on the 144,000 and their Gethsemane experience that we just read. They, like Christ in Gethsemane expressed the struggle that raged within:

"Then saith he unto them, My soul is exceeding sorrowful. . ." Matt. 26:38.

Inspiration relates:

"His soul agony. . . convulsed all heaven. They saw their Lord inclosed by legions of Satanic forces, his human nature weighed down with a shuddering, mysterious dread. Everywhere he may look is a horror of great darkness beyond the measurement of human minds. And there was silence in heaven; no harp was touched. Could mortals have viewed the amazement of the angelic host as they watched in silent grief the Father separating his beams of light, love, and glory, from the beloved Son, they would better understand how offensive sin is in his sight."[605]

Not yet had Christ consented to endure rigged courts, false witnesses, unjust scourging's and the cross as Osgood[606] so elegantly illustrated that I will glean from. No one could force Him to take punishment He did not deserve:

---

[603] "And shall not God avenge his own elect, which cry day and night unto Him, though he bear long with them? I tell you that He will avenge them speedily. Nevertheless when the Son of man cometh, shall he find faith on the earth?" Luke 18:7, 8. See also Revelation 14:14, 15.
[604] Ellen White, *Testimonies*, 1:183. [Emphasis mine]
[605] Ellen White, *Signs of the Times*, December 9, 1897.
[606] De Witt S. Osgood, *Preparing for the Latter Rain*, (Ukiah, CA; Orion Publishing, 2005) 51-52.

"And he went a little further, and fell on his face, and prayed, saying, O my Father, <u>if it be possible, let this cup pass from me</u>: nevertheless <u>not as I will, but as thou *wilt*</u>. Matt. 26:39.

"He felt himself becoming separated from his Father by a gulf of sin, so broad, so black, so deep, that his spirit shuddered before it. He clung convulsively to the cold, unfeeling ground, as if to prevent himself from being drawn still farther from God. The chilling dews of night fell upon his prostrate form, but the Redeemer heeded it not. From his pale, convulsed lips wailed the bitter cry, "*O my Father, if it be possible, let this cup pass from me; nevertheless not as I will, but as thou wilt*. It was not dread of the physical suffering that he was so soon to endure, that brought this agony upon the Son of God. He was suffering the penalty of man's transgression, and shuddering beneath his Father's frown. He must not call his divinity to his aid, but, as a man, he must bear the consequences of man's sin, and the Creator's displeasure toward a disobedient subject."[607]

He recoiled as He experienced the black gulf encircling Him and the rays of Infinite Love being retracted from his soul:

"He went away again the second time, and prayed, saying, O my Father, <u>if this cup may not pass away from me, except I drink it, thy will be done</u>." Matt. 26:42.

"And prayed the third time saying the same words." Matt. 26: 44.

"If it be possible," how Christ anguished plea pierced the heart of Infinite Love! But no answer came from the skies as at His baptism. God's silence told the suffering Saviour, "Impossible!"

In the garden there were two wills, the Father's and the Son's. Would Jesus refuse the cup or offer the Father a *surrendered will*:

"There was the hiding of the Father's face from his dear Son. Humanity staggered and trembled in that trying hour. It was anguish of soul beyond the endurance of finite nature. It was woe condensed that brought from the trembling lips of the noble sufferer these words: "Now is my soul troubled." "O my Father, if it be possible, let this cup pass from me; *nevertheless, not as I will, but as thou wilt*." Again from his pale lips are heard these words: "O my Father, if this cup may not pass away from me, except I drink it, *thy will be done*." *The awful moment had come which was to decide the destiny of the world*. Angels are waiting and watching with intense interest.

The fate of the world is trembling in the balance. The Son of God may even now refuse to drink the cup apportioned to guilty man. He may wipe the blood sweat from his brow, and leave the world to perish in their iniquity Will the Son of the infinite God drink the cup of humiliation and agony? Will the innocent suffer the curse of God to save the guilty? It was here the mysterious

---
[607] Ellen White, *Review & Herald*, October 9, 1888. [Emphasis mine]

cup trembled in his hand, and the destiny of a ruined world was balanced. The world's Redeemer sees that the transgressors of his Father's law must perish under his displeasure. He sees the power of sin and the *utter helplessness of man to save himself.*

The woes and lamentations of a doomed world come up before him, and *his decision is made. He will save man at any cost of himself.* He has *accepted his baptism of blood*, that perishing millions through him might gain everlasting life."[608]

The surrendered will constitutes the supreme test of obedience! The surrendered will constitutes Christ perfection being imputed to us! Gethsemane's crisis is past; our Gethsemane's crisis is yet future. There are two wills, Christ and ours. Will we refuse the cup or offer Christ a *surrendered will*? Here lies the essence of *victory* for the final generation/144,000.

This then brings us to our next word study.

"Those that *overcome* the *world*, the *flesh*, and the *devil*. . ." [609]

Overcome the **Devil**! Scripture delineates the primary definition below but the 144,000 also overcome the devil during Jacob's time of trouble without seeing death:

"Every martyr of Jesus has died a conqueror. Says the prophet, *"They overcame him* ["*that old serpent, called the devil, and Satan*"] *by the blood of the Lamb, and by the word of their testimony; and they loved not their lives unto the death."* Revelation 12:11, 9."[610]

"Satan endeavors to terrify them with the thought that their cases are hopeless, that the stain of their defilement will never be washed away. *He hopes so to destroy their faith that they will yield to his temptations and turn from their allegiance to God.*"[611]

And our last word study:

Overcome the **World**! We all know the following text well:

"Love not the world, neither the things *that are* in the world. If any man love the world, the love of the Father is not in him." 1John 2:15

However, this does not reflect the real meaning Inspiration is conveying to which the 144,000 are to be subjected to. Here is a text suited to her intended meaning of *overcoming the world*:

---

[608] Ellen White, *Signs of the Times*, August 14, 1879. [Emphasis mine]
[609] Ellen White, *Testimonies to Ministers*, 445. [Emphasis mine].
[610] Ellen White, *Patriarchs and Prophets*, 77 [Brackets in the original] [Emphasis mine]
[611] Ellen White, *The Great Controversy*, 619. [Emphasis mine]

> "For whatsoever is born of God overcometh the world: and this is the victory that overcometh the world, *even* our faith." 1 John 5:4.

And with that our "faith" will be tried to the uttermost:

> "And ye shall be hated of all men for my name's sake: but he that shall endure unto the end, the same shall be saved." Matt. 13:13.

Since the majority of Seventh-day Adventist are going to go out[612] and those that come out of the world are the very ones that are going to come in. Heaven has a proven process for all "that the image of Christ may be perfectly reflected" in them as well before His second coming. Please notice again in the sequence of events when this image of Christ is to be perfectly reflected contrary to popular belief of LGT as the flames of affliction from persecuting world-lings are about to consume them. Satan's allurements of the world hold no attractions to the followers of Christ so now Satan turns the world against them with his entire detestation known only to the prince of darkness to force them to renounce their "faith":

> "*Jacob's history* is also an assurance that God will not cast off those who have been deceived and tempted and betrayed into sin, but who have returned unto Him with true repentance. While Satan seeks to destroy this class, God will send His angels to comfort and protect them in the time of peril. The assaults of Satan are fierce and determined, his delusions are terrible; but the Lord's eye is upon His people, and His ear listens to their cries. Their affliction is great, *the flames of the furnace seem about to consume them*; but the Refiner will bring them forth as *gold tried in the fire*. God's love for His children during the period of their *severest trial* is as strong and tender as in the days of their sunniest prosperity; but it is needful for them to be placed in the *furnace of fire; their earthliness* [fires of affliction] *must be consumed, that the image of Christ may be perfectly reflected.*"[613]

Nevertheless we must remember the Saviors promise when all must stand without a mediator:

> "I will keep thee from the hour of temptation, which shall come upon all the world." Revelation 3:10."[614]

Now Satan turns the tables around, instead of focusing on the enticements of the world, he now turns the world against the church as we illustrate as best as human language allows the intensity of the conflict the final generation/144,000 are to be confronted with:

---

[612] Ellen White, *The Great Controversy*, 608.
[613] Ellen White, *The Great Controversy*, 621. [Emphasis mine].
[614] Ellen White, *The Great Controversy*, 619.

> "As the defenders of truth refuse to honor the Sunday-sabbath, some of them will be thrust into prison, some will be exiled, some will be treated as slaves. To human wisdom all this now seems impossible; but as the restraining Spirit of God shall be withdrawn from men, and they shall be under the control of Satan, who hates the divine precepts, *there will be strange developments. The heart can be very cruel when God's fear and love are removed.*"[615]

The cruelty that is then to confront the final generation/144,000 from Satan's arsenal in order to force them to renounce their "faith" will come about from the "strange developments" that has been no stranger to Satan. Nevertheless, the final generation/144,000 remember the words of their Captain as the "cords" are being let down in their behalf.

We have been amply warned of what we are to encounter under the loud cry but many like the disciples have turned a deaf ear when Jesus said to His disciples again and again in so many words, I am going to Jerusalem to be crucified. Words they did not want to hear and did not retain and it left them totally unprepared for their hour of temptation and nearly destroyed their "faith." Remember, to be forewarned is to be forearmed:

> Rev. 20:4 "And I saw thrones, and they sat upon them, and judgment was given unto them: and *I saw* the souls of them that were beheaded for the witness of Jesus, and for the word of God, and which had not worshipped the beast, neither his image, neither had received *his* mark upon their foreheads, or in their hands; and they lived and reigned with Christ a thousand years."

> "Christ warned his disciples in regard to what they would meet in their work as evangelists. He knew what their sufferings would be, what trials and hardships they would be called upon to bear. He would not hide from them the knowledge of what they would have to encounter, lest trouble, coming unexpectedly, should shake their faith. 'I have told you before it come to pass,' he said, 'that, when it is come to pass, ye might believe.' Their faith was to be strengthened, rather than weakened, by the coming of trial. They would say to one another, "He told us that this would come, and what we must do to meet it."[616]

> "We have a living Saviour, and he has not left us in the world to fight the battles alone. No, but He has not flattered us (either).... He tells us.... "that whosoever killeth you will think that he doeth God service" (John 16:12)

> This is a terrible deception that comes upon the human mind. *But here He has shown you the plan of the battle. He tells you what you are to meet*: "We wrestle not against flesh and blood, but against principalities, against powers,

---

[615] Ellen White, *The Great Controversy*, 608. [Emphasis mine]
[616] Ellen White, *Review and Herald*, April 20, 1911.

against the rulers of the darkness of this world, against wickedness in high places" (Ephesians 6:12)[617]

"At the *eleventh hour* the Lord will call into his service many faithful workers. Self-sacrificing men and women will step into the places made *vacant by apostasy and death*. To *young men* and *young women*, as well as to those who are *older*, God will give power from above. With converted minds, converted hands, converted feet, and converted tongues, *their lips touched with a living coal from the divine altar*, they will go forth into the Master's service, moving steadily onward and upward, *carrying the work forward to completion*."[618]

"We need not be surprised at anything that may take place now. We need not marvel at any developments of horror. Those who trample under their unholy feet the law of God have the same spirit as had the men who insulted and betrayed Jesus. Without any compunctions of conscience they will do the deeds of their father the devil."[619]

"Many will fall at their post, betrayed and condemned by their fellowmen."[620]

"The two armies will stand distinct and separate, and this distinction will be so marked that many who shall be convinced of the truth will come on the side of God's commandment-keeping people. When this grand work is to take place in the battle, prior to the last closing conflict, many will be imprisoned, many will flee for their lives from cities and towns, and many will be martyrs for Christ's sake in standing in defense of the truth."[621]

"How much of evil would be averted, if all, when falsely accused, would avoid recrimination, and in its stead employ mild, conciliating words."[622]

Lest we fail to mention and be blindsided here as well, we must unmask a myth that declares after the latter rain has fallen there will be no more martyrdom. That supposition is totally false. Inspiration has clearly spelled it out in *Early Writings,* 279, the seal of protection of Rev. 7:1-4 and Eze. 9:1-6 as described in *Early Writings* 71, does not take place until *after* the latter rain *after* the loud cry of Rev. 18:1-5 when the third angel's message is closing, just before the close of probation, just before the falling of the seven last plagues. It is only after the close of

---

[617] Ellen White, *Ms* 49, 1894. [Emphasis mine]
[618] Ellen White, *Youth Instructor*, February 13, 1902. [Emphasis mine]
[619] Ellen White, *Selected Messages*, 3:416.
[620] Ellen White, *Letter*, 230, 1907.
[621] Ellen White, *Selected Messages*, 3:397.
[622] Ellen White, *Signs of the Times*, May 12, 1881.

probation that God will not allow anymore martyrdom for this is a heaven-ordained method to vindicate the truth and convince others of the truth:

> "If the blood of Christ's faithful witnesses were shed at this time, [during the seven last plagues] it would not, like the blood of the martyrs, be as seed sown to yield a harvest for God. Their fidelity would not be a testimony to convince others of the truth; for the obdurate heart has beaten back the waves of mercy until they return no more. If the righteous were now left to fall a prey to their enemies, it would be a triumph for the prince of darkness."[623]

> "Whenever persecution takes place, the spectators make decisions either for or against Christ."[624]

> "There is no necessity for thinking that we cannot endure persecution; we shall have to go through terrible times."[625]

For the sake of clarification again, this means we may call all probationers who have received of the latter rain may rightly be called the "final generation." Those probationers yet living when the seal[626] of God (Eze. 9:1-6) is being administered that have not experienced death when probation closes may rightly be called the 144,000 and they will be alive to see the glorious second coming of Christ in all His glory and in the glory of His Father!

In my years of research I have come across some of the most amazing finds. There is one infamous find that stands out far and above all others. I came across this when I was researching in the archives of Nazi and papal documents pertaining to the ties between the Catholic Church and the Third Reich of the Nazi regime in relation to the Jews. Also the capitulation of the Protestant churches to the Third Reich and their aftermath. From that research it became evident, without dispute from the primary sources that the origin of antisemitism against the Jews rest solely with the Roman Catholic Church. She is fully responsible through her smear campaigns of hate and through her councils, bulls and anti-Jewish polemics even among the legal codes of the barbarians that converted to Catholicism to restrict and demonize the Jews. It then resonated with me when I recalled two statements from Inspiration that I had read previously that now demanded a better look behind the scenes. I share this because many are truly delusional of what an enemy we are so soon to confront that never fatigues. A enemy that boast it "never changes" and will be relentless to bring about our destruction in that we forsake our "faith" and let go of the arm of the Almighty. The only thing glorious about the second coming is the second coming! All prophesied events just prior to the second coming will be nothing short of a horror show. The two quotes I referenced provided below pertain to the Jews and the Seventh-day Adventist:

---

[623] Ellen White, *Great Controversy*, 634.
[624] Ellen White, *Review & Herald*, December 20, 1898.
[625] Ellen White, *Review & Herald*, December 20, 1898.
[626] See my book, Heidi Heiks, *King of the Noth* (Teach Services, 2009), for a Biblical understanding of the three sealing's of the saints. An exposition of Daniel 11:40 – 12:1.

> "Misled by the false statements of Haman, Xerxes was induced to issue a decree providing for the massacre of all the Jews "scattered abroad and dispersed among the people in all the provinces" of the Medo-Persian kingdom. Verse 8. A certain day was appointed on which the Jews were to be destroyed and their property confiscated. Little did the king realize the far-reaching results that would have accompanied the complete carrying out of this decree. *Satan himself, the hidden instigator of the scheme, was trying to rid the earth of those who preserved the knowledge of the true God.*"[627]

However, when the Jewish nation rejected Christ they were met with a perpetual curse:

> "Barabbas, the robber and murderer, was the representative of Satan. Christ was the representative of God. Christ had been rejected; Barabbas had been chosen. Barabbas they were to have. In making this choice they accepted him who from the beginning was a liar and a murderer. Satan was their leader. As a nation they would act out his dictation. His works they would do. His rule they must endure. *That people who chose Barabbas in the place of Christ were to feel the cruelty of Barabbas as long as time should last. . . . a perpetual curse*"[628]

Seventh-day Adventist at large had no idea that when they joined this church they had enlisted as soldiers to be sent straight to the front lines in a moment's notice:

> "The whole world is to be stirred with enmity against Seventh-day Adventists, because they will not yield homage to the papacy, by honoring Sunday, the institution of this antichristian power. *It is the purpose of Satan to cause them to be blotted from the earth, in order that his supremacy of the world may not be disputed.*"[629]

Will we buckle under the enormous pressure that is so soon to confront us? That depends, wholly upon our foundation. Will we still be arguing and promoting a gospel that provides no victory for the recipient? Or will we unify and present to the world a message of hope that brings peace to the inner man? It is now left with each and every one of us as to which procession we now enlist under!

Satan has and will use means little dreamed of among God's people, methods most insurmountable. Incidentally As illustrated in my *King of the North* book the four prophetic steps Satan takes against God's people at the end of time that Ellen White saw and recorded. She noted the escalating severity of the methods to be used against them to compel them to forsake their allegiance to Jesus. Ironically, it was *the same four steps, in the same chronological order used*

---

[627] Ellen White, *Prophets and Kings*, 600-601. [Emphasis mine]
[628] Ellen White, *The Desire of Ages*, 739. [Emphasis mine]
[629] Ellen White, *Testimonies to Ministers*, 37. [Emphasis mine]

against the Jews in Nazi Germany that is to be used by Satan *again* in his last *final solution* attempt against the church. "Hate" will have a new defined meaning among the 144,000 before the second coming, just as it has with the Jews.

Hitler was fully aware of the hundreds of years of persecution, hate and oppression of the German Jews. He also knew that it would be clever politics to appeal to the general mood of anti-Semitism which was always encouraged during this period anyway. On the occasion of the negotiations with the Vatican for the Concordat in 1933 Hitler traced:

> "His anti-Semitism to the Catholic Church, which had also always considered the Jews as pests and which because of the moral dangers involved had forbidden Christians to work for Jews. For this reason the Church banished the Jews to the ghetto."[630]

All too well the German people had learned the lessons of intolerance, cruelty and torture which Rome had so diligently taught:

Papal and Nazi Anti-Jewish Legislation

CANONICAL LAW	NAZI MEASURE
Prohibition of intermarriage and of sexual intercourse between Christians and Jews, Synod of Elvira, 306	Law for the Protection of German Blood and Honor, September 15, 1935 (RGB1 I, 1146.)
Jews and Christians not permitted to eat together, Synod of Elvira, 306	Jews barred from dining cars (Transport Minister to Interior Minister, December 30, 1939, Document NG-3995.)
Jews not allowed to hold public office, Synod of Clermont, 535	Law for the Re-establishment of the Professional Civil Service, April 7, 1933 (RGB1 I, 175.)

---

[630] (From the minutes of June 7, 1933, on the conference which had taken place on April 26, 1933, between Bishop Dr. Bermig, General Vicar Prelate Dr. Steinmann, and Hitler, quoted by F. J. Raddatz in "Summa iniuria oder durfte der Papst schweigen?" Rowohlt, 1963).

Jews not allowed to employ Christian servants or possess Christian slaves, 3d Synod of Orleans, 538	Law for the Protection of German Blood and Honor, September 15, 1935 (RGB1 I, 1146.)
Jews not permitted to show themselves in the streets during Passion Week, 3d Synod of Orleans, 538	Decree authorizing local authorities to bar Jews from the streets on certain days (i.e., Nazi holidays), December 3, 1938 (RGB1 I, 1676.)
Burning of the Talmud and other books, 12th Synod of Toledo, 681	Book burnings in Nazi Germany
Christians not permitted to patronize Jewish doctors, Trulanic Synod, 692	Decree of July 25, 1938 (RGB1 I, 969.)
Christians not permitted to live in Jewish homes, Synod of Narbonne, 1050	Directive by Göring providing for concentration of Jews in houses, December 28, 1938 (Borman to Rosenberg, January 17, 1939, PS-69.)
Jews obliged to pay taxes for support of the Church to the same extent as Christians, Synod of Gerona, 1078	The "Sozialausgleichsabgabe" which provided that Jews pay a special income tax in lieu of donations for Party purposes imposed on Nazis, December 24, 1940 (RGB1 I, 1666.)
Prohibition of Sunday work, Synod of Szabolcs, 1092	

Jews not permitted to be plaintiffs, or witnesses against Christians in the Courts, 3d Lateran Council, 1179, Canon 26	Proposal by the Party Chancellery that Jews not be permitted to institute civil suits, September 9, 1942 (Bormann to Justice Ministry, September 9, 1942, NG-151.)
Jews not permitted to withhold inheritance from descendants who had accepted Christianity, 3d Lateran Council, 1179, Canon 26	Decree empowering the Justice Ministry to void wills offending the "sound judgment of the people," July 31, 1938 (RGB1 I, 937.)
The marking of Jewish clothes with a badge, 4th Lateran Council, 1215, Canon 68 (Copied from the legislation by Caliph Omar II [634-44], who had decreed that Christians wear blue belts and Jews, yellow belts.)	Decree of September 1, 1941 (RGB1 I, 547.)
Construction of new synagogues prohibited, Council of Oxford, 1222	Destruction of synagogues in entire Reich, November 10, 1938 (Heydrich to Göring, November 11, 1938, PS-3058.)
Christians not permitted to attend Jewish ceremonies, Synod of Vienna, 1267	Friendly relations with Jews prohibited, October 24, 1941 (Gestapo directive, L-15.)
Jews not permitted to dispute with simple Christian people about the tenets of the Catholic religion, Synod of Vienna, 1267	
Compulsory ghettos, Synod of Breslau, 1267	Order by Heydrich, September 21, 1939 (PS-3363.)

Christians not permitted to sell or rent real estate to Jews, Synod of Ofen, 1279	Decree providing for compulsory sale of Jewish real estate, December 3, 1938 (RGB1 I, 1709.)
Adoption by a Christian of the Jewish religion or return by a baptized Jew to the Jewish religion defined as a heresy, Synod of Mainz, 1310	Adoption by a Christian of the Jewish religion places him in jeopardy of being treated as a Jew, Decision by Oberlandesgericht Königsberg, 4th Zivilsenat, June 26, 1942 (*Die Judenfrage [Vertrauliche Beilage]*, November 1, 1942, pp. 82-83.)
Sale or transfer of Church articles to Jews prohibited, Synod of Lavour, 1368	
Jews not permitted to act as agents in the conclusion of contracts between Christians, especially marriage contracts, Council of Basel, 1434, Sessio XIX	Decree of July 6, 1938, providing for liquidation of Jewish real estate agencies, brokerage agencies, and marriage agencies catering to non-Jewish (RGB1 I, 823.)
Jews not permitted to obtain academic degrees, Council of Basel, 1434, Sessio XIX	Law against Overcrowding of German Schools and Universities, April 25, 1933 (RGB1 I, 225.) [631]

This is just a *small* sampling of the legislation from these two entities confirming "these have one mind" and who truly controls them! When Hitler legally came to power in 1933, *everything* was ready for the last act of the drama.

We now want to step behind the diabolical scenes of Satan's workings in what I believe will be a tactic reenacted from what I read from Ellen White's writings and of the mob mentality when it's granted unfettered restraint. Satan's plan consists of phase II of the *Final Solution* that

---

[631] Raul Hilberg, *The Destruction of the European Jews*, (Chicago, IL: Quadrangle Books Inc; 1961), 5-6.

has already been tried and proven. This will bring about the near utter annihilation of the church and therefore the need to bring in the 11th hour workers to finish the work to completion.

Our story takes us back in time to Nazi Germany. Climbing the ladder in Christian virtue is a process. Likewise, when humanity chooses to climb down to the bottom rung of the ladder it's a conditioning process as well. Some may argue this section is not necessary but with where we are at in time and place of world events and an unenthusiastic church, I fully disagree. Someone has to warn the people of what to really expect, someone has to reveal the magnitude of the ordeal and how to prepare for it, do they not? I make no apology!

War brings out the best in a few people but also the worst in others. Such was the case with the, Reserve Police Battalion 101, a unit of the German Order Police in World War II. For those who have researched into the primary sources of Nazi Germany know for one that the personnel of the death camps were rather small. The personnel needed to round up and deport or shoot Polish Jewry was not. Thanks to the law office of the State Prosecutor (Staatsanwaltschaft) in Hamburg who has conducted a decade-long (1962-1972) investigation and legal prosecution of Reserve Police Battalion 101. At that time most of the men were from Hamburg and still lived there. Christopher R. Browning and Daniel Jonah Goldhagen were fortunate enough to see the original court records and study the interrogations of 210 men of nearly 500 of which I will glean from. Browning was given their real names but had to promise not to disclose their names. However the names of the battalion commander, Major Wilhelm Trapp, and the three company commanders, Captain Wolfgang Hoffmann, Captain Julius Wohlauf, and Lieutenant Hartwig Gnade, appear in other documentation in archives outside of Germany and therefore may be used and will serve our purpose well.

What is extraordinary about Reserve Police Battalion 101 is that they were middle aged family men of working and lower-middle-class background from the city of Hamburg. Ages were from 33 to 48 and none belonged to the SS. Considered too old to be of use in the German army they were drafted instead into the Order Police. Most were raw recruits with no previous experiences in German occupied territory. The battalion was divided into three companies, each of approximately 140 men when at full strength. They arrived in Poland three weeks earlier. It was the very early hours of July 13, 1942 and it was still very dark. Each policeman received extra ammunition and additional boxes were loaded onto the trucks as well. They were headed for their first major action. Just as the sky had begun to lighten the convoy met its destination just outside of Jozefow. The town was quiet and among its inhabitants were 1800 Jews. Battalion commander, Major Wilhelm Trapp then gave the order:

This assignment was not to his liking but came from the highest authorities. The battalion had now been ordered to round up these Jews. The male Jews of working age were to be separated and taken to a work camp. The remaining Jews-the woman, children, and elderly were to be shot on the spot by the battalion. This is how Reserve Police Battalion 101 began its infamous career. Once the killings began, however, the men became increasingly brutalized as the thousands of dead began to multiply. As in combat, the horrors of the initial encounter eventually became routine, and the killing became progressively easier. The men were now accustoming to the blood, tissue and brain matter that would cling to their uniforms. These men knew how to clear out the ghettos as they always left a trail of blood that identified their sport. These men knew how to transport multiplied thousands of prisoners onto the train cars to the concentration camps with no food, water or sanitary measures provided. These men knew how to round up Jews from towns, villages and the cities and execute them in the city square or unmarked graves in the woods. Ordinary men who became professional killers! In this sense, brutalization was not the cause but the effect of these men's behavior.

This in turn easily prepared Reserve Police Battalion 101 for what was called the, "Harvest Festival". Erntefest massacre was the culmination of Himmler's crusade to destroy Polish Jewry in accordance with the wish of the Fuhrer and at the silence of the Catholic Church. Members of Reserve Police Battalion 101 participated in virtually every phase of the Erntefest massacre in Lublin. In that day alone their harvest yielded almost a 1000 dead with a victim total of 42,000 Jews sent to the Treblinka concentration death camp. For a battalion of less than 500 ordinary men, their body count throughout the war was at least 83,000 Jews. Hitler's war effort yielded 6 million Jews whose only crime was being a Jew. Keep in mind this was all accomplished when the Spirit of God was still restraining the hearts and minds of men; the 144,000 will not have that privilege!

Historians are agreed that if the Jews would have stuck together instead of having multiple divergent religious splinter groups that resulted in a mass array of disunity among themselves their outcome would have been very different if they would have simply united. Is it possible for Seventh-day Adventist to learn from history?

Stationed only ten meters from the grave sites at Lublin, Heinrich Bocholt, of First Company witnessed first-hand the killing procedure as it was transcribed in his own words:

> "From my position I could now observe how the Jews were driven naked from the barracks by other members of our battalion. . . the shooters of the execution commandos, who sat on the edge of the graves directly in front of me, were members of the SD. . . Some distance behind each shooter stood several other SD men who constantly kept the magazines of the sub machine guns full and handed them to the shooter. A number of such shooters were assigned to each grave. Today I can no longer provide details about the number of graves. It is possible there where many such graves where shooting took place simultaneously. I defiantly remember that the naked Jews were driven directly into the graves and forced to lie down quite precisely on top of those who had been shot before them. The shooter then fired off a burst at these prone victims. . . How long the action lasted, I can no longer say with certainly. Presumably it lasted the entire day, because I remember that I was relieved once from my post. I can give no details about the number of victims, but there were an awful lot of them."[632]

---

[632] Heinrich BL. HW 467-68.

"Observing the killing from a greater distance was SSPF Sporreberg, who circled above the camp in a Fieseler Storch airplane as the Poles watched from the rooftops."[633] All the while two loudspeaker trucks provided the music in a futile attempt to drown out the steady noise of gunfire with business as usual.

While I have left out the grizzly graphics of multiplied hundreds of accounts I have accumulated over the years from the primary sources of the Nazi war machine. None compare to how ordinary men and woman who had been law-abiding citizens find their way down to the bottom rung of the ladder as Reserve Police Battalion 101 did just that in the following account. This brings us to the infamous climax if you will, of just how far down Satan can take fallen humanity and perfect it into a well-orchestrated frenzy and mob mentality.

Captain Julius Wohlauf, commander of First Company, Reserve Police Battalion 101 had returned to Hamburg for a previous scheduled weeding on June 29, 1942. He then quickly caught up with his comrades, while his wife delayed a bit. She (Frau Wohlauf) later joined him and the Battalion shortly after their first major killing in Jozefow. Captain Julius Wohlauf and Lieutenant Paul Brand had their wives by their sides when they were killing in Poland.

Wohlauf's wife attended the day-long killing operation that the entire battalion conducted at Miedzyrzec on August 25. The roundup, the driving of the Jews from their homes to the market square, was perhaps the most brutal and licentious of all those that the Police Battalion 101 conducted. The men left hundreds of dead Jews strewn about the streets. The scene at the market square was also among the most gruesome. Some of the notable features included the Germans forcing the Jews to squat for hours in the burning sun so that many fainted, and shooting any Jew who did nothing more than stand up. The market square became littered with the dead.[634] Such shootings naturally included many children, who found it particularly difficult to remain immobile in such discomfort for hour on end. The Hiwis and some of the Germans in the Miedzyrzec's German Gendarmerie also used the occasion to satisfy their lust for cruelty. They entertained themselves by flogging Jews with whips.[635] Not only was Frau Wohlauf a party to all this, but so were the wives of some of the locally stationed Germans, as well as a group of German Red Cross nurses.[636] Frau Wohlauf, if conforming to her usual practice, probably carried that symbol of domination, a riding whip, with her.[637] That day Frau and the other German woman got to observe firsthand how their men were purging the world of putative Jewish menace, by killing around one thousand and deporting ten thousand more to their deaths.

---

[633] ZStL, 208 AR-Z 268/59 (Staatsanwaltschaft Wiesbaden, 8 Js 1145/60, indictment of Lothar Hoffmann Hermann Worthoff, KdS Lublin case):633-35.
[634] F.B. Hoffmann, p. 1583.
[635] J.F. Hoffmann, p. 2232; for the Gendarmerie's involvement, see G.G., Hoffmann, p. 2183.
[636] For the nurses, see F.M. Hoffmann, pp. 2560-2561; for the wives, see the statement of one of the wives, L.L. Hoffmann, p. 1293. That German Red Cross nurses also observed the scene at the market square is known because they complained about the killing of the children, who had done nothing more than stand up at the market square. The perpetrators apparently had no hesitation in letting these women, these agents of healing and succor, observe the mass slaughter.
[637] H.F. Hoffmann, p. 2172

When not rounding up towns and villages of Jews, Police Battalion 101 would be found roaming the countryside for escaped prisoners that they called the Juden-jagd, or "Jew hunt" in order to make the region judenfrei, or "free of Jews." Other tactics used by Police Battalion 101 during deportations when many Jews had apparently been hiding tenaciously. After the trains left, the Security Police employed a ruse to lure the surviving Jews from their concealment. It was announced throughout the ghetto that new identity cards would be issued. Anyone who reported for his card would be spared; anyone found without one would be shot immediately. Hoping at least for another brief respite between deportations, desperate Jews emerged from their hiding places and reported. After at least 200 Jews had been collected, they were marched outside of Lukow and shot on November 11. Another group was collected and shot on November 14.[638]

The irony of it all is that Captain Julius Wohlauf, Commander of First Company, Reserve Police Battalion 101 and his new wife who was four months pregnant, Frau Wohlauf decided to spend their honeymoon with Police Battalion 101 in plundering towns and villages and murdering Jews!

Few Seventh-day Adventist have realized that we have come full circle to 1933 all over again. Like Hitler, The National Reform movement which is one and the same as the, Religious Right, Christian Reconstructionism a Protestant movement that upholds "Dominion Theology" has been sitting at her Mother's table drinking the wine of Babylon and is also learning the lessons of intolerance, cruelty and torture which Rome had so diligently taught. This time however it is not just one nation in league with Rome, no, this time it's "all the world wondered after the beast." (Rev. 13:3):

> "The persecutions of Protestants by Romanism, by which the religion of Jesus Christ was almost annihilated, will be more than rivaled when Protestantism and popery are combined."[639]

Let that quote sink in please.

The National Reform movement, the Religious Right, Dominion Theology and Christian Reconstructionism are essentially all one and the same ideology. And what is that? I can only briefly share some of this research and documentation at this time for again this would necessitate another book running in another direction but I will provide some stimulating facts for the reader's edification. In short, many adhere to Rousas Rushdoony's and Gary North's

---

[638] Brustin-Berenstein, table 10, list only one November shooting in Lukow, of 200 Jews. The testimony of the policemen indicates that there were two. The Burger judgment, 20-21, confirms two Lukow shootings, on November 11 and 14, each with 500 victims-a rare case in which a German court estimates casualties higher than do other sources.

[639] Ellen White, *Selected Messages*, 3:387.

writings in the concept that Christians are Biblically mandated to occupy all secular institutions and this has become the central unifying ideology for the Christian Right. They want the United States to be a Christian theocracy. For them the Constitution and Bill of Rights are merely addendums to Old Testament Biblical law. Dominionist Dream is to Repeal the 1st Amendment, *Talk To Action*, December 16, 2005.

They claim that Christian men with specific theological beliefs are ordained by God to run society. Christians and others who do not accept their theological beliefs would be second-class citizens.

Dominists seek to re-interpret the U.S. Constitution so that it conforms to their Biblical Worldview. Mathew Staver, founder of Liberty Counsel declares it's time to get Jesus into the judicial mix:

> "Now we're working to establish Liberty University School of Law, which will open its doors in August 2004. We are going to teach lawyers to think in a biblical, Christian world view."

According to dominionists, the Bible has supremacy over the U.S. Constitution. In a 2002 address to the Society of Catholic Social Scientists in Ann Arbor, Mich., federal judge James Leon Holmes, appointed in July, 2004, affirmed the supremacy of the Bible:

> "Christianity transcends the political order and cannot be subordinated to the political order."

The principle of separation of church and state has no place in his vision for the future:

> "The final reunion of Church and state will take place at the end of time, when Christ will claim definitive political power of all creation, inaugurating an entirely new society based on the supernatural."

Rob Boston reports in Church and State, November, 2004:

> "Despite the Christian Coalition's best efforts, those pesky federal courts keep upholding the Bill of Rights and the separation of church and state. But not to worry, the group has a plan to fix that: take away the right of the courts to hear those cases in the first place. This bold gambit, called "court stripping," is all the rage among the Religious Right these days."

According to acclaimed journalist and television host Bill Moyers:

> "True, people of faith have always tried to bring their interpretation of the Bible to bear on American laws and morals ... it's the American way, encouraged and protected by the First Amendment. But what is unique today

is that the radical religious right has succeeded in taking over one of America's great political parties. The country is not yet a theocracy but the Republican Party is, and they are driving American politics, using God as a battering ram on almost every issue: crime and punishment, foreign policy, health care, taxation, energy, regulation, social services and so on."

Dominionism is therefore a tendency among Protestant Christian evangelicals and fundamentalists that encourages them to not only be active political participants in civic society, but also seek to dominate the political process as part of a mandate from God.

This highly politicized concept of dominionism is based on the Bible's text in Genesis 1:26:

> "And God said, Let us make man in our image, after our likeness: and let them have dominion over the fish of the sea, and over the fowl of the air, and over the cattle, and over all the earth, and over every creeping thing that creepeth upon the earth." (King James Version).

> "Then God said, 'Let us make man in our image, in our likeness and let them rule over the fish of the sea and the birds of the air, over the livestock, over all the earth and over all the creatures that move along the ground." (New International Version).

They love the NIV! The vast majorities of Christians read this text and conclude that God has appointed them stewards and caretakers of Earth. As Sara Diamond explains, however, some Christians read the text and believe, "that Christians alone are Biblically mandated to occupy all secular institutions until Christ returns." That, in a nutshell, is the idea of "Dominionism."

This brings us to a quote from Ellen White that prophesied over 100 years ago about this movement and its ideology when *fully developed* will be "intolerant" and manifest the same spirit and intent of Rome. We were also informed it will crush "liberty of conscience" and it will produce "legislation" that will bring about the "Mark of the Beast":

> "*The National Reform movement*, exercising the power of religious *legislation*, will, *when fully developed*, manifest *the same intolerance and oppression that have prevailed in past ages*. Human councils then assumed the prerogatives of Deity, crushing under their despotic power liberty of conscience; and imprisonment, exile, and death followed for those who opposed their dictates. If popery or its principles shall again *be legislated into power*, the fires of persecution will be rekindled against those who will not sacrifice conscience and the truth in deference to popular errors. This evil is on the point of realization."[640]

---

[640] Ellen White, *Testimonies*, 5:712. [Emphasis mine]

Like Hitler when he came to power, this legislation is already on the books just waiting for the last act of the drama to unfold! Rousas Rushdoony's and Gary North's writings has become the unified legislation for the Christian Right as portrayed in, "The Institutes of Biblical Law."[641] This is a work that consisted of three volumes. Volume I was completed in 1973, Volume II in 1986 and Volume III in 1999 with nearly 1900 pages combined. There is so much that needs to be said, exposed and countered, but that would necessitate another book in another direction. Therefore, we will confine this presentation solely to some of the laws and stipulations pertaining to the central issue, their Sunday Law legislation and their manipulating methods behind it to implement the Mark of the Beast. All quotes will be taken from, "The Institutes of Biblical Law" Vol. I and all references will be designated only by the page number. All emphasis, lowercase or otherwise will be presented just as it is, in the original:

THE INSTITUTES OF BIBLICAL LAW

"The pattern of the sabbath is God's creation rest; the goal of the sabbath is man's redemption rest."[642]

"The sabbath asserts the principle of freedom under God, of liberty under law, God's law. It summons man to obedience to the ordinance of rest in order to free man from himself and from this work."[643]

"Now to examine the sabbath laws more specifically, it is at once apparent that, while the principle of the sabbath remains basic to Biblical law, the specific form of sabbath observance changed radically in terms of the new covenant in Christ.

First, the sabbath in the Old Testament law was not primarily a day of worship but a day of rest. The pattern of weekly worship did not exist in the Old Testament law. The synagogue introduced it in the inter-testamental period, and the New Testament clearly practiced it and urged it (Heb. 10:25). In the Old Testament, worship was family centered, and woven into the fabric of daily life."[644]

"Third, there is not a trace of the maintenance of the sabbath penalties in the church after the resurrection. Because the early disciples and members were Jews, they continued for a time to observe the Old Testament sabbath (Acts

---

[641] Rousas John Rushdoony, The Institutes of Biblical Law, (The Presbyterian and Reformed Publishing Company, 1973) Vol. I. (Three appendices by Gary North)
[642] Ibid. 128.
[643] Ibid. 129.
[644] Ibid. 130.

13:14-26; 16:11-13; 17:2,3; 18:1,11). But the Christian day of worship was the first day of the week, the day of resurrection as well as of Pentecost (Matt. 28:1; Mark 16:1,2,9; Luke 24:1; John 20:1-19; Acts 20:6-8; 1 Cor. 16:1,2)."[645]

"Fourth, not only is the legal status of the sabbath altered, but the day of rest has been changed from the Hebrew sabbath to the Christian day of resurrection. The Deuteronomic law (Duet. 5:12-15) made clear that the Hebrew sabbath celebrated the deliverance from Egypt: "And remember that thou wast a servant in the land of Egypt, and that the LORD thy God brought the out thence, through a mighty hand, and by a stretched out arm; therefore the LORD thy God commanded thee to keep the sabbath day" (Duet. 5:16). The Hebrew redemption was thus celebrated in the sabbath; the Christian Sabbath commemorates Christ's triumph over sin and death, and hence it is celebrated on the day of resurrection, the first day of the week. To reject this day is to reject Christ's redemption and to seek salvation by another inadmissible way."[646]

"Fifth, the Hebrew sabbath and the modern Saturday cannot be equated. As Curtis Clair Ewing has clearly shown, the calendar of Israel does not permit such an identification. The calendar of Israel at Sinai was a solar calendar, and it is not to be confused with the modern Jewish solar-lunar calendar of A.D. 359. Ewing has called attention to the unfortunate translation at times of "moon" for "month," thus creating some confusion. There are three sabbaths spoken of in scripture: the creation sabbath; the Hebrew sabbath, which commemorated the deliverance from Egypt; and the Christian sabbath, which is "kept in commemoration of Christ's finished resurrection and is the only sabbath that remains."8 As Ewing points out, the fourth commandment orders remembrance, because it recalls the creation sabbath, God's rest, as the pattern of the covenant rest. . . In Deuteronomy, they are not commanded to remember, since it is not the pattern of the creation sabbath in view, but they are commanded to keep the sabbath, in commemoration of the deliverance of Israel from Egypt:"[647]

"Jesus said, "The sabbath was made for man, and not man for the sabbath: Therefore the Son of man is Lord also of the sabbath" (Mark 2:27-28). The sabbath was made for the true and perfect man, Jesus Christ, who is therefore Lord of the sabbath; it was therefore also made for the redeemed of Christ, for covenant man, and as a principle of life and regeneration to him.

---

[645] Ibid. 131.
[646] Ibid. 133.
[647] Ibid. 134.

To understand the meaning of this, it is perhaps necessary to do two things, first, to remember that the principle purpose of the sabbath is not worship but rest."[648]

"Chruchmen who limit the meaning of the sabbath, or who feel it is obeyed in worship and inactivity, have no knowledge of its meaning."[649]

"The sabbath is God's covenant sign with man, declaring God's grace and God's efficacious work unto salvation, so that man can rest, "forasmuch as ye know that your labour is not in vain in the Lord" (1 Cor. 15:58).[650]

"The commandement does not merely require a cessation of work but "remember….to keep it holy" (Ex. 20:8)."[651]

"The essence of the sabbath is our rest in Christ, and our growth in the knowledge of that salvation by His grace.

"The point of difference between Israel's sabbath and the Christian sabbath is not only in the day but in the end of the old restrictions. The first day of the week was a work- day in Palestine and also throughout the Roman Empire. The church normally met on the evening of the first day, because the members worked during the day. On one occasion, a sleepy member fell out of the window and was killed (Acts 20: 7-12). Obviously, if work on the Lords day was still illegal, the New Testament would have had much to say concerning it. The old law was clearly altered here. The duty now, as stated by St.Paul, was "not forsaking the assembling of ourselves together, as the manner of some is" (Heb. 10:25)."[652]

"In a Christian state, it cannot be made anything resembling the sabbath of Israel. It must be a day of rest, and of peace and quiet, but the basic emphasis is on the authority of God, knowledge of Him, and rest in his government and salvation. The shifting emphasis from the meaning of the sabbath to quibbling about regulations for the Sabbath is certainly no honor to the Sabbath. The words of St. Paul in Colossians 2:16,17 remain true: if no man is to judge us with respect to the sabbaths, we then are similarly to judge none."[653]

"In a sabbath- oriented society, the provident man, having lived debt-free, finding rest in Christ, and able both to work and to relax, has a peace and joy in

---

[648] Ibid. 138.
[649] Ibid. 144.
[650] Ibid. 146-7.
[651] Ibid. 150.
[652] Ibid. 153.
[653] Ibid. 154.

life lacking in phrenetic generation. But, fourth, since all law has reference to the future, and is in essence a plan for the future, the sabbath law is a plan for the world's tomorrow."[654]

"Third, we have seen that the principle is life for life, i.e., a punishment proportionate to the crime. This crime has no reference to the criminal or his mentality but only to the nature of the act. If death is the penalty for animals on the principle of life for life, then this is certainly true for men. Thus on this principle, Biblical law has no plea of not guilty by reason of insanity. Neither is there any privileged status before the law of a minor. Murder requires the death penalty whether the offender is an animal, an "insane" man, a child, or a feeble minded person."[655]

"Augustine, interpreting the Sabbath as an allegory of the believer's rest in Christ from the bondage of sin, a rest to be made perfect in eternity."[656] [657]

[The Death Penalty]

"If we Accept the principle that it is wrong for us to hire another person to commit a crime for our benefit and his profit, then certain implications follow. Sabbath violations were capital crimes. If strict sabbatarian's regard Old Testament provisions as binding on Christians, then it is as wrong to hire a man to violate the sabbath as it is to hire someone from murder, Inc. to kill a neighbor. The execution of the crime and the guilt of the hiring party are in both cases equal. Capital crimes are major ones. If the Hebrew sabbath is morally binding today, its implications and applications are equally binding. I have heard Christian people charge their fellow Christians with a violation of the sabbath because the latter have dared to go out to a restaurant after church services are over. The same supposedly holds for those who purchase food in a supermarket on the sabbath. Why should this be a violation? Clearly, only on the grounds that it is a violation of the Sabbath to encourage anothers violation of the Sabbath by paying him to remain open for business. If the standards of the Hebrew sabbath are binding, then entering a place of business on the sabbath is morally a capital crime, and an abomination in the sight of God.

---

[654] Ibid. 157.
[655] Ibid. 231.
[656] On Augustine and Irenaeus, see Knappen, ibid., p. 443. Calvin's viewpoint can be seen in his Commentary on Hebrews, chap.4;cf. Tracts and Treatises (Grand Rapids: Eerdmans, 3 vols., 1958), II, 61-62. His ambivalence in the tracts stands in contrast to his more rigid exegesis of Exodus 20: 8 ff.
[657] Ibid. 825.

Therefore, pastors and elders must tell their flock to refrain from entering into trade of any sort on the sabbath."[658] [659]

Scalia's article in *First Things* is about the death penalty. He writes:

"Indeed, it seems to me that the more Christian a country is, the *less* likely it is to regard the death penalty as immoral."

The textbook, *Americas's Providental History* views the death penalty as "the backbone of civil government." The book goes back to the time God brought Noah through the flood:

"When God brings Noah through the flood to a new earth, He re-establishes the Dominion Mandate but now delegates to man the responsibility for governing other men in order to protect human life. He does this by instituting capital punishment - the backbone of civil government."

This concludes our *short* sample of the legislation projected for the papal (Sunday) sabbath and some of the mentality and reasoning of the men behind it.

Therefore, these quotes are worth contemplating so we are not disillusioned of what we are to meet and to the intensity of the conflict that will test the "faith" of those to whom compose the 144,000:

"The Sunday movement is now making its way in darkness. The leaders are concealing the true issue, and many who unite in the movement do not themselves see whither the under-current is tending. . . They are working in blindness. They do not see that if a Protestant government sacrifices the principles that have made them a free, independent nation, and through legislation brings into the Constitution principles that will propagate papal falsehood and papal delusion, *they are plunging into the Roman horrors of the Dark Ages.*"[660]

"There is soon to open before us a period of overwhelming interest to all living. The controversies of the past are to be revived; new controversies will arise. The scenes to be enacted in our world are not yet even dreamed of. Satan

---

[658] The utter confusion of many sabbatarian pastors is seen in their prohibition against paying for any book bought from the church's book room on a Sunday. The book (s) may be taken home but not paid for until Monday or later. An economic transaction made on credit is not regarded as an economic transaction if the church bookroom is concerned. However, a purchase of gasoline or any other item bought on credit on a Sunday is regarded by the same pastors as a flagrant violation of the sabbath. Anyone who can make sense out of these two positions is a rival of the medieval scholastic theologians.
[659] Ibid. 832-3.
[660] Ellen White, *Review & Herald Extra*, Dec. 11, 1888.

is at work through human agencies. Those who are making an effort to change the Constitution and secure a law enforcing Sunday observance little realize what will be the result. A crisis is just upon us."[661]

When a great terror is soon to come upon human beings because *transgression* has reached its limit,[662] a sudden and unlooked-for calamity,[663] God's people should be preparing for what is to break upon the world as an overwhelming surprise. This will play perfectly into the hands of the *Religious Right* and set in motion "the question of enforcing Sunday observance" when it will be "widely agitated."[664] This in turn will bring about the total demise of the U.S. Constitution and implement the legislation already in place for the long sought for theocracy of the *Religious Right*. All the while when:

> "Satan and the man of sin worshiped by the wisdom of this age, while the angel is flying through the midst of heaven crying "Woe, woe, woe, to the inhabiters of the earth." (Revelation 8:13)."[665]

> "We need not be surprised at *anything* that may take place now. We need not marvel at *any developments of horror*. Those who trample under their unholy feet the law of God have the same spirit as had the men who insulted and betrayed Jesus. *Without any compunctions of conscience they will do the deeds of their father the devil.*"[666]

> "Houses and lands will be of no use to the saints in the time of trouble, *for they will then have to flee before infuriated mobs. . ."*[667]

There will be no sympathizers to lean on; it will be by faith and faith alone:

> "That night I dreamed that I was in Battle Creek looking out from the side glass at the door and saw a company marching up to the house, two and two. They looked stern and determined. *I knew them well* and turned to open the parlor door to receive them, but thought I would look again. The scene was changed. The company now presented the appearance of a *Catholic procession*. One bore in his hand a cross, another a reed. And as they approached, the one carrying a reed made a circle around the house, saying three times: "This house is proscribed. The goods must be confiscated. They have spoken against our holy order." Terror seized me, and I ran through the house, out of the north door, and found myself in the midst of a company,

---

[661] Ellen White, *Testimonies*, 5:753.
[662] Ellen White, *Testimonies*, 8:28.
[663] Ellen White, *Christ Object Lessons*, 412.
[664] Ellen White, *The Great Controversy*, 606.
[665] Ellen White, *1888 Materials*, 2:485.
[666] Ellen White, *Selected Messages,* 3:416. [Emphasis mine]
[667] Ellen White, *Early Writings*, 56. [Emphasis mine]

some of whom I knew, but I dared not speak a word to them for fear of being *betrayed*. I tried to seek a retired spot where I might weep and pray without meeting eager, inquisitive eyes wherever I turned. I repeated frequently: "If I could only understand this! If they will tell me what I have said or what I have done!"

I wept and prayed much as I saw our goods confiscated. *I tried to read sympathy or pity for me in the looks of those around me*, and marked the countenances of several whom I thought would speak to me and comfort me if they did not fear that they would be observed by others. I made one attempt to escape from the crowd, but seeing that I was watched, I concealed my intentions. I commenced weeping aloud, and saying: "If they would only tell me what I have done or what I have said!" My husband, who was sleeping in a bed in the same room, heard me weeping aloud and awoke me. My pillow was wet with tears, and a sad depression of spirits was upon me."[668]

Heaven has also given us explicit instruction for those who come before the world court and what to expect and not let passion arise:

"The character of the judge in the parable, [Luke 18:1-8] who feared not God nor regarded man, was presented by Christ to show the kind of judgment that was then being executed, and that would soon be witnessed at His trial. *He desires His people in all time to realize how little dependence can be placed on earthly rulers or judges in the day of adversity*. Often the elect people of God have to stand before men in official positions who do not make the word of God their guide and counselor, but who follow their own unconsecrated, undisciplined impulses.

In the parable of the unjust judge, *Christ has shown what we should do*. "Shall not God avenge His own elect, which cry day and night unto Him?" Christ, our example, did nothing to vindicate or deliver Himself. He committed His case to God. *So His followers are not to accuse or condemn, or to resort to force in order to deliver themselves.*

When trials arise that seem unexplainable, we should not allow our peace to be spoiled. However unjustly we may be treated, let not passion arise. By indulging a spirit of retaliation we injure ourselves. We destroy our own confidence in God, and grieve the Holy Spirit. There is by our side a witness, a heavenly messenger, who will lift up for us a standard against the enemy. He

---

[668] Ellen White, *Testimonies*, 1:578. [Emphasis mine]

will shut us in with the bright beams of the Sun of Righteousness. Beyond this Satan cannot penetrate. He cannot pass this shield of holy light."[669]

"In the last scenes of this earth's history, war will rage."[670]

However, we must remember:

> "The Father's presence encircled Christ, *and nothing befell Him but that which infinite love permitted* for the blessing of the world. Here was His source of comfort, and it is for us. He who is imbued with the Spirit of Christ abides in Christ. The blow that is aimed at him falls upon the Saviour, who surrounds him with His presence. *Whatever comes to him comes from Christ*. He has no need to resist evil, for Christ is his defense. *Nothing can touch him except by our Lord's permission*, and "all things" that are permitted "work together for good to them that love God." Romans 8:28."[671]

> "The time is right upon us when there will be sorrow that no human balm can heal."[672]

> "Soon the dead and dying will be all around us."[673]

There will be no question that the devil has and will be taunting all with death, doubt and guilt and any other device that he can muster up lest we should renounce our "faith" in Christ as Ellen White has so adequately illustrated in these closing pages but we have this assurance:

> "*If we surrender our lives to His service*, we can *never* be placed in a position for which God has not made provision."[674]

> "*Never give up your faith and hope in God. Cling to the promises*. Do not trust in your feelings, but in the naked word of God. Believe the assurances of the Lord. Take your stand upon the plain thus saith the Lord, and rest there, feeling or no feeling. Faith is not always followed by feelings of ecstasy, but hope thou in God. *Trust wholly in Him*."[675]

---

[669] Ellen White, Christ Object Lessons, 171-2. [Emphasis mine]
[670] Ellen White, *Review & Herald*, October 19, 1897.
[671] Ellen White, *Thoughts from the Mount of Blessing*, 71. [Emphasis mine]
[672] Ellen White, *Review & Herald*, March 14, 1912.
[673] Ellen White, *Review & Herald*, September 1, 1849.
[674] Ellen White, *Christ Object Lessons*, 173. [Emphasis mine]
[675] Ellen White, *Letter* 159, 1905, 2-3. [Emphasis mine]

Matt. 28:20 "Teaching them to observe all things whatsoever I have commanded you: and, lo, I am with you alway, even unto the end of the world. Amen."

APPENDIX

Consider the following additional quotes please as they are instrumental in our Christian walk that will help keep in focus the big picture. These are pertinent word definitions for clarity and continuity:

Justification

"Knowing that a man is not justified by the works of the law, but by the faith of Jesus Christ, even we have believed in Jesus Christ, that we might be justified by the faith of Christ, and not by the works of the law: for by the works of the law shall no flesh be justified." Gal. 2:16.

"The only way which he [the sinner] can attain to righteousness is through faith. By faith he can bring to God the merits of Christ, and the Lord places the obedience of His Son to the sinner's account. Christ's righteousness is accepted in place of man's failure, and God receives, pardons, justifies, the repentant, believing soul, treats him as though he were righteous, and loves him as He loves His Son."[676]

Sanctification

". . . Sanctification . . . is nothing less than a daily dying to self, and daily conformity to the will of God . . . Paul's sanctification was a constant conflict with self. Said he, 'I die daily.' His will and his desires every day conflicted with duty and the will of God. Instead of following inclination, he did the will of God, however unpleasant and crucifying to his nature."[677]

[In sanctification Christ's character is imparted (or conveyed to the believer and becomes a part of his person). Thus his personality is changed. He receives a "new nature"]

---

[676] Ellen White, *Review & Herald*, November 4, 1890.
[677] Ellen White, *Testimonies*, 4:299.

Legalism

"If Satan can succeed in leading man to place value upon his own works as works of merit and righteousness, he knows that he can overcome him by his temptations, and make him his victim and prey."[678]

"Jesus pointed out the power of false teaching to destroy the appreciation and desire for truth. "No man," He said, "having drunk old wine straightway desireth new: for he saith, The old is better." All the truth that has been given to the world through patriarchs and prophets shone out in new beauty in the words of Christ. But the scribes and Pharisees had no desire for the precious new wine. Until emptied of the old traditions, customs, and practices, they had no place in mind or heart for the teachings of Christ. They clung to the dead forms, and turned away from the living truth and the power of God.

It was this that proved the ruin of the Jews, and it will prove the ruin of many souls in our own day. Thousands are making the same mistake as did the Pharisees whom Christ reproved at Matthew's feast. Rather than give up some cherished idea, or discard some idol of opinion, many refuse the truth which comes down from the Father of light. They trust in self, and depend upon their own wisdom, and do not realize their spiritual poverty. They insist on being saved in some way by which they may perform some important work. When they see that there is no way of weaving self into the work, they reject the salvation provided.

A legal religion can never lead souls to Christ; for it is a loveless, Christless religion. Fasting or prayer that is actuated by a self-justifying spirit is an abomination in the sight of God."[679]

"Circumstances cannot work reforms. Christianity proposes a reformation *in* the heart. *What Christ works within, will be worked out* under the dictation of a converted intellect. The plan of *beginning outside and trying to work inward has always failed, and always will fail.*"[680]

"As the leaven, when mingled with the meal, *works from within outward*, so it is by the renewing of *the heart* that the grace of God works to transform the life. No mere external change is sufficient to bring us into harmony with God. There are many who try to reform by correcting this or that bad habit, and they hope in this way to become Christians, but they are beginning in the wrong place. *Our first work is with the heart.*

---

[678] Ellen White, *Review & Herald*, September 3, 1889.
[679] Ellen White, *The Desire of Ages*, 279-280.
[680] Ellen White, 20*MR* 112. [Emphasis mine]

A profession of faith and the possession of truth in the soul are two different things. The mere knowledge of truth is not enough. We may possess this, but the tenor of our thoughts may not be changed. The heart must be converted and sanctified.

The man who attempts to keep the commandments of God from a sense of obligation merely--because he is required to do so--will never enter into the joy of obedience. *He does not obey*. When the requirements of God are accounted a burden because they cut across human inclination, we may know that the life is not a Christian life. *True obedience is the outworking of a principle within*. It springs from the *love of righteousness*, the *love of the law of God*. The essence of all righteousness is loyalty to our Redeemer. This will lead us to do right because it is right--because right doing is pleasing to God."[681]

The Will

"The tempter has no power to control the will or to force the soul to sin."[682]

"Satan knows that he cannot overcome man unless he can control his will."[683]

"The will is the *governing power in the nature* of man, bringing *all the other faculties* under its sway. The will is not the taste or the inclination, but it is the *deciding power* which works in the children of men unto obedience to God or unto disobedience."[684]

Surrender

"There are some who are seeking, always seeking, for the goodly pearl. But they do not make an *entire surrender of their wrong habits*. They do not *die to self* that Christ may live in them. Therefore they do not find the precious pearl."[685]

"Implicit belief in Christ's word is true humility, true self-surrender."[686]

---

[681] Ellen White, *Christ Object Lessons*, 97-98. [Emphasis mine]
[682] Ellen White, *The Great Controversy*, 510.
[683] Ellen White, *Temperance*, 16.
[684] Ellen White, *Testimonies*, 5:513.
[685] Ellen White, *Selected Messages*, 1:399.
[686] Ellen White, *The Desire of Ages*, p. 523.

"When the soul surrenders itself to Christ, *a new power takes possession of the new heart.* A change is wrought which man can never accomplish for himself. *It is a supernatural work, bringing a supernatural element into human nature.* The soul that is yielded to Christ becomes His own fortress, which He holds in a revolted world, and He intends that no authority shall be known in it but His own. A soul thus kept in possession by the heavenly agencies is impregnable to the assaults of Satan . . . . The only defense against evil is the indwelling of Christ in the heart through faith in His righteousness. Unless we become vitally connected with God, we can never resist the unhallowed effects of self-love, self-indulgence, and temptation to sin. *We may leave off many bad habits, for the time we may part company with Satan; but without a vital connection with God, through the surrender of ourselves to Him moment by moment, we shall be overcome.*"[687] [Surrender and death to self equal the same thing.]

Death to Self

"Knowing this, that our old man is crucified with him, that the body of sin might be destroyed, that henceforth we should not serve sin." Romans 6:6.

"Always bearing about in the body the dying of the Lord Jesus, that the life also of Jesus might be made manifest in our body. For we which live are always delivered unto death for Jesus' sake, that the life also of Jesus might be made manifest in our mortal flesh. So then death worketh in us, but life in you." 2 Corinthians 4:10-12.

"Words cannot describe the peace and joy possessed by him who takes God at His word. Trials do not disturb him, slights do not vex him. Self is crucified."[688]

Conversion

"True conversion is followed by a desire to share Jesus.--A man is no sooner converted than in his heart is born a desire to make known to others what a precious friend he has found in Jesus; the saving and sanctifying truth cannot be shut up in his heart. The Spirit of Christ illuminating the soul is represented by the light, which dispels all darkness; it is compared to salt, because of its

---

[687] Ellen White, *The Desire of Ages*, 324.
[688] Ellen White, *Messages to Young People*, 98.

preserving qualities; and to leaven, which secretly exerts its transforming power."[689]

"There are few really consecrated men among us, few who have fought and conquered in the battle with self. Real conversion is a decided change of feelings and motives; it is a virtual taking leave of worldly connections, a hastening from their spiritual atmosphere, a withdrawing from the controlling power of their thoughts, opinions, and influences. The separation causes pain and bitterness to both parties. It is the variance which Christ declares that He came to bring. But the converted will feel a continual longing desire that their friends shall forsake all for Christ, knowing that, unless they do, there will be a final and eternal separation. The true Christian cannot, while with unbelieving friends, be light and trifling. The value of the souls for whom Christ died is too great.

He "that forsaketh not all that he hath," says Jesus, "cannot be My disciple." Whatever shall divert the affections from God must be given up. Mammon is the idol of many. Its golden chain binds them to Satan. Reputation and worldly honor are worshiped by another class. The life of selfish ease and freedom from responsibility is the idol of others. These are Satan's snares, set for unwary feet. But these slavish bands must be broken; the flesh must be crucified with the affections and lusts. We cannot be half the Lord's and half the world's. We are not God's people unless we are such entirely. Every weight, every besetting sin, must be laid aside."[690]

Character

"The character is revealed, not by occasional good deeds and occasional misdeeds, but by the tendency of the habitual words and acts."[691]

"Actions make habits, and habits, character . . ."[692]

"Thus actions repeated form habits, habits form character, and by the character our destiny for time and for eternity is decided."[693]

The Flesh

---
[689] Ellen White, *Testimonies*, 4:318-319.
[690] Ellen White, Testimonies, 5:82-83.
[691] Ellen White, *Steps to Christ*, 57, 58.
[692] Ellen White, *Fundamentals of Christian Education*, 194.
[693] Ellen White, *Christ's Object Lessons*, 356.

"The lower passions have their seat in the body and work through it. The words "flesh" or "fleshly" or "carnal lusts" embrace the lower, corrupt nature; the flesh of itself cannot act contrary to the will of God. We are commanded to crucify the flesh, with the affections and lusts. How shall we do it? Shall we inflict pain on the body? No; but put to death the temptation to sin. The corrupt thought is to be expelled. Every thought is to be brought into captivity to Jesus Christ. All animal propensities are to be subjected to the higher powers of the soul. The love of God must reign supreme; Christ must occupy an undivided throne. Our bodies are to be regarded as His purchased possession. The members of the body are to become the instruments of righteousness."[694]

Born Again

"How, then, are we to be saved? 'As Moses lifted up the serpent in the wilderness,' so the Son of man has been lifted up, and everyone who has been deceived and bitten by the serpent may look and live. *'Behold the Lamb of God, which taketh away the sin of the world.'* John 1:29. The light shining from the cross reveals the love of God. His love is drawing us to Himself. If we do not resist this drawing, we shall be led to the foot of the cross in repentance for the sins that have crucified the Saviour. Then the *Spirit of God through faith produces a new life in the soul.*"[695]

"When the Spirit of God takes possession of the heart, it transforms the life. . . . *The blessing comes when by faith the soul surrenders itself to God.* Then that power which no human eye can see creates a new being in the image of God. . . . Its mystery exceeds human knowledge; yet *he who passes from death to life realizes that it is a divine reality.*"[696]

"The new birth is a rare experience in this age of the world. This is the reason why there are so many perplexities in the churches. Many, so many, who assume the name of Christ are unsanctified and unholy. They have been baptized, but they were buried alive. Self did not die, and therefore they did not rise to newness of life in Christ."[697]

---

[694] Ellen White, *Adventist Home*, 127-8.
[695] Ellen White, *The Desire of Ages*, 175-176.
[696] Ellen White, *The Desire of Ages*, 173.
[697] Ellen White, *Manuscript* 148, 1897.

[The born-again experience necessitates a complete surrender, a dying to self, before a new creature can be born by the power of God. We had no choice in the first birth, but the new birth must be by our choice.]

Faith

"Faith is the only condition upon which justification can be obtained, and faith includes not only belief but trust." Selected Messages, book 1, p. 389.
[Faith is taking God at His word.]

New Nature

"A new nature is imparted. Man is renewed after the image of Christ in righteousness and true holiness."[698]

"The Holy Spirit implants a new nature, and molds through the grace of Christ the human character, until the image of Christ is perfected. This is true holiness."[699]

"The old nature of the disciples often appeared. Often their natural characteristics strove for the mastery. But Jesus was ever presenting before them that these must be given up, emptied from the soul, that he might implant a new nature therein."[700]

"Self--the old disobedient nature--must be crucified, and Christ must take up His abode in the heart. Thus the human agent is born again, with a new nature."[701]

"The power of truth is to transform heart and character. Its effect is not like a dash of color here and there upon the canvas; the whole character is to be transformed; the image of Christ is to be revealed in words and actions. A new nature is imparted. Man is renewed after the image of Christ in righteousness and true holiness."[702]

---

[698] Ellen White, *Letter 2a*, 1892
[699] Ellen White, *Upward Look*, 27.
[700] Ellen White, *Review & Herald*, October 5, 1897.
[701] Ellen White, *Signs of the Times*, July 26, 1905.
[702] Ellen White, *1888 Materials*, 1065.

Victory

"Let no one despair of gaining the victory. Victory is sure when self is surrendered to God."[703] [Unless one is totally surrendered, he cannot possibly overcome his sins]

"Satan assailed Christ with his fiercest and most subtle temptations, but he was repulsed in every conflict. Those battles were fought in our behalf; *those victories make it possible for us to conquer.*"[704]

Obedience

"We should never forget that *love*, the *love of Christ*, is the *only power that can soften the heart and lead to obedience.*"[705]

Man Proves His Utter Inability

"Without the divine working, *man could do no good thing.* God calls every man to repentance, yet *man cannot even repent* unless the Holy Spirit works upon his heart."[706]

"You *cannot* control your impulses, your emotions, as you may desire; but you can control the will."[707]

"Were it possible to force upon you with a hundredfold greater intensity the influence of the Spirit of God, it would not make you a Christian. . . You are not able, of yourself, to bring your purposes and desires and inclinations into submission to the will of God."[708]

---

[703] Ellen White, *MS* 2, 1903.
[704] Ellen White, *The Great Controversy*, 510. [Emphasis mine]
[705] Ellen White, *Review & Herald*, Nov. 25, 1890. [Emphasis mine]
[706] Ellen White, *Testimonies*, 8:64. [Emphasis mine]
[707] Ellen White, *Testimonies*, 5:514.
[708] Ellen White, *Thoughts from the Mount of Blessing*, 142.

We invite you to view the complete
selection of titles we publish at:

www.TEACHServices.com

Scan with your mobile
device to go directly
to our website.

Please write or email us your praises, reactions, or
thoughts about this or any other book we publish at:

info@TEACHServices.com

11 Quartermaster Circle
Fort Oglethorpe, GA 30742

TEACH Services' titles may be purchased in bulk for
educational, business, fund-raising, or promotional use.
For more information, please e-mail:

BulkSales@TEACHServices.com

Finally, if you are interested in seeing
your own book in print, please contact us at:

publishing@TEACHServices.com

We would be happy to review your manuscript for free.

www.ingramcontent.com/pod-product-compliance
Lightning Source LLC
Chambersburg PA
CBHW081212230426
43666CB00015B/2719